Louis de Sainte-Marthe, Giovanni Francesco Loredano, Francis Sandford

A genealogical history of the kings of Portugal

Louis de Sainte-Marthe, Giovanni Francesco Loredano, Francis Sandford

A genealogical history of the kings of Portugal

ISBN/EAN: 9783337149987

Printed in Europe, USA, Canada, Australia, Japan

Cover: Foto ©ninafisch / pixelio.de

More available books at **www.hansebooks.com**

A Genealogical History
OF THE
KINGS
OF
PORTUGAL.

And of all those Illustrious Houses that in Masculine Line are branched from that Royal Family.

CONTAINING

A DISCOURSE

Of their several Lives, Marriages, and Issues, Times of Birth, Death, and Places of Burial.

With their Armes and Emblazons according to their several alterations, as also their Symboles and Mottoes.

All Engraven in Copper-Plates.

Written in *French* by
SCEVOLE and LOVIS DE SAINCTE-MARTHE,
Brethren, and Advocates in the Court of Parliament
of *PARIS*,
Unto the Year, M. DC. XXIII.

Rendred into *English*, and continued unto this present Year, M. DC. LXII.

By FRANCIS SANDFORD, *Rouge-Dragon*,
Pursuivant of Armes.

LONDON,
Printed by E. M. for the Author, ANNO, 1662.

TO THE MOST
Glorious Monarch,
CHARLES II.
KING of *GREAT BRITAIN, FRANCE,* and *IRELAND,* &c.

Royal SIR!

Hose *Presents* which in themselves are rich and beautiful, cannot lose any thing of their esteem, though tendred by the meanest hand; the Diamond falls not under its true value, when found among the low-prized Pebbles: Nor will (I hope) this *History* (which with all due Reverence I presume to lay at Your *Majesties* Feet) be thought worthless, although presented to the greatest of Kings, by the least and lowest of his Subjects.

Yet my presumption bears with it a more extensive Modesty, than to possess me with a belief, that what I now bring, can, as far as it is any thing of mine, be worthy the least regards of Majesty. For it's Worth Consists in it self; and being a *Genealogical History* of a *Royal House* Indubitably Descended from our English Kings, cannot I hope find a less Gracious Acceptance from our Great *Monarch*, than it hath formerly done from His most Christian *Majesty*, in Favour of those who but disputably have maintained it to be a Branch of the Royal Stem of *France*; but it may much more engage Your acceptance, when Your *Majesty* considers, that out of this Renowned

The Epistle Dedicatory.

nowned Stock Your *Majesty* hath made choice of Your most Excellent Queen.

For from *Philippa* the daughter of the great Duke of *Lancaster*, *John* of *Gaunt*, descended that numerous issue, which hath since supplyed PORTUGAL for above Three hundred years with a Succession of Heroick and Valiant Kings, and was not discontinued, but by the Power of the *Castillians*, under *Philip II, III, IV.* Kings of *Spain*, and hath been as miraculously restored in the Person of *K. John IV.* so that as King *John I.* much augmented the Glory of that Nation by allying himself with *England*, another King *John* hath no less renewed it, not more by redeeming his Kingdom out of the hands of Ambitious Seisers, than in being Father to that Daughter, by whom in the Persons of Your Royal *Majesty*, and our Gracious Queen KATHERINE, a second and much firmer union is contracted between these two so antiently allied Crowns.

But here, *Dread* SIR, I do conclude (lest I should too long disturb Your Royal thoughts,) with those Prayers which all good Subjects are bound to make; That as the *Portugueses* have acknowledged that *Match* with *England*, to be the most happy and fortunate that ever any of their Kings contracted, both for the strength, and glory of that Kingdom; So that Heaven would likewise give Your *Majesty* as numerous, and as glorious an issue by this second *Match*, that Generations to come may have cause to Bless that Day wherein a *Monarch* of *Great Britain* did Espouse an *Infanta* of PORTUGAL. Thus prayes,

YOUR MAJESTIES most Faithful,

and most Obedient, Subject and Servant,

FRANCIS SANDFORD.

Rouge-Dragon, Pursuivant at *Arms*.

The TRANSLATOR to the READER.

I Need not a better Authority for the Reputation of this History, then to inform you, That the first Part thereof, from Henry Count of Portugal, to Anthony Prior of Crato, with the Second Book, containing the Pedigrees of the Royal House of Braganza, and other Princes of the Blood of Portugal, is Translated out of the Genealogical History of the Royal House of France, written by Scevole, and Lovis de Sainctc-Marthe, Persons Eminent for their Knowledge in Antiquity, and most exact in the Descents of the Kings of France, and no less curious in this of Portugal, as being a Branch of that Royal Stem.

The later Part, continued from Anthony, to the Sixth Year of the Reign of King Alphonso VI. being this present Year, One thousand six hundred threescore and two; is taken out of the Letters of Francisco Loredano, a Noble Venetian, and an Able Statesman, employed Ambassador from that Republick, to most of the Princes and Potentates of Europe; Englished by an Ingenious young Gentleman, not long since.

To these French and Italian Authors, I have made several Additions out of Don Antonio de Sousa de Macedo, a Portuguese, concerning the several Changes of the Arms of that Kingdom; The Ceremonies used at the Coronations and Burials of the Kings of Portugal, from Conestaggio an Italian; And the Modern Additions to the Descents of the Younger Houses, either out of Nicholaus Rittershusus, a Germain, or from the faithful Report of some of the Nobility of the Portugal Nation.

Having chosen rather to make use of Authors that were strangers, and unbiassed with Interest, than Natives of that Kingdom, both for the Satisfaction of my Reader, and also because the Exploits of that Warlike and Industrious People, would seem from their own Relations almost incredible: For if we consider the small Beginnings out of which they have gained such vast Territories, we cannot but confess, That they have out-done most of the greatest Conquerors; for those with mighty Armies subjected the Old World, but these with small Numbers, have not only carried Victory to the East, but found out New Worlds to Conquer: So that the Dominions of Alphonso the first King of Portugal, are not the Tenth part of those Kingdoms possessed by King Alphonso VI.

If I have too much made use of the French Idiome in this Translation, most Gentlemen will (I presume) pass by that Errour, it being almost impossible to meddle with that Language, and not to receive some Impressions thereby. The Errours of the Press, I have entred on the other side of the Leaf in the Errata, which I would intreat you to Correct; and then I hope you will find the Satisfaction expected in the perusal of this History. Farewel,

F. S.

WE having perused this Book, which is for the most part a Translation out of *French*, of a *Genealogical History of the Kings of Portugal*, do not find that the same doth materially vary from the Sense of the *Authors*; nor that there is in it any thing contrary to the Rules of Armory.

EDWARD WALKER Garter,
Principal King of Arms.

WILLIAM DUGDALE
Norroy, King of Arms.

ERRATA.

Page 1. line 32. for Idolatrous, read Idolators. p. ibid. l. 36. for Histories, r. Historians. p. 2. l. 12. for Father, r. Brother. p. 3. l. 43. after to be built (add) in that Cathedral. p. ibid. l. 44. to, an Epitaph, (add) in Latine. p. 5. l. 36. to, Confine this Princess (add) his Mother. p. 7. l. 31. for 1186. r. 1185. p. 8. l. 17. to, who dyed (add) without Issue. p. 19. l. 43. to, some Historians (add) of *Castille*. p. 27. l. 33. for *Alphonso VI*. r. *Alphonso IV*. p. 36. l. 16. for eracinuted. r. irradicated. p. 55. l. 10. for Forty, r. Threeand Forty. p. 61. l. 34. for *Calicut*, r. *Calicut*. p. ibid. l. 35. for so named, r. of that Denomination. p. 81. l. 3. blot out Blessed. p. 94. l. 18. for 1510. r. 1580. p. 105. l. 4. for *Missal*, r. *Missel*.

This Book is to be sold by the Author, Francis Sandford, *at his Lodgings next door to the* Heraulds-Office, *upon* St. Bennets-hill: *Or by* Edward Mottershed, *Printer, living upon the aforesaid Hill, over against* Doctors Commons.

The Genealogy of t

1. HENRY OF BOURGONGNE Count of PORTUGA
before his Father, and Grand-son of ROBERT OF FRANCE Du
and Grand-child of HUGH CAPET, both Kings of FRANCE.

2. URACCA Countess of *Tristamare*. — ALPHONSO I. o of PORTUGAL, d

3. URACCA Queen of *Leon* and *Galicia*. — SANCEO I. of the of PORTUGAL,

4. ALPHONSO II. of the name, third King of PORTUGAL. He died A° 1233. — FERDINAND of *Portugal*, Count of *Flanders*. — PETER King of *Majorca*.

5. SANCEO II. of the name, fourth King of PORTUGAL, dyed *Anno* 1246. without issue. — ALPHONSO III. King of PORT *Anno* 1279.

6. DIONYSIUS or DENIS, sixth King of PORTUGAL, dyed *Anno* 1325 — ALPHONSO of *Por* Lord of *Portalegre*.

7. CONSTANCE Queen of *Castille*. — ALPHONSO IV. of the name, seventh King of PORTUGAL, dyed 135. — ALPHONSO of *Portugal*, dyed without issue. — ISABEL Lady of *Biscay*.

8. ALPHONSO, DIONYSIO and JOHN, dyed all young. — PETER, eighth King of P TUGAL, deceased *Anno*

9. FERDINAND, ninth King of PORTUGAL, dyed *Anno* 1383. — DIONYSIO of *Portugal*, eldest Son, dyed young.

10. BEATRIX of *Portugal*, Q. of *Castille*. — ALPHONSO dyed, aged Ten years. — EDWARD, eleventh King of PORTUGAL, dyed *Anno* 1438. — PETER, Duke of *Cerimbra*. — HEN *Visco* the

11. ALPHONSO V. of the name, twelfth King of PORTUGAL, ob. 1481. — LEONOR Wife to the Emperour *Frederick* III. — JANE Queen of *Castille*. — FERDI- NAND D. of *Visco*. — PETER elected King of *Arragon*. — JOHN Duke *Conim*

12. JOHN II. of the name, thirteenth King of PORTUGAL, dyed *An.* 1495. — JOHN Prince of *Portugal*, dyed young. — JANE took upon her Religious Habit. — JOHN Duke of *Visco*, dyed young without issue. — JAMES slain by his Brot

13. ALPHONSO Prince of *Portugal*, dyed young, without issue. — ISABELLA wife of the Emperour *Charles V*. — BEATRIX Dutchess of *Savoy*. — MICHAEL Prince of *Portugal* & Castille, dyed young. — JOHN II of th fifteenth K. of P GAL, dyed *Ann*

14. PHILIP II. King of *Spain*, seized upon the Kingdom of PORTUGAL, and was Nineteenth King. — JOHN Prince of *Portugal*, died *An.* 1554. — MARY Princess of *Spain*. — ISABELLA & BEATRIX dyed young. — ANTHO eighteen TUGAL

15. PHILIP III. of the name King of *Spain*, was twentieth King of PORTUGAL — SEBASTIAN sixteenth King of PORTU- GAL, was slain in *Affrica*. S. *prole*. 1578.

16. PHILIP IV. of the name, King of *Spain*, now Reigning, 1662. who possessed the Kingdom of PORTUGAL until the Year, 1640.

17. KATHERINE of *Portugal*, dyed in her Infancy. — JOHN II. of that name, Duke of *Braganza*, by th states, was Crowned King of PORTUGAL, *Anno*

18. THEODOSIUS Prince of *Portugal*, dyed in his youth. — ALPHONSO VI. of the name, Three and twentiet of PORTUGAL, who Reigneth at present, 166

Kings of Portugal.

:ond Son of HENRY OF BOURGONGNE that dyed
IRGONGNE, which ROBERT was Son of ROBERT,
n the Year, One thousand one hundred and twelve.

, King 36.		THERESA Wife of *Ferdinando Mendez.*
nd King 1212.		THERESA Countess of *Flanders.*
THERESA Queen of *Leon.*	MAUD Queen of *Castille.*	SANCE an Abbess.	BLANCHE. BERENGA-RIA.
ie, fifth dyed	FERDINAND of *Portugal*, Infant of *Serpe.*		LEONORA Queen of *Denmark.*
	FERDINAND of *Portugal*, dyed young.	BLANCH of *Portugal*, Abbess of *Lornano.*
STANCE marri- Nounez Gon- de Lara.	MARY wife of *Tel-lez* son of *Alphonso* Infant of *Moline.*	ISABELLA the younger married to *John-Alphon-so* Lord of *Albuquerque.*
	MARY Queen of *Castille.*	LEONORA Queen of *Arragon.*
ortugal, La- of *Tortosa.*	JOHN I. of the name, tenth King of POR-TUGAL, a Natural Son, deceased *Anno* 1433.
of ·of ·ist.	JOHN Grand Ma-ster of the Order of St. *James.*	FERDINAND great Master of the Order *d'Avis.*	ISABEL Dutchess of *Bourgongne.*	ALPHONSO First Duke of *Braganza*, a Natural Son.
ES of al	ISABEL Queen of *Portugal.*	JAMES, G.M. of the Order of St. *James.*	ISABEL Queen of *Castille.*	BEATRIX Dutchess of *Visco*, Mother of King *Emanuel.*	FERDINAND I. of the name, second Duke of *Braganza.*
o, 'I.	EMANUEL fourteenth King of PORTUGAL, dyed *Anno* 1521.	LEONOR wife of *John II.* King of *Portugal.*	ISABEL married to *Ferd.II.* of the name Duke of *Braganza.*	FERDINAND II. of the name, third Duke of *Braganza.*
EWIS of ortugal,).of *Beia.*	FERDINAND of *Portugal*, dy-ed *S.'prole.*	HENRY the Cardinal, seventeenth K.of POR-TUGAL, *ob.S.p.* 1580.	EDWARD Infante of *Portugal.*	JAMES fourth Duke of *Braganza.*
tard, OR- 1595.	EDWARD D. of *Vimarana*, dyed young.	MARY marri-ed to *Alex.D.* of *Parma.*	KATHERINE wife of *John I.* of the name, Duke of *Braganza.*	THEODOSIUS I. of the name, fifth Duke of *Braganza.*
NUEL rtugal.	CHRISTOPHER of *Portugal.*		PHILIPPA LOUISA.	JOHN I. of the name, sixth Duke of *Braganza.*
				THEODOSIUS II. of the name, seventh Duke of *Braganza.*
onsent of the three E- name of JOHN IV.	EDWARD of *Portugal*, dyed in Prison at *Millan.*		ALEXANDER of *Portugal.*
PETER Infante of *Portugal.*	JANE of *Portu-gal*, dyed young.		KATHERINE of *Portu-gal*, Queen of *England.*

HENRY

Of Bourgongne Count of Portugal.

CHAP. I.

PORTU-
GAL.

*D'argent a la
Croix d'Azure.*

PORTU-
GAL.

Mong so many Kings and Princes, who draw their Source and Original from the House of *FRANCE*, and that have in several parts of the World given testimony of their Pietie, joyned with apparent Valour, in their Wars against the *Sarazens, Moors, Turks*, and other *Infidels*, the generous Prince HENRY OF BOURGONGNE Son of *Henry*, and grandson of *Robert* of *France*, Duke of *Bourgongne*, whose Father was King *Robert*, hath rendred his memory so much the more illustrious and famous, as being a worthy Son, an imitator of his Fathers virtues, and the Establisher and Founder of the Kingdom of PORTUGAL. He was the first that swayed the Scepter, and who hath given Original to twenty Kings, who have there since reigned for the space of neer five hundred years, with such power, that they have by the force of their own Armes, Conquered and Subjected to their Dominion several Kingdoms and strong holds in *Affrick*, *Persia*, *East-India* and *America*, which hath facilitated the means to Civilize those people that were heretofore wholly barbarous, and of Idolatrous and Mahumetans, to convert them to Christianity. So that we must acknowledge, that these Princes (originally of the most august Family of the French Kings) have very much merited from the Christian Religion.

Several Histories of *France, Portugal, Castille*, and other Nations have very much laboured to finde out and discover from what Countrey, and what House

Party de CASTILLE. *De gueules a un Chasteau d'or.*

Dom. Anto De Sousa Lusit. Liberat. fol. 767. Appen. Cap. 3. *Henricus portavit Crucem in vexillis. Inquiunt Doctor Fra. Seraphin, de Freitas de just. Imper. Lusit. A siat. C. 18 n. 17, &c. qui notavit Crucem fuisse cœruleam deducto colore ex domo Ducum Burgundiæ, ac Regum Galliæ uti de ille princeps procedebat. Cuncē portavit vel rex sua particulari pietate, vel quod illis temporibus Crucem pro insignibus so ebant portare qui fuerunt in sancto bello Hierusalem, in quo ipsi fuit, ut narrant. Maris dial 2 C. 3. post imed; Blandan in Monarch Lu sit. 1. 3. lib 8. C. 2.*

HENRY of BOURGONGNE

House this Prince HENRY deduced his Original. His extraction having been unknown for a long time, and concerning which there hath been almost as many Opinions as Writers. Some have written that he descended from an Emperour of *Constantinople*, others from a King of *Hungary*, some from *William* Count of *Bourgongne*, brother of *Raymond* Count of *Outre-Soane*, and others also from *Guy* Count of *Vernœil* in *Normandy*, brother of this *William*. Furthermore there are that report, that he was son of *Henry*, Duke and Earl of *Limbourg*, and Duke of *Lorraine*. Lastly, others (which have followed the Error of *Richard* of *Vassebourg* a Modern Historian) are of Opinion that *William* was his Father, who was called Baron of *Joinville*, whom they make to be Governor of *Lorraine* in the absence of his Father the great *Godfrey* of *Buillon* elected King of *Jerusalem*.

Aux Antiquitez de la Gaule Belgique.

But all these Opinions, and Imaginary descents, have been worthily refuted by *Theodore Godefroy* Advocate in the Court of Parliament of *Paris*, in a Treatise which he hath published of the Original of the Kings of PORTUGAL; having first revived this Opinion, and clearly justified by proofs and undeniable reasons, that they are descended in Line Masculine from the Royal House of FRANCE by this HENRY the chief of his Branch.

And he groundeth principally upon the Authority of the Fragment (which yet remaineth) of an old Latin History of *France*, which begins at the decease of King *Robert*, and is continued to the Reign of *Philip* the first; An History composed by a Monk of the Abbey of Saint *Benedict Lez Fleury* upon the *Loir* in the Diocess of *Orleance*, who lived in the time of the same HENRY; This Fragment (with other Historians) hath been published at the end of the last Age by the Learned *Peter Pithou*.

Fragm. Hist. à Rege Roberto ad Philipp. I.

Note here the terms of this Ancient Author which hath been translated: *Our design is not here to mention how many times the King Andefonse* (he is called also *Alphonso* the VI. King of Castille and Leon) *generously behaved himself against the Saraxins, nor the number of the Battels in which he hath vanquished them. It's he which wrested from them, and subjected to his Empire the strong City of* Toledo. *He espoused* Constance *daughter of* Robert *Duke of* Bourgongne, *and had a daughter by her which he gave in marriage to* Raymond *Count of* Outre-Soane. *As for his other daughter begotten out of marriage, He espoused her to* HENRY *one of the sons of the sons of the same Duke of* BOURGONGNE, *and upon the Confines of* Spain, *opposed them both against the Agarenes*. He nameth also the Infidels under whose yoke *Spain* at that time mourned, and of which they possessed a good part.

This is the more to be credited, for that the Historian who wrote it, was co-temporary with the Prince of whom we speak, as may be gathered by other Passages of his History.

Jo. Mariana Hist. Hisp. lib. 10 cap. 1.

Several give unto HENRY the Title and Quality of Count of PORTUGAL, and agree in this Point, that he was established Earl thereof in the year *One thousand fourscore and ten*, by the King of *Castille* his Father in Law, who gave him this County in Dower, in hope (as this King did verily believe) he would war upon the Moors in *Portugal*, as *Hugh* the first of the name Duke of *Bourgongne* his elder brother had done in *Arragon*; in which he was not deceived; for he served as a Rampire to check the course of those Barbarians. But it is otherwise to be presumed, and that the same Queen of *Castille Constance*, who was Aunt by the Fathers side of this HENRY, and lived in the time of the marriage, might have contributed her recommendation for the attainment of this Province of *Portugal* in Dower: and Note also

Th. Godefroy.

1090

Count of PORTUGAL. 3

<small>Years of CHRIST.</small> also that the Count of *Outre-Soan*, who espoused the other lawfully begotten Daughter of the same King, as we have said, had in Marriage with her only a summe of money.

Godefroy is not only of this opinion, for it was also followed by *Jaques Augustus de Thou* President in the Court of Parliament, in the History of his time; by *Prudencio de Sandoval* Bishop of *Pampelona* in *Navarre*, and Historiographer of *Philip* the III. King of *Spain* in the History of *Ferdinand* I. and other Kings of *Castille*; by *Andrew du Chesne* the Kings Geographer in the Histories of *Bourgongne* and *Vergy*; as also by *Antonio de Vasconcellos* a Portugues, of the Order of *Jesus*, and Rector of the University of *Evora*, in the Latine History of the Kings of *Portugal*, which he hath written in a most elegant Stile.

This natural Daughter of King *Alphonso*, and of *Ximena de Gusman* wife of HENRY OF BOURGONGNE, was named TERESA OF CASTILLE. He left *France* in the Year One thousand fourscore and nine, accompanied with a good number of Lords for the succour of the King of *Castille*, among which there are named seven Counts; the principal of which were *Raymond* the son of *William* Count of *Bourgongne*, *Raymond* of St. *Gilles*, and *Toulouse*, this HENRY (who by mistake is sirnamed of *Lorraine* in the History) *Rotrou de Perche*, and *William* Viscount of *Melun*; they are all said to be at the same Battel; for which cause some suppose it had the appellation of the *Seven Counts*: But the Histories of *Spain* speak otherwise.

<small>*Duarte Nunez en Chron. des Reis de Port.*</small>

1089.

<small>*Chronique MS. de S. Denys.*</small>

The Count HENRY Ordered the City of *Conimbra* for his principal residence and that of his Court; and the City of *Braga* for Metropolitane of the other Churches. He vanquished and put to flight some Moorish Kings at *Visco* and *Lamego*, and seized also upon *Lisbonne* (it hath since been the Capital City of the Kingdom) which not long after they recovered again.

<small>*Vasconcellius An acephalæosi I.*</small>

But this great Prince being impatient of repose without honour (if we credit some Authors) undertook the Crossiade with *Godfrey* of *Bullon* and other Princes for the recovery of the *Holy Land*, where he performed wonders. Being upon his return from this Voyage (of which some make a doubt) he vigorously continued his War against the *Moors*, nor did his great age cause him to discontinue the performance of his Martial Affairs. And lastly, he dyed at the Siege of the City of *Asturia* in the Year One thousand one hundred and twelve; being then aged about Threescore and ten years, yet there be some that extend the Course of his Life to a longer period. He was inhumed in the Cathedral Church of the City of *Braga*, which is one of the chief of the Kingdom of *Portugal*. In the Year One thousand five hundred and thirteen, *Diego de Sousa* being then Bishop (who was descended from Prince HENRY) caused a Chappel to be built, in which he reposed the bones of this Prince, and wrote an Epitaph, which declared him to be Son of a King of *Hungary*. But *Edward Nunez*, a judicious and learned person, hath with reason refuted the error of this Original. He often nameth TERESA, Queen, as being a Kings Daughter. She deceased about the Year One thousand one hundred and thirty. Her body lieth near unto that of her Husband Count HENRY. Although the greater number of Writers give her the Qualification of a Natural Daughter; there is an Author of this Time, famous, and well read in the knowledge of the *Portugal* Antiquities, who assures us that in the Ancient Chronicles in Manuscript, she is called the Daughter of the Queen *Ximena*

1097.

<small>His Death: 1112.</small>

<small>*Duarte Nunez.*</small>

<small>*Vasconcellius.*</small>

<small>*Duarte Nunez.*</small>

<small>In his Chronicle of *Portugal*.</small>

<small>*Andr. Resendius.lib.4. Antiquit.Lusit,*</small>

B 2   de

HENRY of BOURGONGNE, &c.

Dom. Anton. de Sousa denieth that *Teresa* was a Bastard, and also writeth that her younger Sister *Uracca* usurped the Kingdom of *Castille* against her. These are his words:

Tharasia mater Alphonsi primi Regis lusitaniæ, filia erat Legitima, & natu major Alphonsi 6. Regis Legionis & Castellæ cumq; pater mortuus fuerit sine filio masculo, ut est notorium, ipsa extabat heres Legitimi Regnorum ejus, Quæ tamen Uracca soror junior usurpavit, quapropter inter utrumq; orta sunt bella. Appen. ad Lusit. Lib Cap. 4. Actio Prima.

de *Gusman* lawful Wife of King *Alphonso*, and also *Nunez* and *Vasconcellos* seem to be of the same opinion, which is confirmed by the quality of *Ximena*, who was descended from one of the most Illustrious Houses of *Spain*. The History of *Portugal* hath been written by several Authors, and in several Languages, among others, by *Edward Galvan*; *Stephen Garibay*; the same *Nunez* or *Nonius Leo*, a *Portugal* Lawyer; *John de Maris*; *John de Barros*; *Lopez de Castagneda*, *Damiano de Goez*; *Hierosme Osorio* Bishop of *Silva*; *John Mariana*, the same *Vasconcellos*; *Hierosme Francchi Conestaggio*; *Joseph Texera*, *Theodore Godefroy*, and others, who have conjointly treated of the History of *S P A I N E*.

Years of CHRIST.

Children of HENRY OF BOURGONGNE
Count of PORTUGAL, and of TERESA OF CASTILLE his Wife.

2. **A**LPHONSO, Count, afterwards first King of PORTUGAL continued the Posterity.

2. **U**RACCA OF PORTUGAL, Wife to *Veremond Paatz de Trava* Count of TRASTEMARE.

Nunez. Vasconcellius.

2. **T**ERESA, others name her SANCE OF PORTUGAL, married to FERDINAND MENDEZ a Puissant Lord in *Gallicia*.

Her Marriage.

Natural Children of HENRY OF BOURGONGNE
Count of PORTUGAL.

2. **P**ETER Bastard of PORTUGAL, made a Journey into *France* in the Year *One thousand one hundred seven and forty*; and reported unto King *Alphonso* his Brother, the Miracles performed by St. *Bernard* Abbot of *Clervaux*. He incited this King to Found the rich Monastry of *Alcobace*, into which this PETER retired, and there passed the rest of his dayes in great humility, where he was also entombed.

1147.

ALPHONSO.

2. ALPHONSO I.
KING OF PORTUGAL.
CHAP. II.

1113.

His Birth.
4094.

TO the Count of Portugal, *Henry* of *Bourgongne*, and the Countess *Teresa* of *Castille* his wife, succeeded this Prince their Son; and was born at *Guimareans* in the Month of *July*, in the Year One thousand fourscore and fourteen, who did more and more augment the glory of this Family.

Being only Eighteen years old at the death of his Father, he was, by some of the *Portugals*, judged too young to undergo and manage those grand Warres, begun as well against the *Moors*, as those of *Leon*; and therefore they endeavoured to marry *Theresa* Widow of the defunct, to the Count of *Trastamare*; who upon this occasion should undertake the Government of *Portugal*. But the young Prince ALPHONSO not suffering it, opposed him with so much courage, that having Vanquished the Count, he was constrained to with-draw. And nevertheless by the Agreement afterwards setled betwixt them, he caused him to marry his Sister *Uracca* of *Portugal*, as we have said before, by which we may presume, that the Marriage of *Teresa* with the Count of *Trastamare* was only proposed. It's true, which we add, That ALPHONSO so ill resented his intended Deprivation from the Government, that it urged him to confine this Princess to a Prison, in which she finished her life. Whereupon not long after began that cruel Warre with *Alphonso* VII. King of *Castille* and *Leon*, his Cousin; from which nevertheless he ever came off with honour; and, according to some, wounded this King in a Battel, put the flower of his Nobility to the Sword, to the number of seven Earls that accompanied him, and took the Queen of *Castille* his wife prisoner. Whom some believe to be, (as it's probable she was) the Mother of ALPHONSO.

Afterwards the Count of *Portugal* directed the course of his War against *Ismar* and four other Infidel Kings, whom he defeated at *Ourique* in a pitch-

---

PORTUGAL.

D'argent a cinq escussons d'Azure perie en Croix, Chacun chargé de cinq besans d'argent posé en sautoir avec un point de sable.

PORTUGAL.

Party de MAURIENNE *ou Savoye.*

D'or a l'aigle de sable ... bté & becqué de gueules.

Vignier suit l'an. 1147.

Vasconcellos

ALPHONSO I. King of PORTUGAL.

Garibay.
Mariana.
Nunez.
Vasconcellos.

ed field, and also that Puissant Army by them raised, some Historians write, that upon the day of battel our Lord Jesus Christ appeared in the Aire in that form he was Crucified, who bowing his body downward, and casting his eyes on the ground, expressed these words, *ALPHONSO, thou shalt overcome in this sign*; which came to pass, for the five *Sarazen* Kings were kill'd upon the place, in memory of which signal Victory, to the end there might remain a perpetual mark thereof to Posterity.) ALPHONSO changed the *Azure-Cross*, which he did before bear in a *silver field* for his Armes, into five *Escocheons* also *Azure*, every one of them charged with *five pence* of *silver*, and this in commemoration of the *thirty pieces of silver* for which our Lord was sold by the *Jews*. In the same Year of our Salvation, *One thousand one hundred and nine and thirty*, in pursuit of the same Victory, those of the Army of ALPHONSO, acknowledged and saluted him for King at *Conimbra*, leaving the name of Duke, which he had before changed into that of Count.

The Arms of Portugal are changed.

Nunez Vignier.

1139.

And. Favine. Lib. 6. C. 18. Alphonso Henriquez first King of Portugal, having conquered from the Moors the City of E- vora Anno 1147. there placed a Garison, or number of brave-spirited Knights to defend it, who made themselves known under the name of *Fellow-Brethren of St. Mary of Evora*.

The same King *Alphonso* not long after gave them the strong Castle d' *Avis*, and therefore the Knights of this Order were called, *Brethren d' Avis*, who preserved the memory thereof in their Armes, which they took thus.

D'or a la Croix Fleurdelisse de Synople, & en pointe deux Osteaux ainsi que des Corbeaux de sable.

Robt. de Monte.

La Orden de Avis tuuo su principio en el anno de 1147. en tiempo del Rey Dom Alonso primero Rey de Portugal. Llamose al principio la Cavalleria de Ebora, porque tuuo su Convento en la Ciudad d'este nombre, Su primer Maestre sellamo Dom Ferdinando Monteiro; despues succedio en el Maestrado Dom Fernand, Yannes n qui el Rei Dom Alonso de Portugal dio el Castillo de Avis anno 1161. y siendo alli uns la dado el Convento primero, sellamo DE AVIS. Y so por señal una Cruz como la de Alcantara, y por Armas la misma Cruz en Campo d' Oro, y al pie della dos Aves negras por alusion del nombre de AVIS. Thus much out of *Dom Damiano a Goes, Radez de Andrada*, and the Count of *Lansarote*, in his Nobility of *Andaluzia*.

Memorable was that Assembly Convened by this King *Alphonso* in the City of *Lamego*, consisting of the three Estates of the Kingdom, where were made many Laws which they justly account their Fundamentals, as unalterable as those of the *Medes* and *Persians*, made Sacred by the observation of them, both by Prince and People; among which it was enacted; First, That the said King *Alphonso's* son, Grandson, and so forward, should reign after him for ever. But if the King have only daughters, the eldest should be Queen after her father, upon condition she be married to a Native of *Portugal*, and that he be a Noble-man, who shall not take upon him the name of a King, until he hath a son born, nor wear a Crown on his head, nor take the right-hand of his Wife.

But the last clause is most to be considered, which my Author hath faithfully transcribed out of the said Laws.

Sit ista lex in sempiternum quod Prima Filia Regis accipiat maritum de Portugale, ut non veniat Regnū ad Extraneos; & si nupserit cum Principe extraneo, non sit Regina: quia nunquā volumus nostrum Regnum ire de Portugalensibus qui nos sua fortitudine Reges fecerunt, sine Adjutorio alieno, per suam fortitudinem, & cum sanguine suo.

Nunez, Vasconcellos.

This Law was put in execution after the death of *Ferdinando* the 9th King of that race; for *Donna Beatrice*, his daughter being married to *John* the first of the name, King of *Castille* a Forrein Prince, was excluded, and *John* the first King of *Portugal*, though illegitimate, was advanced to the Throne on from his Mother the Countess *Teresa*.

In the mean time an Army composed of divers Nations, viz. *English, Flemmings, Normans* and *Lorrainois*, being embarqued in *England*, and bound for *Jerusalem*, to give succour to the Christians under the Conduct of *William Longespe* Duke of *Normandy* (my Author meaneth Earl of *Salisbury*) passed by the coast of *Spain*, where making some stay, at the instance of King ALPHONSO, they besieged and took the City of *Lisbonne* which the *Moors* possessed, the Siege having continued five months; They were at length defeated by the Christians, who delivered this City into the hands and power of ALPHONSO, he also Conquered from them the Cities of *Leiria, Santarem, Evora, Elvas, Beja,* and several other Towns and Fortresses, which make at present the better part of the Kingdom of *Portugal*, which he annexed to the Province situate between the Rivers of *Dourho* and *Minho*; and that of *Tarsos Montes*, as also a part of *Estremadura* (where are *Braga, Conimbra, Visco,* and other Cities) Provinces which descended to him by succession

1147.

Now

ALPHONSO I. King of PORTUGAL.

Years of Christ.
1179.

Now fell out the dispute betwixt *Ferdinando* King of *Castille* and *Leon*, and his Father-in-law King ALPHONSO, about the City of *Badaios*, which the Castillian urged belonged unto him, as being enterprised upon the *Moors*; being come to blows, the King of *Portugal* having by an accident been hurt before the fight, fell within the power of the King of *Castille* his Enemy, but afterward a peace being concluded betwixt them, the *Portugues* remitted unto *Ferdinand* part of the Province of *Galicia*.

Idem.

1181.

His success was more propitious in the Enterprise he undertook against *Alboiac* King of *Seville*, whom he also subdued, and after the Victory obtained, instituted a Military Order, called, *Of the Eagle*; The device was *An Eagle Purple enfermed within a Circle Or*.

Vasconcellos.

After all these Warres ALPHONSO had attained to a very great age, nevertheless he ceased not to exercise himself in his Martial affairs, with his Valiant Son, who seconded him in his high and generous Enterprises.

But that hindred not his inclination to Piety, and the erection of several Churches and Monasteries, among others he Founded that of St. *Croix* at *Conimbra*, which he so richly endowed, and with so stupendious a revenue, that the famous University of this City hath a sensible apprehension thereof, and that it is at this day the most Famous and Flourishing of all *Spaine*. ALPHONSO also Founded the Monasteries of St. *Bernard* of *Alcobace*, and of St. *Vincent* near *Lisbonne*, in the same place where he encamped at the Siege thereof. In short, the *Portugal* Historians give him the reputation of having Built and Founded an hundred and fifty Churches and Religious Houses.

Idem.

His Death.
1186.

In fine, this great Prince being aged Fourscore and eleven years, and after he had Reigned Six and forty, departed out of this life into a better, in the same City of *Conimbra*, the Ninth day of *December*, in the Year *One thousand one hundred fourscore and six*, (and not two years before, as some believe) and lieth in this Church of St. *Croix*. King *Emanuel*, one of his most Illustrious Successors, erected for him (a long time after) a most Magnificent Tomb.

Nunez.

His Marriage.
1146.

There are divers opinions among Authors, about the House from which Queen MAUD wife of ALPHONSO did descend, whom he married in the Year *One thousand one hundred and six and forty* (and not two years before, as some are of opinion.) For those which write the History of *Portugal* and *Savoy*, say that she was Daughter of *Amides* the second of the name, Count of *Savoy* or *Maurienne*, and of *Maud* Daughter of the Count of *Albon* (they would say *Viempoü*) his second Wife. But *Hierosme Surita* writes, that she was Sister of *Peter*, Count of *Lara* and *Mollina*, and Daughter of *Henry*, Count of *Lara*, and of *Ermensinda* Vicountess of *Narbonnay*: An opinion which is reproved by *Nunez*. And nevertheless it may be that he married both the one, and the other; certain it is, that Queen *Maud* dyed in *Anno One thousand one hundred threescore and eighteen*, and was interred with her Husband.

Nunez.
Pingonius.
Dami. a Gorz.
Vasconcellos.

In the Hist. of Arragon.

1178.

G2 *Children*

ALPHONSO I. King of PORTUGAL.

Children of ALPHONSO I. KING OF PORTUGAL, and of MAUD OF SAVOY his Wife.

3. **HENRY PRINCE OF PORTUGAL** dyed young; There is mention made of him in a Letter which the King his Father wrote to St. *Bernard*, Abbot of *Clerveaux* in *Bourgongne*.

3. **SANCHO** first of the name, succeeded his Father, and was King of Portugal.

3. **URRACCA OF PORTUGAL**, Queen of LEON, was married unto *Ferdinand* II. of the name, King of LEON and *Galicia*; And notwithstanding she had a son by him which carried the name of *Alphonso*, and was King of *Leon* after his Father, yet this Marriage was dissolved by the Pope, because of the proximity of blood betwixt them.

LEON. D'argent au lyon de pourpre. Party de PORTUGAL. Comme cy devant.

Her Marriage.

3. **TERESA OF PORTUGAL**, Countess of FLANDERS, whom the *Flemmish* Historians call MAUD: and this name was given her when in the Year One thousand one hundred fourscore and four, she was espoused to *Philip* of *Alsace* Count of *Flanders*, who dyed at the Siege of *Ptolemais* or *Acre* in *Syria*, in the War against the Infidels in the Year One thousand one hundred and ninty one. During his absence the Queen Countess MAUD (for so is she called by *Rigord* and other Historians, as being the Daughter of a King, and the Wife of a Count) did with great prudence govern his Estates and Seigneuries.

After the death of *Philip*, she was re-married (and was first wife) unto *Eudes* III. Duke of *Bourgongne*, but was divorced by the Authority of the Church. TERESA lived to a great age, and afterwards dyed the sixth day of *May*, in the Year One thousand two hundred and eighteen, by an accident that hapned unto her near the City of *Furnes*. For her Coach falling into a Fenne, she could not be drawn out until she expired; since which time this place hath been called *The Queens Ditch*. Her body was first inhumed in the Monastery of *Dunes*, and afterward removed to the Abbey of *Clervaux*; It's probable it was so ordered, because she was issued from the Ancient Dukes of *Burgundy* by the King her Father. This Princess is much commended for her great Courage and Prudence, she made *Adam*, Bishop of *Tourohenne* the Executor of her last Will and Testament. She also had the happiness to see her Nephew *Ferdinand* of *Portugal* established in the County of *Flanders*.

Some write, that the eldest Daughter of King ALPHONSO, was *Maud*, who espoused *Raymond* the son of *Raymond*, Count of *Barcelona*; but the more judicious are of opinion, that this alliance is not creditable.

FLANDERS. D'or au lyon de sable. Party de PORTUGAL. In gest. Philippi Aug.

Her Marriage.

1184.
1191.

Ma. Gr. History of Flanders. Em. Sueyro. Nunez.

Her Death.
1218.

Idem.

Bastard Children of ALPHONSO first of the name, King of PORTUGAL.

3. **ALPHONSO OF PORTUGAL**, Knight of the Order of St. *John* of *Hierusalem* at *Rhodes*, a man Couragious, witness several high enterprises he undertook: but he quit this Order near the end of his life, and returned

Vasconcellos.

SANCEO I. *of the name*, &c. 9

<small>Years of
CHRIST.</small> returned into *Portugal*, where he dyed in the Year *One thousand two hundred and seven*, some by mistake, name him *Pedro Alphonso*.

3. **TERESA OF PORTUGAL**, married unto **SANCEO NUNEZ**, <small>*Nunez.*</small> by whom he had issue *Uracca Sancez* married unto *Goncalo de Sousa*, created by King *Sanceo* the first Count of **MENDEZ**, and from him is descended the Illustrious Familie of **SOUSA** in *Portugal*.

3 SANCEO I.
Of the Name, KING of PORTUGAL.

CHAP. III.

<small>PORTUGAL

Comme cy devant.</small>

1185.

His Birth
1154.

IF *Alphonso* the first was a GREAT and MAGNANIMOUS King ; this his Son and Successor did not degenerate ; For (in the Judgement of many) he seemed to be equal in Piety towards God , in Prudence and Ingenuity in the management of his Estate, and in Martial Prowesse , of which he gave a sufficient proof at the famous Combat of *Seville*, against the *Sarazens*, of whom there fell so great a number, that the River of *Betis* was for some space of time made red, and tinctured with their Blood.

He took his first Breath at *Conimbra* the Eleventh day of *November* , in the Year *One thousand one hundred and four and fifty*.

<small>PORTUGAL
Party de
ARRAGON:
*D'or a quatre
pal's de gueules.*

Nunez.</small>

Before he came to the Crown, two *Mahumetane* Princes having besieged the City of *Badaios*, he came to the relief thereof so opportunely, that he raised the Siege, and afterwards gained a memorable Victory. He performed several other Noble adventures. But most miraculous was that Trophie he obtained upon the Puissant King of *Marocco*, *Miramolin*. For neither the assistance of thirteen other Kings, wherewith he was accompanied , nor the infinite number of *Sarazens* his followers, (and who had besieged **SANCEO** in *Scalube*,) could hinder him the gaining a Victory upon

<small>*Vasconcellos.*</small>

D so

SANCEO I. of the name,

so many Enemies conjured to the Ruine of him, and also of his House.

After so many Warres, observing *Portugal* to be almost Desert, and the Land unmanured; He favoured so much labouring men, and rendred himself so great a Proficient in the Knowledge of Agriculture, that he was ordinarily called THE LABOURER, as if he had been the whole course of his life exercised in this Employment, although indeed he was intirely born a son of *Mars*. A great lover he was of Architecture, and took the care to re-build several Cities and Castles ruined by those Warres.

It fell out, that a Fleet of Ships composed of *Danes*, *Frisons*, and *Hollanders*, having put to Sea (as at other times) bound for the *Holy Land* to Warre upon the Infidels, were by foul weather driven into the Port of *Lisbonne*; And then SANCEO (as his father had done before him) so ordered it, that they assisted him in the Reduction of the City of *Silva* in the Kingdom of the *Algarbies*, a place at that time most flourishing, and strongly Fortified; which hath since been made the Metropolis of that Kingdom.

But as the Time and the Affairs of the World are often crossed by sinister events, it hapned that another *Miramolin*, also King of *Marocco*, came and assaulted *Portugal*, committing several Ravages and Spoyles, and there leaving the marks of a most sad desolation, unfortunately followed with Rain and Inundations, then with extream Drouths, Famine, and other contagious diseases, which swept away so great a number of people, that *Portugal* was reduced to a miserable estate, for the space of eight or ten years: So that the *Moors* took advantage by these calamities to seize upon several Cities and places. Accidents which caused King SANCEO to contract a League with them for the space of five years, during which time there fell out another Warre betwixt him and the King of *Leon*, all which misfortunes hindred his Voyage beyond Sea, which he had resolved against the Infidels; having only sent to the oppressed Christians some pieces of Money. This League being ended, the *Sarazens* began again their incursions.

The last memorable Action of War performed by King SANCEO, was the Prise of the City of *Elva* from the *Moors*, which they had possessed a long time, and not long after he dyed in the Year *One thousand two hundred and twelve*, being aged eight and fifty years, and having Reigned seven and twenty. He was interred in the Church of St. *Croix*, where King *Emanuel* raised a Tomb for him like unto that of his father. He left behind him great Treasure, and remarkable summes of money, of which (by his Testament, which he had made two years before his death) he disposed for Legacies to his Children, and several Churches.

In the Year *One thousand one hundred fourscore and one*, the same King SANCEO was conjoyned in Marriage with DOULCE, or ALDONSE OF ARRAGON, daughter of *Raymond Berengarius*, Earl of *Barcelona*, and of *Petronella* daughter and Heir of *Raymer* King of *Arragon*. The which Queen DOULCE dyed in the Year *One thousand one hundred fourscore and eighteen*. After her Death the King her Husband suffered himself to be transported to unlawful Loves, and had several Bastards. Which incontinence did somewhat eclips the lustre of those Virtues with which he was adorned.

Children

Idem.

History of *Flanders*.

Vasconcellius.

Nunez.
Vasconcellius.

Nunez,
Sarita.
Vasconcellius.

Nunez.

Years of CHRIST.

1189.

1200.
His Death, 1212.

His Marriage.
1181.

1198.

Children of SANCEO I. King of PORTUGAL, and of DOULCE OF ARRAGON his Wife.

4. **A**LPHONSO II. King of PORTUGAL, succeeded his father King *Sanceo*.

His Birth. **F**ERDINAND OF PORTUGAL Count of FLAN-
1186. DERS, born in the Year *One thousand one hundred fourscore and*
His Marri- *six*. The Queen *Teresa*, called *Maud* of *Portugal* Countess of *Flanders* his
age. Aunt by the Fathers side, procured his Marriage with JANE Countess
1211. of FLANDERS, eldest Daughter and Co-heir of Count *Baldwin*,
who was also Emperour of *Constantinople*; In the right of which Marriage
contracted in the Year *One thousand two hundred and eleven*, the Prince
FERDINAND stiled himself Count of *Flanders*. This Marriage
was made also at the instance and perswasion of *Philip Augustus* King of
France, supposing thereby to make a Friend of this Prince, who promised to remit and render into the possession of *Lewis* Count of *Artois*, the
Kings eldest Son, the Towns of *Aire* and St. *Omer*. But FERDI-
NAND being in possession of the County of *Flanders*, it repented him,
that his promises should deprive him of the right which he pretended to have
to those Towns that he had quitted; This caused him to be more easily induced by the Princes and Barons of his Countrey to alienate himself from
the affection of the King of *France*, and to adhere to the pernitious designs
of his enemies.

So it was, that this Great Monarch having put to Sea with a considerable force to pass into *England*, all the Princes and Barons of *France* shewed
themselves ready and willing to accompany him, except the Count of *Flanders*, who freely declared, that he would not move, except the King would
first restore to him the Towns he had from him. And although he had recompence offered him for the same Towns, yet he returned home with the
demonstration of ill-will against *France*. This caused the King (who would
not suffer so rash a boldness from his Vassal,) to set Sail streight for *Flanders* with that Army he had prepared for *England*, and had so happy success
in this Action, as to subdue the Count to his obedience, and in a small time
to gain a notable Victory upon his Army. By this means the Cities of. *Cas-
sel*, *Ypre*, *Bruges*, and *Gaunt*, and the rest of *Flanders* was reduced into the hands of the King, where he left his Garisons. But he had no
sooner turned his back, but the Count FERDINAND re-entred
with a fresh Army, at the sight of which all the same Cities were again
surrendred.

Sometime after, the *Flemmings* continuing in their disaffection, resolved to revenge themselves upon the King, and to that purpose joyned their
power with the Emperour *Otho IV.* King *John* of *England*, and other
1214. Princes, enemies of the same King *Philip*; But at their Rencounter, which
was near unto *Bonines*, the *French* behaved themselves with so much resolution, that they carried a glorious Victory, by so much the more signal,
because several Princes and Grandees were there made Prisoners, among o-
thers this Count of *Flanders*, who was conducted to the Castle of the *Louure*
at *Paris*, in Triumph, and had the unhappiness to see the *Parisians* rejoyce at
his mis-fortune, and at his arrival to entertain him with scorn and dirision.

Marginalia:
PORTUGAL
Escartelle de
FLANDRES.
D'or au Lyon
Rampant de
sable.

PORTUGAL.
Party de
FLANDRE.

Rigord.
G. Brito in
Philippo.

Mejer.
Marchant.

Rigord.
P. Aemilie.

He

SANCEO I. of the name,

History of France.

Nunez.

He was a Prisoner until the beginning of the Year *One thousand two hundred seven and twenty*, when Queen *Blanch* of *Castille* his Couzin, and Mother of St. LEWIS (having for that purpose made use of all occasions that presented themselves during her Regency) restored him to his liberty, and sent him back into his own Countrey, with intention to oblige him hers, in opposition to the Revolted Princes. So that those Authors misapprehend, who have written that FERDINAND dyed a Prisoner. For six years after his release, his death hapned in the City of *Noyon*, in the Year *One thousand two hundred thirty and three*, being seven and forty years old, his body was deposited at *Marquettes* near unto the City of *Lisle*, an Abbey of Monks of the *Cistertian* Order, and his heart intombed in the Church of our Lady in the same City of *Lisle*, where you may read this Epitaph.

Years of CHRIST. 1227.

His death. 1233.

> *FERNANDI proavos Hispania, Flandria Corpus,*
> *Cor cum visceribus continet iste locus.*

Mejer. Marchantius, Sueyro. Pinzonius.

The Countess JANE of FLANDERS his Widow espoused for her second Husband, in the Year *One thousand two hundred two and thirty*, *Thomas* second of the name, Count of *Maurienne* and *Piedmont*, son of *Thomas* Count of *Savoye*, which *Thomas* in the right of the Princess his Wife, used also the Title and appellation of Earl of *Flanders* and *Henault*.

1232.

She finished her dayes in the Year *One thousand two hundred four and forty*, having Founded several Hospitals, Churches and Religious Houses in the Cities of *Bruges*, *Gaunt*, *Ipre*, and *Lisle*, the Church of the *Beguinees* in the same City of *Bruges*, the Abbey of *Marquettes* above-mentioned, and the *Cordileires* and *Jacobines* at *Valenciennes*, which are so many famous Monuments of her Piety.

1244.

Daughters of FERDINAND OF PORTUGAL, and of JANE, COUNTESSE OF FLANDERS, his Wife.

In Tabat:o Genealog.

5. MARY OF FLANDERS was promised to *Robert*, Count of *Artois*; whom she never married. *Hierosme Henninges* is mistaken, saying, That *she was married to* Thomas of Savoye *son of Count Thomas*. For it was *Jane* her Mother, as we have before expressed.

BEAUJEU.

D'or au lyon de sable, au lambel de gueules de trois pieces.

Party de FLANDRE *qui est de mesme sans le Lambel.*

5. SIBILLE OF FLANDERS, whose Husband was *Guiccard* III. of the name, Lord of *Beaujeu*, as writeth *Claud Paradine* in his *Genealogical Alliances*, who reports, That *there is mention made of her in the Records of the Church of Beaujolois*; adding also, That *she dyed in the Year One thousand two hundred six and twenty*. But this *Guiccard* being deceased Ten years before, as the same Author notes; it's not to be credited, that he had Children by SIBILLE, as he would perswade us, that *he had three*; For the Marriage of *Ferdinando* father of the Princess, was Consummated but five years before the decease of *Guiccard*, and SIBILLE

Her Marriage.

Her Death. 1226.

King of PORTUGAL.   13

Years of CHRIST.

BILLE was at that time too young. Indeed *Andrew de Chesne* seems to doubt whether she were the Daughter of *Ferdinand*, saying, That *if she was of the House of* Flanders, *she might be Sister of* Philip *of* Alsace *Count of Flanders*.

Here follow the Children of SANCEO I. King of PORTUGAL.

4.
His Birth. 1187.

PETER OF PORTUGAL, King of MAJORCA, and Count of *Urgel*, was born in the Year *One thousand one hundred fourscore and seven*; being come to age, whether it were for the displeasure that hapned between him and the King of *Portugal Alphonso* II. his elder Brother, or the desire he had to Travel, and to profit himself by the conversation of strangers, is not certainly known; but depart the Kingdom he did, and was sometime in the Court of the *Miramolin* King of *Morocco*.

His Marriage. 1211.

From thence he took his journey into *Arragon*, where he espoused *Aremburga* Countess of *Urgel*, a rich Heiress, in whose right he was Lord and Count of *Urgel*, and other rich Seigneuries. She dyed without issue in the life-time of her Husband, and for testimony of the conjugal love she did bear to this Prince, she gave him her County, with the right she had in the City of *Valedolit*, and in some other Lordships she possessed in the Kingdom of *Galicia*. But because that *Ponce de Cervera* pretended to the County of *Urgel*, and those other Seigneuries, PETER parted with them all to his Cousin *James* King of *Arragon*, Sirnamed the Conquerour, Son of King *Peter*, who had received him with affection, and also in recompence gave him some Lands in *Arragon* for his Portion and lawful Appennage, which appertained unto him in the right of his Mother the Queen of *Portugal Doulce* of *Arragon*.

Now, *James* having a desire to appropriate to himself this County of *Urgel*, came to a Treaty with Prince PETER OF PORTUGAL, by which he made it over to this King of *Arragon*, with the other Lands in *Galicia*, and in exchange this King gave him the Kingdom and Isle of *Majorca*, and the others adjacent. But the *Moors* of this Countrey having rebelled, and King PETER observing that the King of *Tunes* was preparing a powerful Army for their assistance against him, and finding himself not capable to resist them, made another exchange with the King of *Arragon*; For he having returned him the Kingdom of *Majorca*, *James* remitted him the Cities and Places of *Segorbia*, *Morella*, and others.

His Death. 1235.

The same Prince PETER gave assistance to *William Mongriu* Archbishop of *Saragoca*, with which he subdued the Isle of *Juica* or *Ebuse*, in the Year *One thousand two hundred five and thirty*, about which time he likewise dyed.

PORTUGAL MAJORCA
Escartelle, Au 1. & 4. D'or a quatre pais de gueulles, l'Escu brisé d'un bande aussi de gueulles. Au 2. & 3. de PORTUGAL

PORTUGAL MAJORCA *Escartelle de* URGEL

Hier. Zurita in his Hist. of *Arragon*.

Nunez.
Vasconcellius.

History of *Portugal*.

4.
His Birth. 1189.

HENRY OF PORTUGAL came into the World in the Year *One thousand one hundred fourscore and nine*, and died young in the life-time of King *Sanceo* I. his Father. He lieth in the Abbey of St. *Croix* at *Conimbra*, in the Sepulchre of his Fathers.

4.

TERESA OF PORTUGAL, Queen of LEON, was married unto ALPHONSO King of LEON her Cousin,

E   Son

15 SANCEO I. of the name,

LEON.
D'argent au lyon de pourpre.

Party de PORTUGAL.

Jo. Mariana de reb. Hisp.

Vasconcellius.

Son of King *Ferdinando* II. which Marriage was Consummated without Dispensation.

After the accomplishment of which, there succeeded in *Portugal* several evils and mis-fortunes, the Plague, Famine, and Tempests; Calamities which were attributed to this unlawful Marriage, of which Pope *Celestine* III. being informed, sent into *Portugal*, *William* Cardinal of St. *Angelo* his Legate, who caused the Prelates of this Kingdom, and those of *Leon*, to meet at *Salamanca*, and there was resolved the Divorce and Dissolution of this Marriage; which was done although they had three Children; one Son named *Ferdinand*, who died young, and two Daughters.

After this Dissolution the Princess TERESA resolved to forsake the World, and to incloyster her self in the Nunnery of *Lorvano*, which she restored and enlarged with great Revenues. She there most Piously passed the rest of her dayes, and in the reputation of great Holiness. Also her Tomb having been opened in the Year One thousand six hundred and seventeen, by the Command of the King of *Spain*, *Philip* III. her body was found entire, and her face so ruddy, as if the Princess had been alive, or had departed but some few houres before.

Years of CHRIST.

1617.

4.

CASTILLE
De gueules a un chasteau d'or.

Party de PORTUGAL

Nunez.

Mariana.

MAUD OF PORTUGAL, Queen of CASTILLE, was Wife of HENRY first of the name, King of CASTILLE, eldest Son of *Alphonso* VIII. But they were also separated, because of their proximity of Blood, and that by the sentence of *Momin* Bishop of *Burgos*, and of *Telles* Bishop of *Palencia*, whom the Pope *Innocent* III. had delegated for the *Cognizance* and *decision* of this separation. *Henry* Reigned but a short time, and died by the hurt of a Tile, which, as he was playing with some Lords of his Court, fell with violence upon his head, in the Year One thousand two hundred and seventeen. And deceasing without Children, his Cousin *Ferdinand* III. succeeded him in the Kingdom of *Castille*. After the Dissolution of this Marriage with *Henry*, the Princess MAUD retired into the Monastery of *Arouce* in her Countrey of *Portugal*, which she Founded, and is there interred. If she deceased the second day of *May*, in the Year One thousand two hundred fourscore and ten, as writeth *Vasconcellos*, she attained unto a very great age.

Her Marriage.

1217.

Her Death.
1290.

4. SANCE OF PORTUGAL would never marry, but took upon her Religious Orders, and was Abbess of *Lorvano*. She Founded the Monastery of the Order of St. *Francis* at *Alanquer*; Land which she had for her Portion, or appennage; Her body was ensepultured in the Church of the same place of *Lorvano*.

4. BLANCHE OF PORTUGAL, Lady of *Guadalaiara* in *Castille*, died in that Kingdom, her body was afterwards conveyed into *Portugal* to St. *Croix de Conimbra*.

4. BERENGARIA OF PORTUGAL also was never married, and was educated with her Sister the Queen *Teresa*, in the Abbey of *Lorvano*; she lieth interred also in the same place of St. *Croix de Conimbra*, with her Ancestors.

Bastards

Bastards of King SANCEO I.

4. MARTIN OF PORTUGAL, Count of *Tristemare* in *Galicia*, and two other Counties, was a Knight full of Valour and Courage; Being employed by the King of *Leon* in his Warres, he twice defeated the Armies of the King *Alphonso* II. his Brother. He lieth at *Cosins* of the Order of St. *John*, in the place of *Campos*. He and his Sister *Uracca* were begotten upon *Mary Anez de Fornellos*.

4. URACCA OF PORTUGAL.

4. RODERICK OF PORTUGAL died in a Battel disputed near *Porto*, fighting for the *Portugues*; He is interred in the Monastery of *Grio*; He and his Brother and Sisters, had for their Mother, *Mary Paaez de Ribera*.

4. GILLES SANCEO died, not having been married.

4. TERESA SANCEZ OF PORTUGAL, was espoused unto ALPHONSO TELLEZ the Aged, who built the City of *Albuquerque*.

4. CONSTANCE OF PORTUGAL Founded the Monastery of St. *Francis* of *Conimbra*, upon the River of *Monda*. Her body lieth near unto that of *Sanceo* I. her Father.

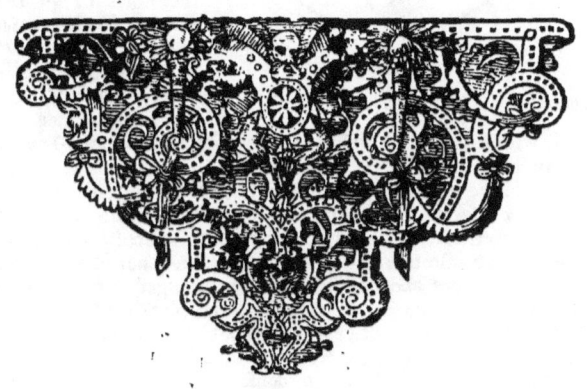

4 ALPHONSO II.
Of the Name, KING of PORTUGAL.
CHAP. IV.

PORTUGAL
Comme cy devant.

PORTUGAL
Party de CASTILLE.
De gueulles au Chasteau d'or.

Vasconcellius.

Nuñez.

Vasconcellius.

His King was born upon the day of the Feast of St. *George*, the three and twentieth of *April*, in the Year, *One thousand one hundred fourscore and five*, and succeeded King *Sanceo* the First his Father, at the Age of Seven and twenty years.

His Birth.
1185.

Following the steps of his Ancestors, he behaved himself Valiantly in several Conflicts against the *Moors*. By the assistance of a Naval Army consisting of those of the *Belgique* Nations, he recovered out of the hands of the *Infidels* the City of *Alcassere de Sal*; which was performed at the instance of *Matthew* Bishop of *Lisbonne*, a man of an holy life.

1217.

In pursuance of which ALPHONSO vanquished the Kings of *Seville*, and of *Jean*, who came to lay Siege to the City of *Juica*.

But if he was plausable in his Military and publick Affairs, he could not avoid the reproach which Posterity hath cast upon him in his History, in what concerned his Domestick, having ill treated his Brothers and Sisters, and his Brother-in-law the King of *Leon*, not suffering them to enjoy the portions and inheritance which belonged unto them, nor performing the Testament and last Will of the King their Father. By reason of which there ensued great Divisions, until that the Pope, unto whom the younger Princes made their recourse, used his Censures and Interdictions against ALPHONSO, and constrained him to submit to Arbitration for the Determination of their Differences, and to undergo the Execution of that Judgement which should be given.

He was tall of stature, of an able body, and so corpulent, that his subjects sirnamed him, *The Gross*, which, it may be, shortned his life; for he
lived

King of PORTUGAL.

Years of CHRIST. His Death. 1233.

lived only Eight and forty years. And after he had Reigned One and twenty years, he expired, *Anno, One thousand two hundred three and thirty*, as *Edwardo Nunez*, and *Antonio Vasconcellos* do note; and not in the Year, *One thousand two hundred twenty and four*, as others have written.

He was inhumed in a Chappel, which he Ordered to be made in the Abbey of *Alcobace*, near unto the Sepulchre of URACCA OF CASTILLE his Wife, Daughter of *Alphonso* VIII. others say IX. of that name, King of *Castille*, and of *Elianor* of *England* his Wife; and Sister of *Blanche* of *Bastille*, Queen of *France*, Mother of the King St. LEWIS. Some years after *George de Mello* Abbot of the Monastery, caused the Corps of King ALPHONSO, and of the Queen his wife, to be transported to the Chappel of St. *Vincent*.

Mariana.

Nunez.

Children of ALPHONSO II. King of PORTUGAL, and of URACCA OF CASTILLE, his Wife.

5. SANCEO II. of the name, King of PORTUGAL, whose Elogie followeth.

5. ALPHONSO OF PORTUGAL III. of the name, first Count of *Bolongne* in *France*, then King of *Portugal*, after his Elder Brother; continued the Posterity.

5. FERDINAND OF PORTUGAL, called the Infant of SERPE, because he was Lord of this place in the Kingdom of *Castille*, espoused SANCE-FERNANDINE DE LARA, Daughter of the Count *Ferdinando de Lara*. This Prince of SERPE is intombed at *Alcobace*, and from them came one only Daughter, who followeth.

PORTUGAL-SERPE

PORTUGAL-SERPE

Party de LARA. Gueulles a deux chaudieres d'or liées sur l'autre chacune chargee de trois traits de sable courbez en fac', avec sept serpenteaux d'or sortant de chaque costé des oreilles des ances, trois en dedans, quatre en dehors.

6. LEONOR OF PORTUGAL, who is said to have been married to a Prince Heir apparent to the Kingdom of DENMARK; He was (as some say) VALDEMAR, Son of another *Valdemar* second of the name, King of *Denmark*, who outlived his Son, deceasing in the Year, *One thousand two hundred one and thirty*; The Father was also allied to this House of *Portugal*, as you shall see hereafter. *Erpold Lindenbruch* in his History of the Kings of *Denmark*, maketh mention of these two Marriages; he corrupteth the name of the Princess LEONOR, whom he calleth *Bormegera*, adding also by mistake, That *she was Sister of the Count of Flanders*. He notes her death to happen in the Year, *One thousand two hundred and twenty*.

1231.

Erpold Lindenbruch in Hist. Daniæ Regum.

1220.

5. VINCENT OF PORTUGAL, fourth Son of King *Alphonso* II. died young.

5. LEONOR OF PORTUGAL their Sister, was (according to some Historians of *Allmaine*,) third wife of VALDEMAR II. of that name, King of DENMARK, who died in the Year, *One thousand*

His Marriage. 1241.

DENMARK. D'or a trois Leopards d'azure couronnez.

F

armes & lam- *sand two hundred and forty one.* Hierosme Henninges reports her to be Si- Years of
pillez de gueul- ster of *Ferdinando* of *Portugal* Count of *Flanders*; but it may be that he CHRIST.
les, le seu seme meaneth Lord of *Serpe.* He addeth that she had by this *Danish* Prince se-
de tours aussi ven Sons, and three Daughters; three of which Sons, *viz. Eric* VII.
de gueules. *Christopher* I. and *Abel,* were successively Kings of *Denmark.* From *Chri-*
Party de *stopher,* descended *Eric* VIII. Father of *Eric* IX. and of *Christopher* II.
PORTUGAL all also Kings of *Denmark.* *Valdemar* IV. Son of this last King, was Father
of *Margaret* Queen of the Potent Kingdoms of *Denmark, Sweden,* and *Norwey.*

Natural Sons of King ALPHONSO II.

5. JOHN-ALPHONSO OF PORTUGAL, finished his dayes in the Year of our Salvation, *One thousand two hundred foure and thirty,* and lieth in the Monastery of *Alcobace.*

Those that have written, that this King ALPHONSO II. had another Natural Son, named *Martin-Alphonso,* are mistaken, for he was Son of King *Alphonso* III. as shall appear hereafter in his place.

PORTUGAL
D'argent au cinq Escussons d'Azure, chacun chargé de cinq besans d', argent.

5. SANCEO II.
Of the Name, KING of PORTUGAL.
CHAP. V.

PORTUGAL
Party de
MARO.
D'argent a l'Abre de Gra-mea de Synople, a deux Loups de sable tra-versez au pied de cest Abre, c'est à dire l'un devant, & l'au-tre d'erriere l'Abre, laquelle est entre ces deux loups a l'Orle de gueules charge de sept Croix en saltoir d'or.

Mong the Children 1233.
of *Alphonso* II. His
and of *Uracca* of Birth.
Castille this
Prince who came
into the World in the Year,
One thousand two hundred and 1207.
seven, the Eighth day of *September,* was the eldest.

Who brought with him from the womb such mortal infirmities, as made most believe, he would sooner arrive at the grave, than the Scepter, the Queen his Mother having tryed all humane remedies, applyed her self to Divine, making a Vow to God, that if he lived past his adolescency, she would make him pass the Hood of Canons Regular of the Order of St. *Augustine,* which she inviolably performed, and from which habit this King

was

King of PORTUGAL.

was firnamed CAPELLO. Also he appeared more apt and proper for a monaſtick and quiet life, than to the exerciſe of War, and the Government of his Kingdom, to which he ſucceeded at the age of Six and twenty years.

Alſo the Queen of *Caſtille Berengaria*, (his Couſin) who had the Government of this Prince, obſerving him to be of a weak Judgement, endeavoured to match him to ſome Lady of an Illuſtrious Houſe, that in defect of her Husband, might be capable of the management of his affairs. But ſome Grandees of the Kingdom oppoſed this deſign, prevented her, and clandeſtinely married him to SANCE-MENTIE-LOPEZ DE HARO, daughter of *Diego-Lopez de Haro*, Lord of *Biſcay*, and of *Uracca* natural daughter of *Alphonſo IX.* King of *Leon*. After which ſeveral of the Prelates having made Remonſtrance to the Pope of the unlawfulneſs of the Marriage, which had been effected without the Diſpenſation of the Holy See; which was required by reaſon of the proximity of blood betwixt the parties, and for that the King alſo continued in the evil Government of his Eſtate, during which time ſeveral miſchiefs had been committed, they ſupplicated Pope *Gregory IX.* for a remedy.

Who ſent therefore his Legate Apoſtolick, the Biſhop of *Sabine*, into *Portugal*, after whoſe departure the oppreſſion, diſorders, and popular Sedition ſtill remained as before; theſe calamities cauſed the Prelates and ſome of the Grandees to make their ſecond application to *Rome*, at what time *Innocent IV.* ſate in the Holy Chair; who Ordered (with a *Salvo* to the Authority Royal, and the Children of King SANCEO, if he ſhould have any) that the Count of *Bolongne*, *Alphonſo* his younger Brother, ſhould take the Reins of the Government, and the adminiſtration of affairs into his hand; as he did accordingly.

But SANCEO unwilling to quit his Kingdom and lawful inheritance, made his recourſe for aſſiſtance to the King of *Caſtille*, who ſent him an Army, with which he entred the field, but with ſo little ſucceſs, that he was forced to disband his Souldiers, and ſecure himſelf by retiring to the City of *Toledo* in *Caſtille*; from which time he addicted himſelf wholly to devotion and a private life, diſtributing Alms to the poor of what he had brought out of *Portugal*, living with great auſterity, and ſupporting his exile and other calamities, with an admired patience and conſtancy. But there were yet among his Subjects thoſe who remained unſhaken in that duty and fidelity which they had ſworne, who made his re-eſtabliſhment their endeavours; but their deſign was interrupted by the news of his death happening in the Year, *One thouſand two hundred ſix and forty*, in the ſame City of *Toledo*; he lieth in the Cathedral Church, his body being interred in a Sepulchre which he had prepared in his life-time.

Some Hiſtorians, and among others *Mariana* in the thirteenth Book of his Hiſtory of *Spain*, extendeth his Life to fifty years, and his Reign to three and thirty, *John Vaſee* ſaith ſix and twenty, but they are both in an errour, for *Edward Nunez* hath made appear in his Chronicle of *Portugal*, who tells us more certainly, that he lived only Nine and thirty years, and Governed thirteen. And dying without iſſue, he had for his Succeſſor to the Crown, his younger brother Prince *Alphonſo*, of whom we have ſpoken.

F 2 ALPHON-

5. ALPHONSO III.
Of the Name, KING of PORTUGAL and the ALGARVES.

CHAP. VI.

PORTUGAL.
D'argent a cinq Escussons posez en Croix d'azure chacun chargé de cinq besans d'argent posé en sautoire à la bordure de gueules chargée de dix Chasteaux d'or.

PORTUGAL
Ancien comme cy devant, sans la bordure de gueules.

Party de
BOLONGNE.
D'or a trois Tourteaux de gueules, 2. 1.

PORTUGAL
Comme cy dessus, aussi sans la bordure.

Party de
CASTILLE.
De gueules a un Chasteau d'or.

Year after this Prince was established Regent of *Portugal*, he ascended the Throne by the decease (without issue) of his elder brother King *Sanceo II*. both sons of King *Alphonso*, also Second of the name, and of *Uracca* of *Castille*, being at that time aged about Six and thirty years. For he was born at *Conimbra* the Tenth day of *May*, Anno, *One thousand two hundred and ten*.

The Queen of *France*, *Blanche* of *Castille*, his Aunt by the Mothers side, entertained him in the Court of her son the King St. *Lewis*, and also procured his Marriage (in the Year, *One thousand two hundred and thirty five* (according to the Historian of *Portugal*, *Nunez*, and not ten years after following the opinion of other Writers) with MAUD OF DAMMARTIN Countess of BOLONGNE; eldest daughter of *Rainaud* Count of *Dammartin* in his own right, and of *Bolongne* in the right of the Countess *Ida* his Wife, which MAUD was at that time Widow to *Philip* of *France*, younger son of King *Philip Augustus*.

This Prince ALPHONSO, after his Marriage, had the Title of Count of *Bolongne*; And gave such notable testimonies of his Virtue, that the Pope elected him Captain of those Knights of the *Cruciada*, who were judged worthy to carry their Valour into the *Holy Land* against the Enemies of our Faith, but he was diverted this Honour, by the necessity of his return into *Portugal*, to put an end to those troubles which were moved by the ambition of those who presumed upon the plyable nature of King SANCEO II. his brother.

Years of Christ.
1246.

His Birth.
1210.

His Marriage.
1235.

After

King of PORTUGAL and the ALGARVES.

Years of CHRIST.

After he was come to the Crown, he found difficulty enough to establish himself, wherefore he was necessitated to reduce some Places by force, and to carry himself severely towards his Nobility.

Nunez.

Home-bred stirs being quieted, he gave his mind to the Building of several Cities of his Kingdom, and also Founded two Monasteries of the Order of the *Jacobines*, one at *Lisbonne*, the other at *Elvas*, and the Abbey of *Nunnes* of the Order of St *Clare* at *Santarem*; and furthermore, he instituted several Fairs for the increase of Commerce with his Neighbours, delighting much in Traffique, and for the encouragement thereof, remitting his Customs.

Mariana. Nunez.

But as all these generous Acts acquired him a grand reputation, yet he also underwent an unhappy scandal, for notwithstanding his lawful Wife the Princess MAUD was then living, he endeavoured to violate the holy Laws of Marriage; For under pretext that this Princess was too old, and so incapable of bringing him Children, he espoused another Wife, (about the Year, *One thousand two hundred and threescore*,) which was BEATRICE OF CASTILLE, natural daughter of *Alphonso IX*. King of *Castille*, and of *Mary Vilena*, daughter of *Peter de Gusman*; some write, that the King of *Castille* gave in Dower to this BEATRICE his daughter, the Kingdom of *Algarves*, a good part of which ALPHONSO III. gained out of the hands of the *Moors*.

His 2d. Marriage. 1260.

In consideration of this alliance, he added to the Armes of *Portugal*, *A Border gueulles charged with seven Castles Or*: Which some believe to be the Armes of the Kingdom of *Algarvie*, the Title of which King ALPHONSO also joyned with that of *Portugal*.

Castella aurea in Campo rubro per circum, sunt Insignia Regni Algarbiorum unici Lusitanio; ea primo posuit Sancius 1. Rex 2 quoniam Algarbia cepit à Sarracenis; sed, eo Regno ad ipsis Infidelibus recuperato, cessarunt Castella; quousq, ALPHONSUS 3. Rex 5. eo iterum obtento, Castellorum restituit circum. Fuit aurem numerus Castellorum diversus usq, ad tempus Johannis 1. qui reformans in omnibus Regium scutum secundùm regulam, reduxit Castella ad septem (qui numerus perstictus) prout apparent hodiè. Dom. Anto. de Sousa. Lusit. Liberat. Appen. Cap. 1.

Vasconcellius.
The Border and Castles are added to the Arms of Portugal.

Now MAUD understanding the design of the King her Husband, to take another wife; From *France* she undertook a journey into *Portugal*, and there made her protestations and opposition against this unlawful Marriage, which ALPHONSO regarded not, but slightly passed over. When this would not move him to Justice, the Princess and her kindred, (of the number of which was the King St. *Lewis*) made their appeal to Pope *Alexander IV*. with whom their complaint and the Princesses tears took such effect, that he first mildly admonished ALPHONSO to receive again his lawful wife, and forsake BEATRIX, but continuing refractory and stubborn, the same Pope thundred out his Excommunications against him and his Kingdom, prohibiting Divine Service throughout all his Dominions, under which Interdiction he lay the space of two years, and to the death of MAUD happening in the Year, *One thousand two hundred threescore and two*, when the Prelates of the Kingdom so carried the matter to Pope *Urban IV*. that he not only removed this Excommunication, but also approved the Marriage; this proceeded principally from the Relation of kindred the said Pope had to the King ALPHONSO, and for the peace and welfare of the Kingdom.

Mariana.

1262.

Nunez.

MAUD having made her last Will and Testament in the Year, *One thousand two hundred forty and one*, bequeathed unto her Husband King ALPHONSO, the Summe of Twenty thousand Livers, beside the right she had to another Summe of Four thousand *l*. due unto her by the

Idem.

G Count

ALPHONSO III. of the name,

Mariana.

Count and Countess of *Flanders*. Also to others she left many pious Legacies, and ordered for the Executors of this her last Testament, *Robert* Bishop of *Beauvais*, her Cousin *Matthew de Trie*, and others; Gifts which were approved by *Gaucher de Chastillon sieur de Monjay* her Kinsman, who had espoused *Jane* her daughter, descended from her first Marriage.

Nunez.
Vasconcellius.

Lastly, King ALPHONSO having lived Threescore and nine years, and Reigned Three and thirty, finished his dayes at *Lisbonne*, the Capital City of his Estate, in the Year, *One thousand two hundred threescore and nineteen*. He received the honour of Sepulture within the Church of St. *Dominick* in the same place; and from thence, ten years after, his body was transported to the Chappel dedicated to St. *Vincent* in the Abbey of *Alcobace*, where lieth also Queen *Beatrix* of *Castille* his Wife.

His Death.
1279.

Traité du droit de succession sur la Portugal de la Royne Catherine de Medicis.

Some are of opinion, that he had by the Countess of *Bolongne* two sons, the elder of which, named after him *Alphonso*, dyed young; the younger called *Robert*, lived in *France*, and was Count of *Bolongne*, from whom are descended the other Earls unto *Jane de la Tour*, who exchanged this County for that of *Lauregais*, and had issue her daughter *Magdelene de la Tour*, Mother of Queen *Katherine de Medicis*, wife of *Henry II*. King of *France*. The same Queen, as being descended from *Robert*, pretended a right to the Kingdom of *Portugal* after the death of the Kings *Sebastian* and *Henry*. And at what time the Estates were assembled to Advise of a Successor to the Crown, she sent her Embassadors also thither to represent her Right and Pretentions, as also did several other Princes upon the same account. At the same time there was published in *France* a Treatise (which is reputed to have for Author *Peter Beloy* afterwards the Kings Advocate in the Court of Parliament of *Toulouse*) concerning the right and lawful succession of the Kingdom of *Portugal* appertaining to this Queen *Katherine*, Mother of the most Christian King *Henry III*.

En Chronica des Reis de Portugal.

But the *Castillian* and *Portugal* Historians, among others *Edward Nunez*, will not admit of this descent of the House of *Bolongne*, nor that ALPHONSO III. had any children by Queen MAUD his first Wife. But to confound this extraction, and to prove it only imaginary, he grounds upon divers Circumstances, and pregnant Conjectures, which he particularly toucheth upon in the Chronicle of the Kings of *Portugal*, by him published in his own Language; Conjectures drawn from the time, as also from the consideration of the Age of the Princess, and the words of her last Testament (in which there is mention made only of her daughter by the first Bed.) And lastly, from the Contents of that Supplication presented by the Prelates to the Pope, intreating his Holiness to give Absolution to their King, and a Dispensation, to the end that he and *Beatrix* might lawfully continue and live together, and that their Children after them might be capable of the possession of their Estates.

1262.

Children of ALPHONSO III. King OF PORTUGAL, and of BEATRIX OF CASTILLE, his second Wife.

6. D IONYSIO OR DENIS King OF PORTUGAL, and the ALGARVES, continued the Posterity.

ALPHON-

King of PORTUGAL and the ALGARVES. 23

Years of CHRIST.
6.
His Marriage.

ALPHONSO OF PORTUGAL, Lord of *Portalegre*, *Chasteauvieux*, *Marvau*, and of *Arouce*, was joyned in Marriage with **YOLAND OF CASTILLE**, daughter of the Infant *Emanuel*, son of *Ferdinando III.* King of *Castille*, and of *Constance* of *Arragon* his Wife. And because that **ALPHONSO** married his daughters to *Castillian* Lords, and would have given them those places of his appennage in *Portugal*, his brother King **DIONYSIO** opposed him. But this difference was at last appeased, by exchange made betwixt the King and this Lord of *Portalegre*, who consented to part with places upon the Frontire of *Castille*, for those that were situate within the middle of *Portugal*. He was inhumed in the Church of St. *Dominick* at *Lisbonne*, and left issue a Son, and four Daughters, which follow.

PORTUGAL OR-TALEGRE.
Party de CASTILLE.
De gueules au Chasteau d'or.

7. **ALPHONSO OF PORTUGAL**, Seigneur of *Leiria*, dyed without Children.

7. **ISABEL OF PORTUGAL**, Wife of **JOHN** Lord of **BISCAY**, sirnamed the *Purblind*.

BISCAY. Comme cy devant.
Party de PORTUGAL.

7. **CONSTANCE OF PORTUGAL**, espoused to **GONCALE-NUNEZ DE LARA**, son of *John Nunez de Lara*, called the *Good*.

LARA.
Party de PORTUGAL

7. **MARY OF PORTUGAL** was conjoyned in Marriage with **TELLEZ** son of *Alphonso*, Infant **OF MOLINA**.

7. **ISABEL OF PORTUGAL**, sirnamed the *Young*, to difference her from her elder Sister of the same name, was married unto **JOHN-ALPHONSO**, Lord of *Albuquerque*, son of *Alphonso-Sanceo*, who was Nephew of *Dionysio* King of *Portugal*.

Here follow the Children of King ALPHONSO III. and of BEATRIX OF CASTILLE.

6. **FERDINAND OF PORTUGAL** dyed young in the City of *Lisbonne*.

6. **BLANCHE OF PORTUGAL**, Abbess of *Loruano*, then of that *Das Holgas* at *Burgos*. This Princess was exceeding rich: For the King of *Castille*, her Grand-father by the Mother, and King *Dionysio* her Brother, gave her the Seigneuries of *Monmor le Vieil*, and *Campo-Major*.

6. **CONSTANCE OF PORTUGAL**, having been with Queen *Beatrix* her Mother in *Castille*, for to visit the King her Grand-father, she there dyed in the City of *Seville*, being young. Her body was brought home, and buried in the Abbey of *Alcobace*.

Natural

Natural Children of ALPHONSO III. King OF PORTUGAL.

6. FERDINAND-ALPHONSO OF PORTUGAL, Knight of the Order of the Templars, lieth at *Lisbonne* in the Church of St. *Blaise*.

6. GILLES-ALPHONSO OF PORTUGAL, was father of *Lawrence-Gilles*, Baily of the Commandrie of the same Church of St. *Blaise*.

6. ALPHONSO-DIONYSIO OF PORTUGAL, espoused MARY DE RIBEIRA, by whom he had *Pedro-Alphonso*, *Roderick*, and *Diego-Alphonso*; and *Garsia Mendez*, Prior of *Alcaceua* of *Santarem*.

> *Diego-Alphonso* son of *Alphonso Dionysio*; married *Yoland Lopez* daughter of *Lopo Fernandez* Lord of *Ferreira*, and of *Mary Gomez Tauiera*, and had issue *Alvaro* and *Lopo Dia*, from which *Lopo* descend those of *Sousa*, which at present are called *Diabos*.

6. MARTIN-ALPHONSO CHICORRO DE PORTUGAL, another natural son of King *Alphonso III.* by a Moorish Woman, hath given original to the Lords so called; some (but erroneously) suppose this MARTIN was son of King *Alphonso II.*

6. LEONOR OF PORTUGAL, Wife of Count GARSIA DE SOUSA, a Nobly qualified Lord, whom his Father-in-law King *Alphonso* honoured with the Title of a Count.

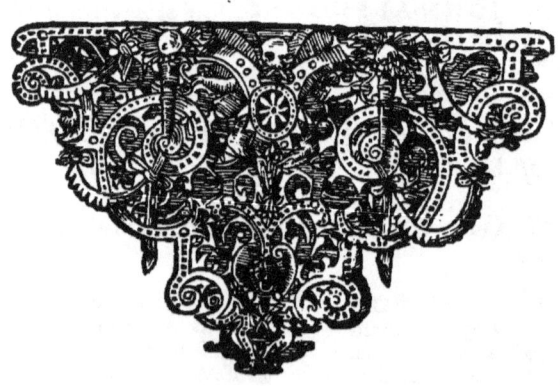

DIONY-

6. DIONYSIO
KING of PORTUGAL and the ALGARVES, firnamed, *Father of his Countrey.*
CHAP. VII.

Years of Christ.

1279.

His Birth. 1261.

TO King *Alphonso* III. succeeded this his eldest son, whom he had by *Beatrix* of *Castille* his second Wife. The time of his Birth was in the Year, *One thousand two hundred threescore and one*, upon the Ninth day of *October*, being the Feast of St. *Dionysius*, wherefore he was called by the name of that great Areopagite.

He was a Prince both Pious, Just, and Liberal, and moreover, so singular an Admirer of Truth, of which he was so Grand and Religious an observer, that he was never known to make breach of his promise, often saying, That, *Nothing was more offensive, than an Untruth.*

He had arrived at the Eighteenth year of his age at the death of his father, at what time he took the reins of the Government into his own hand, when the Queen his Mother fearing that by his too prodigal Liberality and profuseness, he would exhaust the Treasure of the Kingdom, desired to take a part with him in the administration of his affairs. But this, King DIONYSIO would not consent unto, which so much incensed the Queen, that she retired into *Castille*, under pretext of a Religious desire she had to give assistance to the King her father, and being gray with age, she there finished her mortal life, before which nevertheless King DIONYSIO went into *Castille*, where he obtained a reconciliation, and had the happiness to comfort her at her last gasp.

PORTUGAL.
D'argent a cinq Escussons d'Azure chacun charge de cinq besans d' argent peris en sultoir, a la Bordure de gueulles chargee de huict Chasteaux d'or.

PORTUGAL
Party de
ARARGON.
D'or a quatre pals de gueulles.

Nunez

But

DIONYSIO King of PORTUGAL

(margin: Mar. an.) But King *Sancto* of *Castille* making little reckoning of performance of the agreements of Marriage made betwixt his Children, and those of King DIONYSIO, gave ground to that Warre set on foot betwixt them, in the beginning of which *Sancto* deceasing, his Son and Successor continued it, *(margin: Vasconcellius.)* who was so Canvased by the *Portugueses*, that he was constrained to Demand the Peace; which not long after he violated, and so again, to his great prejudice, drew upon himself the just Armes of King DIONYSIO. But their discords ended in another agreement sealed and confirmed by the knot of other alliances of Marriage reciprocally contracted between their Houses of *Castille* and *Portugal*.

(margin: Nunez.) The differences between the Kings of *Castille* and *Arragon*, and *Alfonso de la Cerda*, who pretended to the Kingdom of *Castille*, being put to the Arbiterment of this King DIONYSIO, he shewed the admirable effects of his wisdom in composing their discords, and left them to the enjoyment of a most happy peace.

But the Divisions and Civil Warre happening betwixt him and his son and Successor the Prince *Alphonso*, jealous and envious of the affection which the King did bear to *Alphonso-Sancto* his natural brother, gave him some trouble in his declining years, for though the Bastard had fled into *Castille*, yet this young Prince ceased not to continue discontents towards *(margin: Mariana. Nunez. Vasconcellius.)* his father, who having held the Scepter six and forty years, and lived threescore and four, dyed at *Santarem* in the Year, One thousand three hundred twenty and five, the seventh day of *January*. His body was brought and interred in the Monastery of St. *Dionysius*, called *Odivelles*, Religious of the Order of the *Cistertians*, by him founded, and situate three Leagues from *Lisbonne*. Nor was this the only Foundation of his raising: For the Monastery of *Nunns* of the Order of St. *Clare* at *Conimbra* (which Queen ISABEL OF ARRAGON his Wife Founded, and where she was inhumed,) oweth much to his Liberality.

His Death. 1325.

(margin: Ath. Mirans. Hil. de Costo. Marin. Siculus.) He espoused this Princess in the Year, One thousand two hundred fourscore and two, who was daughter of *Peter III.* King of *Arragon*, and of *Constance*, who had for father *Manfroy* King of *Sicelie*, and for Grand-father *(margin: Vasconcellius. Perpinian.)* by the Mothers side, the Emperour *Frederick II.* ISABEL was born in the Year, One thousand two hundred threescore and eleven. In the whole course of her life, especially in her younger years, she wholly dedicated her self to Piety and Devotion, exercising several works of Charity, principally towards the poor and indigent, and was the instrument of the accord and reconciliation betwixt the Princes her kindred. She vailed her self a Nun of the third Order of St. *Francis*. In fine, as she made a journey into *Castille*, to endeavour an Agreement betwixt her Son the King of *Portugal*, *Alphonso IV.* and the King of *Castille*, *Alphonso IX.* her Nephew, she found out her heavenly rest at *Estremos*, in the Year, One thousand three hundred six and thirty, being aged Threescore and five years. And because there had been several Miracles wrought at her Tomb, it was first beautified by Pope *Leo X.* then in our dayes, and in the Year of *Jubile*, One thousand six hundred and twenty five, Pope *Urban VIII.* Canonized her, and entred her in the Catalogue of Saints, the Five and twentieth day of *May*, being the Feast of the *Trinity*; this was performed at the intreaty of *Philip IV.* King of *Spain*, and of Queen *Elizabeth* of *France* his Wife.

His Marriage. 1282.

1271.

1336.

1625.

Several famous men have written the Life and Actions of this good and Pious Princess, among others *John Peter Perpinian*, and *Antonio Vasconcellos*.

and the ALGARVES.

concellos, Jesuites, and *Aubert le Mire*, grand Dean of the Church of our Lady at *Anuers*; but more particularly than all the rest, *P. Hillarian de Coste*, a Frier Minor of the Order of St. *Francis de Paula*, hath most ingeniously treated thereof.

This King DIONYSIO, in the Year, *One thousand three hundred and eighteen* (others say twenty) Instituted the Military ORDER OF CHRIST, which is the chief of the three Orders of *Portugal*. The Knights live according to the rule of the *Cistercians*, wear a *black Robe*, and upon that a *Cross Pateé Red*, surmounted by a *Plain Cross. White*. This Order was Confirmed by Pope *John XXII*. The King gave unto the Knights the Towns and Lands which the Templars (but a little before abrogated) had in *Portugal*, and for their principal abode, the City of *Tomar*.

This Order of Christus, had Cōmandries not only in Portugal, and Algarue; but in Affrica and the Indies also, and especially in Brasile, which made the Mastership thereof seem so wealthy, that it amounted to the yearly rent of an Hundred thousand Ducates. And this was the reason why it was annexed inseparably (as well as that D' Avis) to the Crown of Portugal; The Kings thereof having taken the Title of Perpetual Administrators of the Orders D' Avis, and of Christus. And. Favine. fol. 188.

A. Favin.
The Order of *Christ* instituted.

This Prince was so great an Admirer of Learning, that he established the Famous University of *Conimbra* in his Kingdom. He was a Lover of *Poesie*, unto which he sometimes addicted himself. And so much favoured Labouring men (by the example of one of his Ancestors) that he bestowed upon them several Immunities and Priviledges, giving them the appellation of *The Nerves of the Earth*. In Brief, His excellent Government, his Ordinances and Rules for the order of Justice, and the Cities and Towns which he either built or restored; did deservedly merit him the name of *Father of his Countrey*. So that whatsoever his Illustrious Predecessors made themselves Renowned for, in Martial Performances, he commanded and acquired by those of Peace, and Policy.

Vasconcellius.

Children of DIONYSIO *King of* PORTUGAL, *and of* St. ISABEL OF ARRAGON *his Wife*.

7. ALPHONSO VI. King of PORTUGAL, continued the Posterity.

7. CONSTANCE OF PORTUGAL, Queen of CASTILLE, was espoused to FERDINAND IV. King of *Castille*, who dyed in the Year, *One thousand three hundred and ten*. He was son of King *Sancho IV*. From this Marriage proceeded King *Alphonso IX*. who by *Mary* of *Portugal* had issue *Peter*, firnamed the *Cruel*, also King of *Castille*. By a Love-Mistress he had several Bastards, among others *Henry* Count of *Tristemare*, who usurped the Kingdom of *Castille* by aide of the *French*. CONSTANCE deceased in the Year, *One thousand three hundred and thirteen*, in the Month of *November*.

Her Marriage.

Her death. 1313.

CASTILLE.
Escartele Au 1. & 4. de gueules au Chasteau d'or. Au 2. & 3. d'argent au lyon de pourpre.
Party de PORTUGAL.

Natural

Natural Children of DIONYSIO King of PORTUGAL.

7. *Vasconcellius.* ALPHONSO-SANCEO Count of *Albuquerque*, was affectionately loved by the King his father, to the great displeasure and jealousie of his lawful Son; who forced him to flie into *Castille*, as we have said; But returning into *Portugal* with a Force, they had some disputes, after which they came to an agreement.

7. *Nunez.* PETER OF PORTUGAL, Count of *Barcellos*, wrote a Book of the Illustrious Houses of *Portugal*; he received the honour of Burial in the Church of St. *John de Tenrouce*.

7. ALPHONSO IV.
King of Portugal and the Algarves.
CHAP. VIII.

PORTUGAL
Comme cy devant.

Party de CASTILLE.

Escartelé au 1. & 4. de gueules au Chasteau d'or; au 2. & 3. d'argent au lyon de pourpre.

The beginning of the Year, One thousand two hundred fourscore and ten, was remarkable in *Portugal* for the Birth of this Prince, which fell out to be at *Conimbra* in the Month of *February*. He came to the Crown at the age of Thirty five years. And either for the tartness of his Disposition, or the grandure of his Courage, was called the *Bold*.

His Birth. 1290.

He still continued in that unwarrantable Hatred towards his brother *Sanceo*, whom by his own Judgement he banished the Kingdom, deprived of his Honours and Dignities, seized upon his Lands, and confiscated his Goods: *Sanceo* was at that time in *Castille*, who by Letters made his application to King ALPHONSO, but his Prayers wrought little effect upon the hard and obstinate heart of his brother; wherefore seeing intreaties would not soften him;

Years of Christ. him, the Bastard resolves to force that with the reason and Justice of his Sword, which his supplications could not obtain, raises an Army, enters *Portugal*, takes several places, and layes the Countrey waste; The King also draws into the Field, where he performs the like acts of Hostility, but at length an agreement was made betwixt them.

The end of this Warre, was the beginning of another Commotion, betwixt the Father-in-law and the Son, this King of *Portugal* and the King of *Castille Alphonso XI.* who being incensed for that the *Portugueses* would marry the Princess *Constance* (daughter of the Infant *John-Emanuel*, descended from King *Ferdinand* of *Castille*, called the *Holy*) to his Son the Prince *Pedro*; These Princes were upon the point of another Cruel Warre, but that Pope *Benedict XII.* and the King of *France, Philip IV.* perfected a reconciliation betwixt them, shewing these two Kings the danger that *Spain* at that time did undergo, by reason of the progress the *Moors* had made, and that their Armies would be better employed against the Enemies of their Faith, the *Infidels*, than in the ruine of themselves; To whom the Holy Queen of *Portugal*, *Isabel* of *Arragon*, having joyned her prayers, things were at last agreed. *Vasconcellim.*

So the two Kings, of Enemies, being made Friends, joyned their Forces against their common adversaries the *Moors*, conducted by *Albohacen* King of *Fez*, and *Joseph* King of *Granada*, who had laid a straight Siege to *Tariffa*, which they resolved to raise maugre the almost numberless number, and (to be imagined) invincible Troops of these Barbarians, they gave them a Field near unto the River *Salado*, in which famous Battel, the two Christian Kings (both ALPHONSO's) engaged them with so indefatigable and undaunted Resolutions, that they obtained a most Famous Victory, and a Glorious Trophy, which hapned in the Year, *One thousand three hundred and forty.* An incredible number of these *Infidels* were killed both upon the Field, and in the pursuit. And if we will believe the *Castillian* Historians, there dyed of them Two hundred thousand, the *Portugal* Histories say Four hundred thousand, with the loss only of twenty of the Christians. These two Kings by this wonderful Victory, gained a grand reputation in the world, and that reputation a security to their estates. The King of *Portugal* took prisoner with his own hands, the son of *Albohali*, then King of *Salamanque*, whom he brought Captive into *Portugal*. *Garibai. Marians. Lib. 16. C. 7. The famous Battel of Tariffa, or Salado, 1340.*

1355. Not long after his arrival, at the instigation of some evil instruments of his Court, he stained his reputation in the cruel Execution of *Agnes de Castro*, of whom his son was most passionately enamoured, taking her as his Wife after the death of the Princess *Constance*; from this Original sprung that most Unnatural Warre betwixt the father and the son, which was looked upon by Historians, as a judgement from God, who had permitted, that ALPHONSO should suffer the same injuries from his son, which he had done to his father. *Nunez.*

His Death. 1357. ALPHONSO IV. dyed at *Lisbonne* in the Month of *May*, One thousand three hundred fifty and seven, after he had performed the Kingly Office, One and thirty years, and five Months; and lived Threescore and seven. He lieth in the Cathedral Church with the Queen BEATRICE OF CASTILLE his Wife, who was daughter of King *Sancto IV.* and of *Mary* of *Molina* his Wife. He was a Lover of Justice; Magnanimous; and resembled in many good parts King *Dionysio* his father, but was far inferior to him in the Virtue of Liberality; he is blamed also for the immoderate love he had to the exercise of Hunting. *Marians. Nunez.*

I   He

30 ALPHONSO IV. *King of* PORTUGAL, &c.

He took for his Device, a Stone, upon which stood an Eagle with his Wings expanded; This was the Soul, ALTIORA PETO, to signifie, that he aspired to High and Celestial things.

Years of CHRIST.

Children of ALPHONSO IV. King OF PORTUGAL, and of BEATRIX OF CASTILLE, his Wife.

Nunez.

8. ALPHONSO OF PORTUGAL, dyed young at *Penelle*, and lieth in the Church of St. *Dominick* at *Santarem*.

8. DIONYSIO OF PORTUGAL, deceased at a year old, and was inhumed in the Church of the Abbey of *Alcobace*, at the feet of King *Alphonso III.* his great Grand-father.

8. JOHN OF PORTUGAL, dyed also in his youth, and was ensepultured at *Odivelles*, (a Monastery of Religious, dedicated to St. *Bernard*) near unto King *Denis* his Grand-father.

8. PETER succeeded his father in the Kingdom OF PORTUGAL, and continued the Line.

CASTILLE.
Escartelé Au 1. & 4. de gueulles au Chasteau d'or; au 2. & 3. d'argent au lyon de pourpre.

Party de PORTUGAL

Mariana. Lib. 16. C. 23.

8. MARY OF PORTUGAL, Queen of CASTILLE, was conjoyned in Marriage with *Alphonso XI.* King OF CASTILLE AND LEON, eldest son of King *Ferdinand IV*. She was espoused unto him in the Year, One thousand three hundred eight and thirty; and they had issue *Peter* the Cruel King of *Castille*. MARY deceased at *Evora*, and was interred in the Chappel Royal, having in her life-time suffered many indignities. For *Alphonso* her Husband forsook her, and bestowed his affections upon *Leonora de Gusman* his Concubine. An History of *Spain* tells us that she dyed in the Year, One thousand three hundred six and fifty. Her too much freedom, and prodigal Carriage to *Martin Tellez* a *Portugal* Lord, was the cause why she was poysoned by her brother, nay, some stick not to say, by her own father. *Alphonso XI*. left this world in the Year, One thousand three hundred and fifty; after he had by the Aid of the King of *Portugal* his Father-in-law, vanquished the Moors at *Teriffa*, as we have before written.

Her Marriage. 1338.

1356.

1350.

ARRAGON.
D'or a quatre pals de gueulles.

Party de PORTUGAL

8. LEONORA OF PORTUGAL, Queen of ARRAGON, had for her Spouse PETER IV. King of ARRAGON, eldest Son of King *Alphonso IV.* and of *Teresa* Countess of *Urgel*. This Marriage was consummated in the Year, One thousand three hundred eight and forty, *Peter* being at that time a Widower, his first Wife was *Mary* of *Navarre*. He deceased at *Barcelona* in the Year, One thousand three hundred fourscore and seven, aged Seventy five years; By this Princess of *Portugal* he had only a daughter named *Beatrix*, who dyed young, and was entombed in the Cathedral Church of *Lisbonne*, near unto the body of *Beatrix* of *Castille* her Grand-mother.

Her Marriage.
1348.

PETER

8. PETER
King of PORTUGAL and the ALGARVES.
CHAP. IX.

1359.

A S this King is a- **PORTUGAL** dored on the *comme cy de-* one side for be- *vant.* ing a most zealous Defender **PORTUGAL.** of his Laws and Ordinances, *Party de* and an observer of Justice MANUEL. with such care, that he banish- *De gueulles à* ed his Kingdom, all those that *un bras ou na-* made breach thereof, and so *turel ailé d'or,* acquired the excellent appel- *mouuant du se-* lation of *The Justicer* : So *cond party, te-* on the other side he is repre- *nant une Espée* hended also, and blamed, to *d'argent garnie* have put them in execution a- *d'or.* gainst the Criminals with such *Escartelé d'* rigor and severity, that he *Argent au lyon* was therefore called the *Cruel. de pourpre cou-* It being remarkable, that at *ronne d'or.* this time there Reigned three Kings in *Spain* that had this same sirname; The other two were *Peter* King of *Castille*, and *Charles* II. King of *Navarre*. But PETER, of whom we speak, was so much transported to the virtue of Liberality (in which he had a community with King *Dionysius* his Grand-father) that he often used this expression, *That a King that let slip one day without the distribution of some Benefit, was not worthy of the Title of the Dignity Royal.*

His Birth. *1320.*

He first saw the light of day in the Year, *One thousand three hundred and twenty*, the Nineteenth day of the Month of *April*; and was also in the Seven and thirtieth year of his age, when his fathers death made his way to the Crown; the end of whose Reign was sad and mournful, occasioned by the death of CONSTANCE MANUEL this his sons Wife, who was Daughter of the Infant *John Manuel* Duke of *Peñafiel*, Marquess of *Vilena*, and Siegneur of *Ascalona*, who was son of the Infant *Emanuel*, issued from *Ferdinand* III. King of *Castille*, as hath been said before. PE- *Nom:* TER

TER had been before married to *Blanche* the daughter of *Peter* King of Y ars of
Castille, whom he repudiated. This Princess CONSTANCE was CHRIST.J
Entombed in the Abbey of St. *Francis* at *Santarem*.

Among the Ladies of Honour which attended her at Court, the principal was *Agnes de Castro*, daughter of *Pedro-Fernando de Castro*, the most
Galibay. Excellently qualified Lord of *Galicia*, and nearly related both to the Kings
Mariana. of *Castille*, and *Portugal*. This Lady being adorned with many beauties
both of body and mind, attracted the Affection of Prince PETER in
the life-time of his Wife *Constance*, and after whose decease he clandestinely married, as he afterwards confirmed by his Solemn Oath.

But some Lords of the Court having conceived a secret envy against
her, supposing her to be instrumental to incite the young Prince to prefer
and agrandize her relations and kindred, perswaded the King *Alphonso IV.*
Duart to put her to death; which was accordingly executed: But the young
Vasconcellios. Prince PETER conceived so great a displeasure and indignation thereat,
that he not only took Arms against his father, but put to cruel torments the
Instruments of this wicked assassination.

During his whole Reign he deported himself so to the Kings his Neighbours, that although they were continually infested with grand Warres and
troubles, with which the Kingdoms of *Castille* and *Arragon* were often afflicted; his Estate on the contrary, had the happiness to enjoy under him a
blessed and happy Peace.

He raised two Proud and Magnificent Tombs in the Abbey of *Alcobace*,
one for himself, the other for *Agnes de Castro*; whose Effigies was to be
seen upon this Monument, adorned with a Royal Diadem, to signifie, that
he owned her for his Queen and Wife; Also he caused Royal Obsequies to
be performed at her Burial.

In fine, when he had ruled the Scepter of *Portugal* for the space of ten
years, seven months, and eight dayes, he expired at *Estremos* in *January*, His death.
in the Year, *One thousand three hundred threescore and seventeen.* He had 1377.
Mariana. for his Device a Star with these words, MONSTRAT ITER,
Nuarq. which he took in Memory of the three Kings, who were conducted by the
Star, going to adore our Lord, at his Nativity.

Children of PETER King OF PORTUGAL, and of CONSTANCE MANUEL his Wife.

9. DIONYSIO OF PORTUGAL, whom some (by error)
name *Lewis*, dyed in his infancy.

9. FERDINAND King OF PORTUGAL, whose History is
contained in the Chapter following.

9. MARY OF PORTUGAL, was married unto FERDINAND OF ARRAGON, Marquess of *Tortosa*, and Lord
ARRAGON. of *Albarazzin*, son of *Alphonso IV.* King of *Arragon*, and of *Leonora* of
D'or a quatre *Castille* his Wife. This Prince was slain in a place called *Chastillon*, by the
p ls de gueulls. command of his Brother, there having several quarrels fell out betwixt
Party de them,
PORTUGAL

and the ALGARVES. 33

Years of *Christ.* 1363. them, and upon a suspicion that he had, that this Prince would attempt the Crown. This violent death hapned in the Year, *One thousand three hundred threescore and three.*   *Mariana. Lib.* 17. C. 8.

Natural Children of PETER King of PORTUGAL, by Agnes de Castro.

9.   ALPHONSO OF PORTUGAL, dyed young.

9.   JOHN OF PORTUGAL was conjoyned in Marriage with MARY TELLEZ, daughter of *Martin-Alphonso Tellez*, and sister to *Elianor*, Wife (or rather Love-Mistress) of King *Ferdinando* of *Portugal* his brother. His Memory is worthy of blame, for having imbrued his hands in the blood of his Wife, whom he put to death under a false pretence that she had forfeited her honour, and violated the Laws of Marriage; An act so much the more mournful and Tragical, as being committed by the Artifice and Machinations of Queen *Elianor*, *Maries* Sister, envious that she had married a Prince of so accomplished a Personage, loved and honoured by all, and into whose hands (after the death of *Ferdinando* his Brother) would fall the Government and Management of the Affairs of the Kingdom; so that the Queen having charged him with no less a Crime than of Designs against the Life of the King; he was forced to flie into *Castille*, where he dyed, being kept a Prisoner by King *John I.* from this Marriage came one Son. *Viz.*
His Marriage.   PORTUGAL TELLEZ. *Nunez.*

10.   FERDINAND OF PORTUGAL, Seigneur of *Eca* in the Kingdom of *Galicia*; was several times married, but last of all unto ISABEL D'AVALOS, daughter of *Peter-Lopez d'Avalos*, son of the Constable of *Castille*, *Ruy Lopez*, by which Wife, and others which he married, and by several Concubines, he had to the number of two and forty children; from some of which are issued the Lords of *Eca*.   D'AUALOS.

The second Wife of JOHN OF PORTUGAL, Natural son of King *Peter*, was CONSTANCE OF CASTILLE, who was also a Bastard-daughter of *Henry II.* King of *Castille*, by whom he had three daughters.   CASTILLE.

10.   MARY OF PORTUGAL, Wife of MARTIN-VASQUEZ DE CUNHA, to whom she brought in Dower the County of *Valence*, and from this Marriage (according to some) the Counts of *Valence* are descended.   CUNHA.

10.   MARY OF PORTUGAL, espoused to the Count, PETER MINHO.   MINHO.

10.   N. OF PORTUGAL, Wife of *Lope-Vasquez de Cunha*.   CUNHA.

The same Prince, JOHN OF PORTUGAL, had also these Bastards following,

10.   ALPHONSO DE CASCAES, married BLANCH DE CUNHA.   CUNHA.

10.   PETER Seigneur *de Guerra*, who hath left a long Posterity.

10.   FERDINAND, Lord of *Braganca*.

9.   DIONYSIO OF PORTUGAL, another Natural Son of King *Peter*, from whom are descended the Lords of *Colmenereio*, and the Counts of *Villar*, as you shall see hereafter in the Descents of the Bastards of the House of *Portugal*.

K   BEA-

34 FERDINAND *King of* PORTUGAL

9. BEATRIX OF PORTUGAL, also a Natural Daughter of King *Peter*, and *Agnes de Castro*, was espoused to SANCEO OF CASTILLE, son of *Sanceo* Count of *Albuquerque*, who was Bastard-Son of King *Alphonso XI.* and of *Leonora de Guzman* his Paramore; they had issue *Uracea* of *Albuquerque*, (afterwards named *Leonora*,) a very wealthy Lady, married to the Infant *Ferdinand* of *Castille*, called *d'Antaguera*; he was King of *Arragon* by Election, and they had two Sons, *Alphonso V.* King of *Arragon* and *Sicelie*, from whom are descended some Kings of *Naples*; and *John* King of *Navarre* and *Arragon*, who hath given original to Kings of these two Monarchies.

Years of CHRIST.

Another Natural Son of PETER *King of* PORTUGAL, *and of* TERESA LAURENS.

9. JOHN King OF PORTUGAL, first of the name, continued the Posterity.

9. FERDINAND
KING of PORTUGAL and the ALGARVES.

CHAP. X.

PORTUGAL.
Comme cy devant.

PORTUGAL
Party de TELLEZ.

Mariana. Vasconcellus.

Mariana.

TO King *Peter* succeeded this Prince his Son, born in the Year of our Salvation, One thousand three hundred and forty, the Twentieth day of *February*; and in the Twenty seventh year of his age he began his Reign, his Father having left him to the enjoyment of a Rich and Flourishing Kingdom.

1377.
His Birth. 1340.

His person was comely, and his aspect pleasant, and most accomplished he had been in all perfections, had it not been that he was unstable and wavering in his Resolutions.

He pretended a right of Succession to the Crown of *Castille* after the death of King *Peter*; as being Great Grandchild of King *Sanceo IV.* and to this end he contracted an alliance with the King of *Arragon*; but to no purpose, for having

having to do with so Valiant a Prince, as was King *Henry II.* Bastard-brother of the same King *Peter*, he discontinued his pretentions.

He gave his promise for the Marriage of *Leonora* daughter of the King of *Arragon*, and contracted the same agreement with the King of *Castille*, to espouse his Daughter also of the same name; but being ill counselled, and continuing in his Levity, he abandoned these honourable and advantageous Marriages, to contract an unlawful one with LEONORA TELLEZ, Daughter of *Martin-Alphonso Tellez*, and of *Aldouce de Vasconcellos*, notwithstanding she was before married to *John-Laurens de Cugna*, under colour that her former Marriage was unlawful, as being contracted without Dispensation, and notwithstanding the propinquity of kindred betwixt the Parties; This gave disgust to several of the *Portugal* Lords, who retired into *Castille*, as did also *Cugna*. *Nunez Vasconcellius.*

The King FERDINAND was yet so rash, as to renew his former Claim and Pretentions to the Kingdom of *Castille*, but *Henry* King of *Castille*, being the more expert Souldier, had much the advantage of him, who entred into the Field, marched into *Portugal*, stormed several Towns, laid waste the Countrey, and at length begirt *Lisbonne* with a straight Siege; But their differences were at last composed in the Conjugal Bed (the ordinary way of reconciliation between the two Royal Houses of *Portugal* and *Castille*) by several Marriages contracted betwixt them.

After the death of *Henry*, FERDINAND renewed his old quarrel against *John* King of *Castille* his Successor, and called in the English to his succour, who were in the end so burthensome, that he was for the second time, enforced to come to an agreement. *History of Castille.*

He begirt the Cities of *Lisbonne* and *Evora*, with strong Walls, and was the first that created the Dignities of *Constable* and *Marshall* in *Portugal*. And dyed in the same City of *Lisbonne*, the Nine and twentieth day of *October*, *Anno*, *One thousand three hundred fourscore and three*, having Reigned Seventeen years, and lived Three and forty. He lieth in the Church of *Santarem*, near unto his Mother *Constance Manuel*. *The Dignities of Constable and Marshal first created in Portugal. Nunez Vasconcellius. Mariana.*

His death. 1383.

He took for his Symbole, a Sword which transpierced two hearts, with these words, CUR NON UTRUNQUE; by which, he would have understood, that by the sagacity of his Judgement, he could penitrate into the most secret thoughts.

Children of FERDINAND *King of* PORTUGAL, *and of* LEONORA TELLEZ.

10. N. OF PORTUGAL, a Son born about the Year, *One thousand three hundred fourscore and two*, to the great joy of the King his father; but that contentment lasted not long; for he dyed within four dayes after his birth.

10. BEATRIX OF PORTUGAL, Queen of CASTILLE, born in the Year, *One thousand three hundred threescore and twelve*: She had been, by King FERDINAND her Father, promised in Marriage to several Princes, among others to *Edward* of *England*, Son of *Edmond* of *Cambridge*, (my Author meaneth, I believe, *Edward* Duke of *York* and *Albemarle*, Son of *Edmond* of *Langley* Duke of *York*) to *Frederick*

Her Birth. 1372.

CASTILLE. *Escartelé Castille & de Leon. Party de PORTUGAL*

Mariana. Lib. 18.
Nuñez.

derick of *Castille* Duke of *Beuevente*, Natural Son of *Henry II.* King of *Castille*, then to *Ferdinand* Son of the same King. But in the end, to knit the Peace of the two Kingdoms of *Castille* and *Portugal* with a firm knot, BEATRIX was first contracted to JOHN King OF CA-STILLE, who was at that time Widower to *Leonor* of *Arragon*, his first Wife, by whom he had children: Then three years after this Contract, in *May*, Anno, *One thousand three hundred fourscore and three*, their Marriage was Solemnized at *Elvas* with great Magnificence, at which the King of *Cyprus*, and *Charles* Prince of *Navarre*, were present.

By reason of this Marriage the King of *Castille* pretended to have a right of Succession to the Kingdom of *Portugal*, after the death of *Ferdinando* his Wives Father, and endeavoured therefore to make himself Master thereof by the force of his Armes.

But that Natural hatred betwixt these two Nations of *Castille* and *Portugal*, was so eradicated, that the *Portugals* would not permit him the Succession; But from this Marriage there came no children. So King *John* of *Castille* dyed in the Year, *One thousand three hundred fourscore and ten*, 1390. leaving issue by his first Wife only, and not by Queen BEATRIX OF PORTUGAL; who being yet young at the time of his death, and having been courted by several other Kings and Princes, yet lived a Widow to the day of her death; and as an admirable example of Continence and Chastity, would not hearken to a second Marriage; saying, That *Ladies Nobly born, and well educated, ought not to be the Wives of two Husbands*.

Years of CHRIST.

A Natural Daughter of FERDINAND King OF PORTUGAL.

10.
CASTILLE.
Party de PORTUGAL

Nuñez.

Vasconcellius.

ISABEL OF PORTUGAL, born in the Year, *One thousand three Hundred threescore and four*; Being Nine years old, was promised in Marriage to the Prince ALPHONSO OF CASTILLE (*Vasconcellos* calls him *Ferdinand*) Count of *Gigion*, and Seigneur of *Norogna*, who was Natural Son of *Henry II.* King of *Castille*; their Marriage was consummated in the Year, *One thousand three hundred threescore and eighteen*, against the grain of *Alphonso*, who was at that time onely Eighteen years old, therefore this Match gave original to many troubles. For King *Henry* his Father moved with displeasure for that he neglected his Wife, deprived him of all his Lands and Seigneuries; So that the Count was constrained to fly to *Avignion*, where he made his complaints to Pope *Gregory XI.* and also to the King of *France Charles V.* Afterwards having rebelled against *Henry III.* he was besieged within his County of *Gigion* with his Wife and Children; And to compose their Differences, *Charles VI.* King of *France*, was chosen Arbitrator, who understanding the injustice of his cause, sent him back to his King, forbidding him the refuge of *France*. Thus afflicted in the Year, *One thousand three hundred fourscore and fifteen*, he secretly retired towards *Rochel*, where his Wife ISABEL and his Children gave him the meeting, and where they had no assistance but what came from the Viscountess of *Thouars*, who gave them the Town of *Marans* for a Habitation. It's to be believed, that some of their Children returned again into *Spain*, among whom was *Peter de Norogna* Arch-bishop of *Lisbonne*, *John de Norogna*, *Ferdinand* Count of *Villereal*, from whom are descended the Houses of *Ville-real*, and of *Meneses*: *Alphonso* had issue also *Sanceo de Norogna* Count of *Odemira*, who had Children. *Alphonso* and ISABEL had also a Daughter named *Constance* of *Norogna*, second Wife of *Alphonso* of *Portugal* first Duke of *Braganca*, but they left no posterity; In Brief, the Illustrious House of *Norogna* in *Portugal*, derive their original from this Marriage.

Her Birth, 1364.

Her Marriage. 1378.

Years of Marriage. The same Count of *Gigion Alphonso* had also three Bastard-children, a-
CHRIST. mong the rest *Martin-Henriquez*, who served *Charles VII*. King of *France*, whom
he sent Embassadour to the King of *Castille*. From him, it's probable, is descended
that Family in the County of *Foix*, who bear the Name and Armes of *Castille*.

9. JOHN I.

Of the Name, KING of PORTUGAL
And the ALGARVES.
Sirnamed, *With the Good Memory*, and Father of his Countrey.

CHAP. XI.

1385.

His Birth.
1357.

THE defect of the birth of this Prince, who was natural Son of *Peter* King of *Portugal*, was in some sort covered, and, as it were, repaired by his singular virtues; Being most Pious, Magnanimous, Liberal and Clement.

The Eleventh day of *April* gave him Birth, which was in the Year, One thousand three hundred fifty and seven, and was but Seven Year old when the King his Father established him Grand-Master of the Knights of the Order *D'Avis*.

In the time of King *Ferdinand* his Brothers Reign, he had been imprisoned at the instance of Queen *Leonora* his Wife, who had contracted envy against him, for having reproved her too free and familiar carriage with the Count of *Andrie*: for which, neither she nor the Count were backward in the procuration of his Death. But God, who hath the disposition of Crowns, had Ordered it other wayes.

PORTUGAL.
D'argent a cinq Escussons d'Azure posés en Croix cheux chargé de cinq besans aussy d'argent posez en saltoir a la Bordure de gueulles chargée de huict Chasteaux d'or.

Party de LANCASTER.

Escartelé au 1. & 4. d'Azure semé de Fleurs de Lis d'or, au 2. & 3. de gueulles a trois Lyons passant guardant d'or; au lambel d'ermine brochant sur le tout.

L For

For JOHN found out means to shake off the Bonds of his Captivity; and after the Death of his Brother, this Queen *Elianora* administring the Affairs of State, otherwise than it belonged unto her, and continuing in her unlawful Loves, to the great dissatisfaction of the *Portugues*; They persuaded the Grand-Master to take away the life of this Count, which he did accordingly; by this act acquiring to himself so great an affection, that they Proclaimed him, *Defender and Protector of the Publick Liberty*; and then he was made General in the Warre against *John I.* King of *Castille*, who aspired to the Succession of the Kingdom of *Portugal*, in the right of *Beatrix* his Queen, as we have told you before.

Vignier.

But the people more willing to submit to the Government of a Prince of the Blood of their Natural Kings, than to that of a stranger; And observing the lawful Line of the Heirs-Male to fail in *Ferdinand*, they elected this JOHN his Brother, King, notwithstanding he was born out of Marriage; This was performed in a general Assembly of the Estates of *Portugal*, held in the City of *Conimbra*, in the Year, One thousand three hundred fourscore and four. But this Election suited not with the desires of Prince JOHN, who told them that he was well content with that Honourable Title which had before been given him; But the *Portugues*, besides that hatred they did bear the *Castillians*, considering his rare qualifications, judged him more fit and proper for the Dignity of the Crown, than any other, earnestly entreating his acceptation thereof, as one whom they judged capable of defending them from their Enemies.

1384.

Mariana.

Vasconcellius.
The Battel of *Minberot.*
Froisard.

The Principal of which was the King of *Castille*, who, incited by the Queen of *Portugal*, *Leonor* his Wives Mother, raised a considerable Army, with which he laid a Siege to *Lisbonne*; defended this City was with so much resolution, that after the *Castillians* had sate down before it some months, they were constrained to raise their Camp. Upon their retreat, the *Portugues* animated by the presence of their generous Prince JOHN, fell into the pursuit of them unto *Aljuberot*, where both Armies drew up and began the Fight, and where the *Castillians* were worsted. This notable Victory hapned to be in *August*, Anno, One thousand three hundred fourscore and five. From which year some have computed the time of the Reign of JOHN, and write that he was then Proclaimed King.

1385.

Nunez.

After this generous exploit, gathering the fruit of this his Victory, he conquered from his Enemy, and reduced to his obedience, those Cities and Towns which had been lost in the former Warre. In the mean time the King of *Castille* being deceased, *Henry III.* his Son and Successor having had the sad experience of his Fathers losses, and the new King of *Portugals* successes, was willing to let fall his Fathers pretentions, to hearken to a peace at last concluded betwixt these two Kings, and afterwards continued with King *John II.* Son of this *Henry*.

Godefroy.

Mariana. lib. 20. c. 7.

So that now King JOHN OF PORTUGAL seeing himself in the enjoyment of a happy peace, and also in a good correspondence with his Neighbours: Notwithstanding he was grown in years, that checked not his resolution from aspiring unto high and pious designs; He turned his Armes therefore against the *Moors* and *Sarazens* of *Affrick*, and by the example of his Valiant Sons, subdued the strong Town of *Septe*, which stood as a Rampire opposite to *Spain*, to the great prejudice of the Christians. And considering his Kingdom to be of too small an extendure, to Dignifie the numerous issue he had by his happy Marriage, he projected to acquire them possessions by the force of his Armes, in other Kingdoms. Insomuch that

1415.

that he gave beginnings to those famous Conquests which have since been prosecuted and continued by the illustrious Kings his Successors.

The exercise of his Armes was no *Remora* to impede the progress of his Justice, witness the *Code* of *Justinian*, which he caused to be translated into his own Language, to the end his Subjects might observe it as his Royal Ordinance; And for a Monument of his Piety, he founded the Monastery of the Order of St. *Dominick*, dedicated to the holy Virgin, giving it the name of BATTEL, in remembrance of that signal Victory there gained upon the *Castillians*, and caused it to be built in the same place where he was Conquerour. And because the Cathedral Church of *Lisbonne* was first subject to the Arch-bishop of *Merida*, and then to that of *Braga*; he obtained the erection thereof into an Arch-bishoprick, from Pope *Boniface* IX. which was done in the Year, *One thousand three hundred fourscore and ten*. The Magnificence of this Prince yet appears in those superb Structures of several Palaces and Royal Mansions, which he built in the City of *Lisbonne*, and in those of *Saintre*, *Santlarem*, *Almerin*, and other places. *Vasconcellius.* *Nunez.*

In fine, after so many Heroick performances, King JOHN (whom *Froissard* by mistake calls *Dionysius*) finished the course of his life at *Lisbonne*, the Fourteenth day of *August*, in the Year, *One thousand four hundred three and thirty*, after he had lived Threescore and sixteen years, and Reigned Eight and forty years, Four months, and Nine dayes. His body was with Funeral Pomp (at that time a thing unaccustomed) conducted by men of all Estates, in a Chariot of Triumph, his Sons accompanying it, and deposited in the same Monastery of BATTEL. He was so lamented by his Subjects, that they gave him these glorious Titles, of, *With the good Memory*, and of, *Father of the Countrey*. In short, he had in the course of his life several rencounters and conformities parallel with those of the Valiant *French* Prince *Charles Martel*. *Vignier.* *Vasconcellins.*

This King JOHN OF PORTUGAL united his Forces and Designs against the *Castillians* with *John* of *England*, Duke of *Lancaster*, one of the younger Sons of *Edward III*. King of *England*, who pretended to the Kingdom of *Castille*, in the right of his second Wife *Constance* daughter of King *Peter the Cruel*; this English Prince assisted him with a Fleet well furnished with Souldiers, and more firmly to contract this Alliance, King JOHN (after he had obtained Dispensation from the Pope for the Vow he had made as a Knight of the Order *d' Avis*) espoused PHILIPPA OF LANCASTER his Daughter; this Marriage was Celebrated in the Year, *One thousand three hundred fourscore and seven*; The Duke of *Lancaster* promising himself, that by this course he should more easily make his way to the Kingdom of *Castille*. The Queen PHILIPPA dyed a long time before the King her Husband, about the Year, *One thousand four hundred and fifteen*; during that preparation of Warre which he made for his Voyage into *Affrica*, leaving, with the grief of her Death, a Noble and Flourishing Progeny, which did not degenerate from the Vertues and Excellencies of their Father. *And. du Chesne, in his History of England.* *Nunez.* *Vasconcellins.*

His Device was a Rock, the Chief of which was transpierced with a Sword, held by an Arm issuing out of a Cloud, with these words, ACUIT UT PENITRET; for to signifie, that he exercised his Souldiers to things troublesome and difficult; that they might the more easily perform the high and generous Enterprises.

L 2   *Children*

Children of JOHN I. King OF PORTUGAL, and of PHILIPPA OF LANCASTER, his Wife.

10. **ALPHONSO OF PORTUGAL**, dyed, being aged Ten years, the Two and twentieth day of *November*, Anno, *One thousand four hundred*; and was inhumed in the Cathedral Church of *Braga*.

10. **EDWARD OF PORTUGAL**, Successor to the King his father, continued the Posterity.

10. **PETER OF PORTUGAL**, Duke of **CONIMBRA**, Seigneur of *Mount-Maïour le Vieil*, and Regent of the Kingdom of *Portugal*, was a Prince whose Travels had excellently qualified him; having gained much experience by the frequentation of several people of *Europe*, *Asia*, and *Affrick*; he was in the Court of the Emperour *Sigismond*, and left not unvisited that of the great and renowned *Sythian*, *Tamerlane*; after several dangerous adventures, he returned home, in the Year, One thousand four hundred twenty and eight, when passing through *Castille*, the Inhabitants left their houses to meet him in his journey, reporting what they had seen with wonder, as if a man, fallen from heaven, had come to visit them.

PORTU-GAL-CO-NIMBRA.
Party de ARRAGON.
D'or a quatre pals de gueulles.
Mariana. lib. 24. cap. 16. & l b. 21. cap. 7.

1428.

He was by the *Portugues* so affectionately beloved, that after the Death of King *Edward* his elder brother, the Government of the Kingdom was committed unto him during the Minority of *Alphonso V.* his Nephew; which he managed for the space of Ten years, with great Fidelity and Prudence; when *Alphonso* Count of *Barcellos*, his Natural Brother, a Prince both Ambitious, and Envious, and who by the means of this PETER, had been before exalted to the Dukedome of *Bragança*, most ingratefully opposed him, rendred him a dangerous and obnoxious person unto the King their Nephew; and also charged him with a scandalous accusation, the heads of which were, That he had performed the Office of Regent much to the prejudice of the Kings interest: had got into his own hands the whole treasure of the Kingdom; and that also he designed to ascend the Throne by the Deposition of the King his Nephew. To these Articles the Duke would have answered, and cleared himself, but the King who was willing and apt to believe any thing that might secure him his Crown, being possessed with a prejudicate opinion, would not hear of his Answer; but on the contrary Resolved to take him off. The Duke had timely intelligence thereof, who to avoid the effects of the Kings Anger, and to secure his person, shut himself up in his Town of *Conimbra*; and there finding that he could not be upon the Defensive part, without the Offensive; forgetful of his Duty; put himself into the head of a considerable Army, with which he marched towards *Lisbonne*, resolving to make himself Master thereof, but he fell into the hands of the Ambushes prepared for him by the Kings party; where, after a hot dispute near unto the River *Alfarubérie*, Duke PETER was killed upon the Field, being shot through the Heart with an empoysoned Arrow; which fell out to be, in the Year, One

Nuntz, Vignier.

Mariana. Vasconcellius.

His Death, 1449.

and the ALGARVES.

Years of CHRIST. *One thousand four hundred forty and nine*, and on the Twentieth day of *May.*

His loss nevertheless was much lamented, as being a Prince worthy of a longer life, and better Fortune: He lived unto the age of Seven and fifty years. His body lay the space of three dayes without Burial, until that by the supplication of the Queen of *Portugal* his Daughter, Wife of *Alphonso*, it was brought, and interred in the Monastery of *Battel*, the Sepulchre of the Kings his Predecessors.

This Duke was so much the more Praise-worthy, (following the foot-steps of some Princes of his House) because he joyned the use of his Pen with that of his Sword, he writ several Books both in Prose and Verse, and Translated some Latine Authors into his own Language. There is yet to be seen of his Verses in *Portugal*, which Treat of Morality, and are replenished with Learning, and Precepts of Wisdom.

His Marriage. 1428.
In the Month of *September*, Anno, *One thousand four hundred eight and twenty*, Duke PETER married ISABEL OF ARRAGON, Daughter of *James* of *Arragon*, Count of *Urgel*, and of *Isabel* the Daughter of *Peter IV.* King of *Arragon*, by which Princess he had Six Children, here underneath mentioned.

Mariana. lib. 20. C. 16.

Children of PETER OF PORTUGAL, *Duke of* CONIMBRA, *by* ISABEL OF ARRAGON, *his Wife.*

II.
1450.
PETER OF PORTUGAL elected King of ARRAGON, and Count of *Barcelona*, was eldest Son of *Peter* of *Portugal* Duke of *Conimbra*, and of *Isabel* of *Arragon* his Wife; and was established Constable of the Kingdom of *Portugal* by the Regent his Father, after the decease of his Uncle by the Fathers side Prince *John.*

ARRAGON.
Escartelé de PORTUGAL

1445.
In the Year, *One thousand four hundred five and forty*, he had the Command of an Army committed to him, for the succour of the King of *Castille*, and for the Reduction of some of his Subjects that had rebelled; Afterwards the *Catalonians*, and some of the Grandees of *Arragon* having revolted from the King of *Arragon* and *Navarre*, *John II.* They caused this Prince PETER to return out of *Affrick*, where he fought against the *Moors*, and acknowledged him for King of *Arragon*, and Count of *Barcelona*,

1464.
in *September*, in the Year, *One thousand four hundred threescore and four*; maintaining that these Estates did lawfully belong unto him, as being Son of the eldest Daughter of the Count of *Urgel* descended from the King of *Arragon*: so that PETER was Proclaimed King: And notwithstanding he had assistance from his Cousin *Philip* Duke of *Bourgongne*, yet he could not maintain himself in his Estate, for after the loss of a Field disputed betwixt him, and the Prince *Ferdinand* Son of King *John*, he was constrained to retire to *Mauresa.* But nevertheless he carried still the Royal Title; And on his journey to *Barcelona*, he fell sick at *Granolie*, and

His Death. 1466.
there deceased the Thirtieth day of *June*, in the Year, *One thousand four hundred threescore and six*, some say in the precedent year. His body was inhumed at *Barcelona* in the Church of our Lady, near unto the Sea. It's believed he was poysoned, but some think, that being over-much wearied,

Mariana. Lib. 23. C. 20.

M

JOHN I. of the name, King of PORTUGAL

ed, and troubled at the evil success of his affairs, he dyed with grief, without leaving any Children.

His Device was an Haulk, with these words, MOLESTIA PRO LÆTITIA; signifying thereby, That the honour of the Kingdom which he had accepted of, had been accompanied with more vexation and trouble, than satisfaction and contentment.

Years of CHRIST.

II. PORTUGAL-CONIMBRA.

Escartelé, Au premier de Jerusalem. Au 2. contre escartelé de PORTUGAL & D'ANGLETERRE. Au 3. d'or au lyon de gueules. Au 4. d'argent au lyon aussy de gueules à la queve fourchée. Sur le tout burelle d'argent & d'Azure en lyon de gueulles brochant sur le tout, qui est CYPRE.

JOHN OF PORTUGAL, Duke of CONIMBRA, and Regent of the Kingdom of *Cyprus*, second Son of *Peter* Duke of *Conimbra*, succeeded his Father in this Dutchy; hoping to advance his Fortunes by his Marriage, he espoused CHARLOTE OF CYPRUS, Daughter of *John II.* King of *Cyprus* of the House of *Lusignan*, and of *Helene Paleologus* his Wife, which CHARLOTE was Heir apparent to the Kingdoms of *Cyprus* and *Jerusalem*. But the Prince JOHN her Husband dyed without issue, before the King his Father-in-law. Therefore *Mariana* and other Authors are mistaken, that give him the qualification of *King of Cyprus*. For he was only Regent of this Kingdom, a Title which he had, when in the Year, *One thousand four hundred threescore and six*, he was admitted into the Order of Knights of the Golden Fleece, by *Philip* the *Good*, Duke of *Burgundy*, in the Chapter held at the *Hague* in *Holland*.

1447.

His Marriage.

1466.

His Widow married for her second Husband *Lewis* of *Savoy*, Count of *Geneva*, Brother of *Amides* Duke of *Savoy*, and Son of Duke *Lewis* by *Anne* of *Lusignan* his Wife. In her right he took the Title of King, and possessed himself of the Kingdom of *Cyprus*, but at last he was defeated by his Wives Bastard-brother; and since, this Kingdom hath been usurped by the *Turks*.

II. PORTUGAL-CONIMBRA. *Party de CYPRE.*

Comme cy dessus, fort que en lieu de 2. quartier doit estre mis l'escusson qui est sur le tout.

JAMES OF PORTUGAL, third Son of PETER OF PORTUGAL, Duke of CONIMBRA, &c. turned Souldier in his youth, and was taken Prisoner in that Battel which his Father lost with his life, in the Year, *One thousand four hundred forty and nine*; after he had obtained his liberty, he went to visit his Aunt by the Fathers side, *Isabel* of *Portugal* Dutchess of *Bourgongne*, who sent him to *Rome*, where the Pope *Calixtus III.* created him a Cardinal by the Title of *St. Eustace*, in the Year, *One thousand four hundred fifty and six*, being at that time but young. He was Modest, of a Pregnant Wit, and a good Scholar, which foundations made men hope great things from him, for those Virtues with which he was accomplished. He is reported to be of a temper so chaste, and continent; that falling extream ill, and being counselled by his Physitians to have the knowledge of a Woman for a remedy: He refused, saying, That he would rather dye, than be polluted. He was Arch-bishop of *Lisbonne*, and dyed at *Florence* the Sixteenth day of *April*, Anno, *One thousand four hundred fifty and nine*. His body being interred in the Church of St. *Miniat*, an Abbey of Monks of the Order of St. *Benedict*.

1449.

1456.

Comme cy devant.

Onuphrius. Fr. Ciaconus.

His death. 1459.

II. PORTUGAL *Party de* PORTUGAL.

ISABEL OF PORTUGAL, espoused to the King of *Portugal Alphonso V.* her Cousin, as you may read in his Story.

II. CONIMBRA.

PHILIPPA OF PORTUGAL, another Daughter of *Peter* Duke of *Conimbra*, and of *Isabel* of *Arragon* his Wife, was a Nun in the Abbey of *Odivelles*.

BEA-

and the ALGARVES.   43

Years of CHRIST. 11. Her Marriage.

BEATRICE OF PORTUGAL, was allied in Marriage to ADOLPHE OF CLEUES, Seigneur of *Ravenstein*, a younger Son of *Adolphe* Duke of *Cleues*, and of *Mary* of *Bourgongne* his Wife, from which Marriage descended *Philip* of *Cleues* Seigneur of *Ravenstein*, Lieutenant General in the City of *Gennes* for the King of *France Lewis XII.* his Cousin; afterwards General of a Fleet against the *Turk*: He left no issue.

CLEUES-RAVEN-STEIN.
De gueulles au rais pommetté & Fleuronné d'or, de huict pieces percé d'argent.

Escartelé de BOURGONGNE *qui est contre escartelé as 1. & 4. d'azure à trois Fleurs de lis d'or a la Bordure componneé d'argent & de gueulles. Au 2. & 3. bande d'or & d'azure de six pieces, a la Bordure de gueull: s.*
Sur le tout d'or au Lyon de sable, qui est FLANDRES.
Party de PORTUGAL-CONIMBRA.

Here follow again Children of JOHN I. King of PORTUGAL, and of PHILIPPA OF LANCASTER, his Wife.

10.

1415.

His Death. 1460.

HENRY OF PORTUGAL, Duke of VISCO (fourth Son of King *John*) and Grand Master of the Order of the Knights of *Christ*, hath recommended his Name and Memory to Posterity, for his high designs, and generous performances; for he had the Glory to have undertaken, and happily accomplished many dangerous Navigations. After he had given testimony of his Valour in the Reduction of the strong City of *Septe* in *Affrica*, he resolved to put himself to Sea for the Discovery of the unknown World. And because he might attain to his design with the more facility, he addressed himself earnestly to the study of the Mathematicks, and of Astrology, rejecting the enjoyment of Marriage, as a thing that was altogether incongruous to the designs of a contemplative Life. And that he might more easily apply himself to the Comtemplation of the Starres, he bestowed a good part of his life upon the Cape of St. *Vincent*, because the Aire was there serene and clear, and seldom or never troubled, or overcast with Clouds. In fine, being satisfied in his Judgment, that there were Islands yet undiscovered in the *Atlantique* Ocean, he was resolved to hazard the proof thereof upon his own proper costs & expence: So that first of all he discovered the Isle of *Madera*, so called, because of the Forrests wherewith it was replenished; he peopled it with several Collonies, it having been before a Desert; the next discovery was the *Canaries*, unknown for a long time; in these Voyages he found out also several Ports in the *Atlantique* Sea. Lastly, He so well instructed the *Portugues* in the direction of their Navigations according to the Course of the Stars, that with no less glory, than utility, they have made large Conquest in *Affrick* near unto *Ethiopia*, and of several Isles in the main Ocean, and the *Indies*. And that he might more commodiously attend upon his affairs, towards the end of his life, this Generous Prince established his Habitation at *Sagra* in the Kingdom of the *Algarves*, at the Cape called *Sacra*, from which Port he might with ease send his Ships into the East. But being prevented by death, in the Year, One thousand four hundred and threescore, at the age of Threescore and seven years (*Mariana* adds Ten years more) the progress of his glorious designs was

PORTU-GAL-VISCO.

Step. Garibay.

Nunez. Mariana.

Mariana. Lib. 13. c. 3.

M 2

44 JOHN I. of the name, King of PORTUGAL

was interrupted. He adopted for his Son *Ferdinand* of *Portugal* his Nephew, one of the Children of King *Edward* his elder brother; The Corps of *Henry* was interred within the Church of *Aljuberot*.

Years of CHRIST.

PORTUGAL. Comme cy devant.

PORTUGAL. Party de PORTUGAL-BRAGANCA. Qui est d'argent au Sautoir de gueulles, chargé de cinq escussons de PORTUGAL, un au melieu, & les aultres aux quatre bouts du Sautoir.

10. JOHN OF PORTUGAL, Grand Master of the Order of St. *James*, and Constable of *Portugal*, was fifth Son of *John I.* of the name, King of *Portugal*, and of *Philippa* of *Lancaster* his Wife; he followed the steps of his Illustrious Ancestors, is commended for his Piety and Prudence, and also to have affected the welfare of his Countrey. He married ISABEL OF PORTUGAL, Daughter of his Natural Brother *Alphonso I.* Duke of *Braganca*, and of the Countess of *Barcellos Beatrice*, who was Daughter of *Avarez Pereira*. His decease hapned at *Alcacar de Sal*, about the end of the Month of *October*, in the Year, One thousand four hundred forty and two, and in the Three and fortieth year of his age. As for the Princess ISABEL his Wife, she departed this life in the Year, One thousand four hundred threescore and five, in the place of *Areeval*, where she was to visit her Daughter Queen *Isabel* of *Castille*.

His Marriage.

His Death. 1442.

1465.

Children of JOHN OF PORTUGAL, &c.

Mariana.

11. JAMES OF PORTUGAL, dyed shortly after his Father, some write that he succeeded him in his Honours and Dignities: which others make a doubt of.

CASTILLE. Escartelé de LEON. Party de PORTUGAL.

11. ISABEL OF PORTUGAL, Queen OF CASTILLE, Anno, One thousand four hundred seven and forty, was conjoyned by Marriage unto JOHN second of the name, King of CASTILLE, Son of *Henry III.* and of *Katherine* of *Lancaster* his Wife. He dyed at *Valedolit* the Nineteenth day of *July*, in the Year, One thousand four hundred fifty and four, leaving among other Children, a Daughter named *Isabel* of *Castille*, Wife to the King of *Arragon*, *Alphonso V.* She was a Magnanimous Princess.

Her Marriage. 1447.

PORTUGAL-VISCO. Party de PORTUGAL.

11. BEATRICE OF PORTUGAL, was the Wife of her Cousin FERDINAND OF PORTUGAL, Duke of *Visco*, a younger Son of King *Edward*. This Princess had for her Son, among others, King *Emanuel* of *Portugal*, in the Year, One thousand four hundred threescore and nineteen, she effected the peace betwixt the Kings of *Portugal*, *Alphonso V.* and of *Castille*, *Ferdinand V.* and is much commended by Historians, for her singular Prudence, and grand Authority.

Her Marriage. 1479.

11. PHILIPPA OF PORTUGAL never married.

Vasconcellius.

10. FERDINAND OF PORTUGAL, youngest Son of *John I.* King of *Portugal*, and of *Philippa* of *Lancaster*, Grand Master of the Order *d' Avis*, Seigneur of *Atouguie*, and of *Sauueterre*, was given in

and the ALGARVES. 45

Years of in Hostage by his Brother King *Edward*, to the General of the *Sarazens*
Christ. *Aben Sala*, until that the said King should deliver up into their Hands the
Town of *Septe*, according to the Composition made after the fatal Battel
of *Tangier*. In the mean time *Edward*'s death procured his deliverance, and
although he had Ordered it so in his Will, yet FERDINAND ceased
not to continue in the hands of these Barbarians the space of six years, where
he suffered many hardships; which he underwent with much constancy, and
incredible patience; and was moreover of so holy a life, that he deserved
His Death. to be Registred in the Rubrick of Martyrs. He dyed A°. *One thousand*
1443. *four hundred forty and three*, in the One and fortieth year of his age. His
bones were brought out of *Affrick* into *Portugal*, and reposed in the Abbey
of *Battel*.

10. BLANCHE OF PORTUGAL, eldest Daughter of *John*
I. King of *Portugal*, and of *Philippa* of *Lancaster*, dyed young.

10. ISABEL OF PORTUGAL, second Daughter, was espoused
Her Marriage. in the Year, *One thousand four hundred nine and twenty*, unto PHI- BOUR-
1429. LIP sirnamed the *Good*, Duke of BOURGONGNE, and dyed GONGNE.
in the Year, *One thousand four hundred threescore and thirteen*. *Escartelé*
                                                                                                                                                  Au 1. & 4. de
                                                                                                                                                   FRANCE

a la bordure componnée d'argent & de gueulles qui est BOURGONGNE *moderne*.
Au 2. bandé d'or & d'azure de six pieces, à la bordure de gueulles qui est BOURGONGNE *l'ancien. Party de sable au Lyon d'or, qui est* BRABANT.
Au 3. des mesmes Armes de BOURGONGNE *l'ancien; Party de* LIMBOURG *qui est d'argent au Lyon de gueulles couronné d'or.*
Sur le tout de FLANDRES, *qui est d'or au Lyon de sable. Le tout party de* PORTUGAL.

Natural Children of JOHN I. *of the name, King of* PORTUGAL.

10. ALPHONSO OF PORTUGAL, Duke of BRAGANZA, who
hath given original to that illustrious House, from which the two last Kings of *Portugal* (*John IV*. Father of King *Alphonso VI*. now Reigning, A° 1662.) are descended.

10. BEATRIX OF PORTUGAL, was three times married in *England*;
first to *Thomas Fitz-Allan* Earl of *Arundel*; secondly to *Gilbert* Lord *Talbot*, but
had issue by neither; her third Husband was *Thomas Fettiplace* of *Shefford* in the
County of *Berks*, Esq; by whom she had issue *John Fettiplace*, servant to King *Henry VI*. from whom is descended *Fettiplace* of *North-Denchworth*, *Pusey*, and *Letcombe*,
in the same County.

*Joseph Texera, a Portugues, hath committed a notorious errour (as he hath often done in writing the Genealogies of his Kings) when he reporteth, That King
John I. of the name, beside Blanche and Isabel, had three other lawfully begotten
Daughters*, viz. *Philippa, whom he writeth to be Wife of Eric King of Denmark;
Jane, of Henry III. King of Castille, and Leonora, of the King of Arragon, Peter
IV. For which this Texera is justly reproved by Edward Nunez in that Censure
which he hath published against him.*

                                       N   EDWARD

10. EDWARD
King of PORTUGAL and the ALGARVES.
CHAP. XII.

PORTUGAL
Comme cy devant.

PORTUGAL.
Party d'-
ARRAGON.
D'or a quatre pals de gueulles.

Nonius.
Mariana.
Vasconcellius.

Idem.

Nothing was more to be defired in King EDWARD, but that he had been favoured with better fortune, and a longer life: for he wanted no Virtue, and rendred himfelf by feveral actions, a worthy Succeffor of King *John*, firft of that name, his Father: He had this name given him in memory of *Edward III.* King of *England*, Grand-father to his Mother *Philippa* of *Lancafter*. Having found his Kingdom flourifhing, in peace, rich, and his people Warlike, and well exercifed in Military affairs, by reafon of the former Wars, there was hope that he would have augmented thofe Conquefts made by his predeceffor; But providence permitted this hope to be fruftrated.

1433.

The beginning of his reign was employed in the War of *Affrick*, at the Siege of *Tangier*, which fucceeded not according to his defire; fo that for the accomplifhment of a Treaty, which he made with the *Moors*, into whofe hands he promifed to render in a certain time the City of *Septe*, he was conftrained to give them in Hoftage the Prince *Ferdinand* his Brother, who dyed in their hands; The Eftates of *Portugal* thinking it not reafonable to quit unto thofe Infidels a place of fo great importance.

It was alfo in the beginning of his reign, that the Popes *Martin V.* then *Eugenius IV.* affembled the Council of *Bafil*, at which all the Chriftian Princes were exhorted to give their affiftance; King EDWARD refolved to go thither in perfon. But the grand affairs that at this time lay upon

Years of Christ. on his hands, impeached his Journey. For to supply which default, he sent thither a Solemn Embassade, of which *Alphonso* Bishop of *Porte*, and the Count of *Ouren* were chief. They obtained of the Pope, That from that time forward the Knights of the Military Orders of St. *James*, and St. *John*, should be dispensed for Marriage. As also that the Kings of *Portugal* might from that time be Anointed and Sacred as the Kings of *England* were.

The same King EDWARD. was of a temper couragious, and that which is rare in a Prince, joyned the exercise of Armes with the knowledge of Letters and Sciences; and so earnestly dedicated himself to the study of Philosophy, that he composed many rare and excellent Works; among others, a Treatise of the Administration of Justice, and the Duty of a Prince, another of the Office of the Faithful Councellour, and a third also of the Art of Riding and Managing of Horses. His Eloquence and Piety History makes famous. He was a favourer of Learned men, and of all those that he observed to be excellent in any Art, giving them access to his person, and conferring familiarly with them, for the advantage and information of his judgement. *Marians.*

Among those evils wherewith he was afflicted, that of the Plague was the most fatal, which hapned in his Kingdom, and from which his Royal person it self was not exempted. For he was touched with a contagious Disease upon the opening of a Letter which one sent him from an infected place, suddenly after which he dyed in the Abbey of *Tomar* (whither he had retired to avoid the danger) the Eighteenth day of *September*, in the Year, One thousand four hundred eight and thirty, which was the Seven and thirtieth Year of his age, and the Fifth of his reign; He had his Burial in the Abbey of *Battel*. In the Year, One thousand four hundred eight and twenty, this King EDWARD espoused ELEANOR OF ARRAGON, second Daughter of *Ferdinand* of *Castille*, King of *Arragon* and *Sicilie*, and of *Eleanor* of *Albuquerque* his Wife, the Princess had in Marriage Two hundred thousand Florins. She was then aged Twenty seven years, and not Six and thirty, as writeth *Mariana*; for the *Portugal* Historians note her Birth to be in the Year, One thousand four hundred and one. *Vasconcellius.* *His Death. 1438.* *His Marriage. 1428.* *L. Marin ficulno. Mariana. Lib. 20. Cap. 16. & Lib. 21. Cap. 13.* *Her Birth. 1401.*

By his Testament he ordained his Wife Regent of the Kingdom during the minority of his eldest Son and Successor: to the great dissatisfaction of the Princes his younger Brothers, and also of the people, who would not submit to the Command of a Woman, and more especially of a Stranger, this gave occasion to the Estates of the Kingdom to reject this his Will, and on the contrary to nominate for Regent, *Peter* Duke of *Conimbra*, Brother to the Defunct, at which the Queen conceived so great a displeasure, that she made her complaint to her Brothers, and the King of *Castille*, but in vain, so that leaving *Portugal*, she retired to *Toledo*, where she dyed a sudden death in the Year, One thousand four hundred five and forty, the Eighteenth day of *February*, not without suspition of poyson. Her body was first inhumed in the Abbey of Religious of the Order of St. *Dominique*, founded in the place where she chose her abode, but afterwards transported to that of *Aljubarot*, by the care of the King her Son. *Her death. 1445.*

King EDWARD had for his Device, a Lance environed with a Serpent (the one is the Symbole of Warre, and the other of Wisdom) with this Inscription, LOCO ET TEMPORE; to represent, that War must be prosecuted in time and place, and in such occasions to use Prudence and Discretion.

Children of EDWARD King OF PORTUGAL, and of LEONOR OF ARRAGON, his Wife.

11. ALPHONSO King of PORTUGAL, continued the Line.

11. FERDINAND OF PORTUGAL, Duke of VISCO, grand Master of the Orders of Christ, and of St. *James*, and Constable of *Portugal*, he accompanied King *Alphonso V*. his Brother in his Warres of *Affrick*, at what time he took the Fort of *Alcacer* a Maritime Port. Afterwards he was again sent into *Affrick*, where he performed several acts of Hostility against the *Mahumetans*, among others the prize of the Town of *Anafe*, and then returned Triumphant and Glorious into his own Countrey.

He married his Cousin *Beatrice* of *Portugal*, a younger Daughter of his Uncle *John* of *Portugal*, Grand Master of the Order of St. *James*, and Constable of the Kingdom. She was a Princess prudent and deliberate, it was she that finished the Peace betwixt the two Kings, *Ferdinand* of *Arragon*, and *Alphonso* of *Portugal*, upon the difference they had concerning the Kingdom of *Castille*, as we have told you before. Some Historians write, That the King of *Portugal*, *John II*. Nephew of FERDINAND, put to death this Prince his Father-in-law; But others, better informed, say, That he dyed at *Cetobriga*, above ten years before *John* came to the Crown of *Portugal*, viz. the Eighth day of *September*, Anno, One thousand four hundred threescore and ten, being only Seven and thirty years old, which was the Flower of his age: His Corps was interred at *Badaios* within the Church of the Conception, which had been founded by the Dutchess *Beatrice* his Wife, who there placed a Convent of Nunnes.

Margin notes:
PORTUGAL-VISCO *D'argent a cinq Escussons d'azure posés en Croix chacun chargé de cinq besants d'argent posez en sautoir à la bordure de gueules, aussi chargée de huit chasteaux d'or.*
Escartelé d'ARRAGON. *D'or a quatre pals de gueules.*
PORTUGAL-VISCO Party de PORTUGAL.
1438.
His Marriage.
His Death, 1470.

Children of FERDINAND OF PORTUGAL, Duke of VISCO, and of BEATRICE OF PORTUGAL, his Wife.

12. JOHN OF PORTUGAL, Duke of VISCO after his Father, dyed without issue.

12. JAMES OF PORTUGAL, also Duke of VISCO, succeeded in the Dutchy after the decease of Prince *John* his eldest brother; But because he maliciously conspired against King *John II*. his brother-in-law, he came to a mournful and tragique end. For in the Year, One thousand four hundred fourscore and three, this young Prince, being but in the Twentieth year of his age, was killed by the Kings own hand; which some Authors believe, was done to the intent that way might be made to the Crown for his Bastard-son,

Margin notes:
PORTUGAL-VISCO
PORTUGAL-VISCO *qui est Escartelé de* PORTUGAL & d'ARRAGON.
Mariana. Lib. 24. C. 23. Vasconcellos.

and the ALGARVES. 49

son, *George* Duke of *Aviero* after his decease; But this design took not effect, for the King better counselled, gave the Estate of the Defunct unto his Brother *Emanuel*, and furthermore, appointed him Heir of the Kingdom by his Testament, which he enjoyed accordingly.

Natural Children of JAMES OF PORTUGAL, Duke of VISCO.

13. ALPHONSO OF PORTUGAL was highly advanced, for King *Emanuel* gave him the Dutchy of *Visco*, and Dignified him with the Office of Constable of *Portugal*, which he had in the Year, *One thousand five hundred*, but he dyed four years after, leaving no Children but one only Daughter, named, *comme cy devant.* PORTUGAL.

14. MARY OF PORTUGAL, who was espoused to the Marquess of VILLE-REAL.

12. EDWARD OF PORTUGAL ⎫
12. DIONYSIO OF PORTUGAL ⎬ all Children of *Ferdinand* of *Portugal*, Duke of *Visco*, by *Beatrice* of *Portugal* his wife, and died in their minority.   PORTUGAL-VISCO
12. SIMON OF PORTUGAL ⎭

12. EMANUEL King OF PORTUGAL, youngest son of *Ferdinand* of *Portugal*, Duke of *Visco*, and of *Beatrix* of *Portugal* his Wife, succeeded King *John II.* and continued the Posterity.

Her Marriage.
12. LEONORA was Queen of *Portugal*, as you may observe in the History of *John II.* King of *Portugal* her Husband, by whom she had one only Son, which was Prince *Alphonso*, deceasing before his Father, as shall be discoursed hereafter.   PORTUGAL. *Party de* PORTUGAL-VISCO

Her Marriage.
12. ISABEL OF PORTUGAL, was Dutchess of BRAGANZA; There shall be more ample mention made of this Princess in the Story of *Ferdinand II.* of the name, Duke of *Braganza* her Husband, from this Marriage came three Sons, and one Daughter, *viz. James* of *Portugal* fourth Duke of *Braganza*, who continued the Line, *Philip* and *Denys* of *Portugal*, *Margaret* their Sister dyed young without having been married.   PORTUGAL-BRAGANZA *Party de* PORTUGAL-VISCO

12. KATHERINE OF PORTUGAL, dyed young.

Here are continued Children of EDWARD King of PORTUGAL, and of LEONOR OF ARRAGON, his Wife.

11. PHILIP OF PORTUGAL, being twelve years old, dyed of the Plague at *Lisbonne*.

EDWARD King of PORTUGAL

Years of CHRIST.

11. LEONORA OF PORTUGAL the Empress, was in the Sixteenth year of her age, espoused (A° One thousand four hundred and fifty, and in the City of *Rome*) unto the Emperour *Frederick* III. Arch-Duke of *Austria*, who was eldest Son of Arch-Duke *Ernest*, and of *Zimburge* of *Massovia* his Wife; *Aneas Sylvius*, afterwards Pope under the name of *Pius* II. being at that time principal Secretary to *Frederick*, negotiated this Marriage. The Princess was in the Year following, Crowned Empress by Pope *Nicholas* V. She dyed in the City of *Neustat* in *Austria*, in the Year, *One thousand four hundred threescore and seven*, being aged Three and thirty years, and was entombed in the Monastery of the Trinity, by her founded in the same place.

Her Marriage. 1450.

Her death. 1467.

As concerning the Emperour her Husband, he had undergone a tedious War against the Arch-duke *Albert* his brother, for *Austria*, and also against *Mathias Coruin* elected King of *Hungary*, for that Kingdom; to which he pretended a Right of succession. He departed this life in the City of *Lints* in *Austria*, the Ninteenth day of *August*, A° One thousand four hundred fourscore and thirteen, which was the Four and fiftieth of his Empire, and the Threescore and eighteenth of his age. From this Marriage issued one Son and a Daughter, *viz*. The Emperour *Maximilian* first of the name, Grand-father (by his Son *Philip* also first of that name, King of *Spain*) to the Emperours *Charles* V. and *Ferdinand* I. *Cunegonde* of *Austria*, *Maximilian*'s Sister, was married to *Albert* IV. of the name, Duke of *Bauaria*, and from them those other Dukes draw their original.

1493.

11. KATHERINE OF PORTUGAL, was promised in Marriage, first to *Charles* of *Nauarre* Prince of *Viana*, eldest Son of *John* King of *Nauarre* and *Arragon*; then to *Edward* the Fourth King of *England*. But she espoused neither the one, nor the other, and at last died unmarried at *Lisbonne* in the Abbey of St. *Clare*, A° One thousand four hundred threescore and three, the Twelfth day of *June*. She had the honour of Burial within the Church of St. *Eloy*.

Her death. 1463.

11. JANE OF PORTUGAL, Queen of *Castille*, was conjoyned in Marriage (the Twentieth day of *May*, in the Year, *One thousand four hundred five and fifty*, at *Cordona*,) to HENRY IV. King of *Castille*, eldest Son of King *John* II. and of *Mary* of *Arragon* his Wife. This Marriage was made by the procuration of the King of *France*, *Charles* VII. at that time confederate with the King of *Castille*, who for this purpose sent to the *Castillian* his Embassadour the Arch-bishop of *Tours*. But this Marriage being Celebrated in a time of War, and great trouble, men presaged nothing from the effects thereof but evil events, which accordingly fell out. HENRY and JANE had issue one Daughter, which was *Jane* of *Castille*, (some erroneously call her *Elizabeth*) affianced unto *Charles* of *France*, Duke of *Berry*, then of *Guyenne*, younger Brother to *Lewis* XI. King of *France*; But this Duke being variable and inconstant, abandoned her, and applyed himself to *Mary* of *Bourgongne*, only daughter of *Charles* the *Hardy*, Duke of *Bourgongne*, whom he likewise married not.

Her Marriage. 1455.

So that the Princess of *Castille* had for Husband her Nephew *Alphonso* V. of the name King of *Portugal*, who challenged the Kingdom of *Castille* in the Right of this his Wife, as you shall see more fully hereafter in his

Years of CHRIST.	his History. King *Henry* was reputed in the opinion of the world, uncapable of Children, which gave suspition to many to doubt whether this Princess were really his Daughter, or supposed to be so; nevertheless he owned her by his Testament made before his death, which hapned to be at *Madrid*, A° *One thousand four hundred threescore and fourteen*, in the month of *December*, and in him finished the direct Line of the Kings of *Castille* descended from *Henry* the Bastard; from whom, (being of a couragious and high-flown spirit;) this Prince did much degenerate, who was a person of a weak judgement, and of little Merit.
1474.	
Her death. 1475.	Two years after Queen JANE OF PORTUGAL, his Widow, dyed at *Madrid* in the month of *January*, others more truly report her Death to be in *June*, *One thousand four hundred threescore and fifteen*. She was interred in the Church of St. *Francis*. It's doubted likewise, whether she dyed in Child-bed, or whether her life was shortned by Poyson caused to be given her by the King of *Portugal* her Brother; which last is rather to be believed, because she is taxed to be incontinent, and to suffer her self to be transported to unwarrantable affections.

Marginal: *Idem. Lib.* 23. *Cap.* 11. & *Lib.* 24. *Cap.* 4. & 9.

A Natural Son of EDWARD King of PORTUGAL.

II. JOHN-EMANUEL OF PORTUGAL, was base Son of King *Edward* by *Jane Manuel* Cousin of *Eleanor* of *Arragon*; He was educated with great care, and brought up unto Virtue, by *Nonio Alvarez Pereira* Lord of *Braganca*. After he had approved his Valour in that War against the *Infidels* and *Moors* of *Affrica*; being inspired with devotion, and contempt of earthly things; He forsook the world, and took on him a Religious habit, in the Convent of the *Carmelite* Friers of *Lisbonne*; which he founded, and where he lived most Religiously: Yet afterwards he had given him the Bishoprick of *Septe* in *Affrick*; and then that of *Ingonte*. In fine, King *Alphonso V.* invited him to Court, where he gave him the charge of Master of his Chappel, of whose Wisdom and good Counsel, this King was a strict observer.

Marginal: *Vasconcellius.*

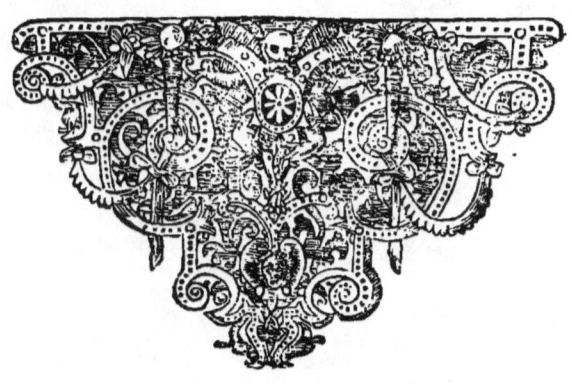

II. ALPHONSO V.

Of the Name, KING of PORTUGAL and the ALGARVES; Sirnamed,

The African.

CHAP. XIII.

PORTUGAL.

D'argent à cinq Escussons d'azur posés en Croix, chacun chargé de cinq besants d'argent posés en sautoir à la bordure de gueulles, chargée de huict chasteaux d'or.

PORTUGAL
Party de
CONIMBRA.

Escartelé Au 1. & 4. de PORTUGAL *au 2. & 3. d'*ANGLETERRE.

PORTUGAL
Party de
CASTILLE.

De gueulles au Chasteau d'or.
Escartelé de LEON *qui est d'argent au Lyon de pourpre.*

O King *Edward* succeeded this Prince, who was his eldest Son, born in the Month of *January*, A° One thousand four hundred thirty and two.

He was but six years old when he succeeded to the Crown. His minority causing great agitations for the Regency, his Grandees having revolted from Queen *Eleanor* of *Arragon* his Mother, who pretended thereto by the Testamentary Will of her Husband; but the Duke of *Conimbra*, Uncle by the Fathers side to the young King, carried it, as we have before written.

And notwithstanding this Prince had prudently and faithfully administred the affairs of State, yet some persons envious at his Virtue, having given the King some evil Impressions concerning him, he was easily induced to Commence a War with the Duke, which he so sharply prosecuted, that he gave a total rout to his Army, and kill'd him upon the Field, which Action was the more unnatural and tragical, because the same Duke had a double relation to this King, both by Affinity, and Blood; for (in the Year, *One thousand four hundred forty and eight*) the Princess ELIZABETH OF CO-
NIMBRA

1438.

His Birth 1432.

His first Marriage. 1448.

King of PORTUGAL and the ALGARVES. 53

NIMBRA his Daughter had been espoused to ALPHONSO. But it often falls out, that Passion, that dangerous Counseller of Princes, shuts her eyes to all manner of Respects.

This War being stifled, the King of *Portugal*, by the example of his Grand-sire and Father, turned his Arms against the *Moors*. He had made a promise to Pope *Calixtus*, to fall upon the *Turk* in *Asia*, and for that purpose had accepted the Crossiade: but the death of that Soveraign Bishop hapning in the mean time, he cancelled that design of assaulting the *Turk*. Nevertheless he resolved to pass into *Affrick*, and to make his way, transported a good Army, besieged the Fort of *Alcacer* near unto *Septe*, which he subdued by fine force, and entred in Triumph. Not long after the King of *Fez* having two several times laid Siege to the same place, it was with so much valour defended by the *Portuguesses*, that they were constrained to retire with shame and prejudice. *Vasconcellius.* *Nonius.*

Four years after ALPHONSO made his second expedition into *Affrica*, but not attended with the former success. Afterward he set Sail the third time for that Countrey, better accompanied than before: For he transported Thirty thousand men, with whom he reduced the strong City of *Arzille*, at the assault of which he gave such proof of his Valour, and became so terrible to the *Infidels*, that they also quit and abandoned the City of *Tangier*. But as he made his entrance into the same City, the loss of his Uncle *Ferdinand* coming into his memory afresh, somewhat allayed the satisfaction he received in the Prize of this place. Also so many memorable and glorious Conquests, acquired him, as another *Scipio*, the Sirname and Title of, *The Affrican*. *Vasconcellius.*

The Queen his first Wife that virtuous Princess, ceased not to bear him still that respect, affection, and honour required, notwithstanding that fatal Difference that had been betwixt him and her father. She deceased at *Evora* in the Month of *December*, in the Year, *One thousand four hundred fifty and six*. *Mariana. Lib. 22. C. 17.*

So ALPHONSO being a Widower, took a resolution to marry a second Wife, and for that purpose cast his eyes upon *Jane* of *Castille* his Neece, Daughter of King *Henry IV.* and of *Jane* of *Portugal* his Sister. Having therefore obtained a Dispensation from Pope *Sixtus IV.* he espoused her in the Year, *One thousand four hundred threescore and fifteen*, others say that it was in the year following; then having been proclaimed Kings of *Castille* after the death of *Henry*; they sent their Summons to *Ferdinand* King of *Arragon*, and his Wife the Princess *Elizabeth* of *Castille* Sister of *Henry*, who pretended to be true and lawful Heir, to desist from the enterprize which they endeavoured upon the Kingdom of *Castille*, maintaining that *Jane* was not Daughter of King *Henry*, for all that he had owned her for such by his Testament, and for his Heir. But this Summons was of little effect, for they ceased not by the strength of their great Forces, and those of their partakers, to maintain themselves in the Title by them usurped, and in their Actual possession. *Vignier.*

This was the reason why the Duke of *Arenal*, and the Marquess of *Villena*, Confederates of the *Portuguesses*, and in whose protection the Father had left his Daughter, with those of their followers, strengthned with some *French* Troops, with the succours of *Alphonso*, took Arms against *Elizabeth*, and endeavoured the seising some places. Upon which motive *Ferdinand* also drew into the Field, and begirt the Castle *Taure* with a strait Siege; To the relief of which the King of *Portugal* came in person with his *Mariana. lib. 24. c. 10.*

his associates; the Armies being come to blows, they disputed it with so much Gallantry, that the *Castillian* lost the day, (according to the *Portugal* Historians, but the Histories of *Castille* agree not in this point;) nevertheless they were not forced to raise their Siege.

The King of *Portugal* having recruited his Army with a good number of Souldiers, came to another engagement with the Army of *Ferdinand*, but the issue of this second Battel was contrary to the other: For he was vanquished, and unfortunately put to flight, which gave an absolute check to the course of his designs, and of ever arriving at his pretentions in *Castille*. Likewise also the Marquess of *Villena*, and other Lords of his party, being suborned, and corrupted with gifts, abandoned him, and ranged themselves on the stronger side, being that of *Ferdinand*.

Vasconcellius.

The *Arragonians* took this advantage; and to confirm their cause, obtained a Bull from the Pope, which he made to be published in *Castille*, by which the Marriage of King ALPHONSO with *Jane*, was declared null, and of no validity, notwithstanding it was Consummated by his Authority, and according to his Rescript: But he declared that, by that his Bull he had been circumvented.

In this extremity the *Portugueses* yet stood upon their guard, hoping to find assistance from the Kingdom of *France*. And to that intent sent their Express to King *Lewis XI*. from whom they only received a fair reception, and good words; for it fell out to be in that nick of time that *Lewis* had made a League with *Ferdinand*, that he might the better prosecute the War with the Count of *Roussillion*, so that the grand affairs that he had at that time against *Charles* Duke of *Bourgongne*, would not permit him to give succours to ALPHONSO; It's the judgement of an Historian of that time, that if he had assisted him, it's very probable he might have brought his Enemy to a Composition, and to that point which he desired.

P. Mathieu en l'Histoire de Louis XI. livre 7.

Philip de Commines.

Then in this despair observing that all things went contrary to his expectation, he designed to perform (as a private and unknown person) the Voyage to *Jerusalem*; where in his youth he had made a Vow to go fight the *Turks*, which he had undertaken, had not he been diverted by the King of *France*. At his return into *Portugal*, he found the Prince his young Son, commanding in the Quality of King, according to that charge which he had given him upon his journey into *France*. *Mariana* reports, that this was by Letters at his departure from *Paris*.

Vasconcellius.

Mariana.

So ALPHONSO constrained to submit to Time and adverse Fortune, looked upon a Peace as the best expedient he could make use of with his enemies, which was concluded at *Alcantara*, in the Year, One thousand four hundred threescore and nineteen, by which he excluded himself from any farther Pretentions to that Kingdom. This Peace was confirmed and Sealed by the agreement of several Marriages contracted betwixt the Children of the Adversary Kings: It being remarkable, that in the Treaty of this Peace, it was particularly declared, That it should continue the space of an hundred and one years; those which effected it, putting, as it's usual so to do, the Incertain for the Infinite. But this limited number proved Prophetical. For the time an hundred and one years, continued from the end of this War, until that in the Year, One thousand five hundred and fourscore, this Kingdom was subdued by *Philip II*. King of *Spain* (descended from *Ferdinand* and *Elizabeth*) against King *Anthony* of *Portugal*, when he rendred himself absolute Master thereof. So that the words and Agreements of the Treaty of Peace, did at last meet with the quality of the Event.

Idem. Lib.24. Cap.20.

Nonius.

Convestaggio au l'ure de l'union de PORTUGAL au Royaume de CASTILLE.

Years of CHRIST.
1476.

1476.

1477.

1479.

Now

King of PORTUGAL and the ALGARVES. 55

Years of Christ.

Now ALPHONSO transported with indignation, that the Queen his Wife had been deprived of that Right which she had to the Kingdom of *Castille*, and vexed with the sinister events that had hapned to his Estate: but principally that his Wife had put on the habit of Religious in the Monastery of St. *Clare* which she had founded at *Santarem*, was carried away with such an extream excess of Melancholly, that it cast him into a violent Disease, and so finished the course of his life at *Sintra*, being the place of his Birth. His decease hapned the Eight (*Mariana* writes the Last) day of *August*, A° One thousand four hundred fourscore and one, having held the Scepter Forty years, and lived Fifty. He lieth at the Royal Abbey of *Battel*, with his Ancestors.

His Death. 1481.

Mariana.

Lib. 14. Cap. 21.

This Prince is commended for his Valour, Sobriety, Continence, and Liberality, as also to have been the first of the Kings of *Portugal*, that placed a Liberary in the Royal Palace, by which we may believe, that in imitation of his Father, he also was a lover of Learning.

Children of ALPHONSO V. *King of* PORTUGAL, *and of* ELIZABETH OF CONIMBRA *his first Wife.*

12. JOHN Prince OF PORTUGAL, dyed young.

12. JOHN II. of the name King OF PORTUGAL, whose Story is comprehended in the Chapter following.

12. JANE OF PORTUGAL, born in the Year, *One thousand four hundred fifty and two*, was desired in Marriage by three great Monarchs, *Maximilian* King of the *Romans* afterwards Emperour first of the name, *Charles VIII.* King of *France*, and *Richard III.* King of *England.* But she refused all these matches; and at what time her Father made his expedition into *Affrica*, being only Eighteen years old, yet had so great a confidence of her Wisdom, that he left her Regent of his Estate in his absence, where she governed his affairs with great care.

Her Birth. 1452.

Vasconcellius

1470.

At his return being transported with a holy zeal, and misprision of the World, she made it her supplication to the King her Father, that he would permit her to pass the Habit of a Nun, and to encloyster her self, her request he granted, and so she went first to *Aveiro*, then to *Odivelles*, where she passed the rest of her life in great Humility. She died at the age of Eight and thirty years, in the Month of *May*, *Anno*, One thousand four hundred fourscore and ten. *Vasconcellos* is very large in the Story of her Life and worthy Actions.

Her death. 1490.

P 2 JOHN

12. JOHN II.

Of the Name, King of PORTUGAL and the ALGARVES, Lord of GUINEE, Sirnamed, *THE GREAT*.

CHAP. XIV.

PORTUGAL
D' argent a cinq Escuissons d'azur pose en Croix chacun chargé de cinq besans d'argent posez en sautoir a la bordure de gueulles chargee de sept chasteaux d'or.

PORTUGAL
Party de PORTUGAL-VISCO
& de PORTUGAL. *Escartelé d'* ARRAGON.

S. a sobuel. fax.

Mong the troubles and infelicities wherewith *Alphonso V.* was afflicted toward the end of his Reign, he had at the least this contentment and happiness, to have a valiant Son, as was this Prince; who first saw the light of day at *Lisbonne*, where Queen *Elizabeth* of *Conimbra* his Mother brought him into the World the Fourth day of *May*, in the Year, *One thousand four hundred fifty and five.*

1481.

His Birth; 1455.

In his younger years he behaved himself with so much Gallantry in the second expedition of *Affrica*, but more particularly at the prize of *Argesille* from the *Moors*, that the King his Father conferred upon him the Order of Knighthood; Afterwards also he gave testimony of a great Courage in the Warre of *Castille*; And upon *Alphonso*'s journey into *France*, he commanded this young Prince to take upon him the Government of his Estate, with the Title of King. At his return his Father perswading him to retain this Title and Royal quality, during his absence in *Affrica*, as a good Son, he refused this proffer, and relinquished the Dignity of King; saying, *That he received a much greater contentment*

Years of CHRIST.

1481.

1483.

tentment to see his Father re-established in his Kingdom, than that he himself had Command of the whole Earth.

The time of his Fathers death being come, he succeeded him, and took in hand the Scepter, when he was of the age of Six and twenty years. No sooner was he mounted upon the Throne, but he caused Justice severely to be administred, without exception, permitting the Judges, and other Ministers of State, to seize upon the Malefactors wheresoever they were to be found, not exempting the Houses of the Grandees it self, notwithstanding that Priviledge, and Antient Custom that might be alledged to the contrary. This caused many of his own Relations wickedly to plot against him, and to hold intelligence, and contrive conspiracies, with the *Castillian* to his ruine. The Chief of these were *Ferdinand* Duke of *Braganza*, and *James* Duke of *Visco*; the contrivances and pernitious designs of the first having been manifestly discovered by his own Letters at his Indictment, so that being convicted, he was condemned, and then publickly executed, and his Goods confiscated; which so much amazed some of them, that they fled into *Castille*.

But for all this the audacity of the Conspirators was such, that they ceased not yet to contrive the death of the King, of which he had information, and not long after got the Duke of *Visco* into his power, where he lost his life, being assassinated by the Kings own hand. The severity of which action, hath by some been called Inhumanity, & Cruelty: but this default was recompenced with several perfections of Body and Soul, with which he was adorned.

He designed to prosecute the high and glorious designs of the King his Father for the Discovery and Conquests of strange Regions, proposing a beginning by the Western Coast of *Ethiopia*, and giving Commission to *John Cane* a *Portugal* Knight, to search out a Countrey which is on the other side the Equator, where being arrived, he found it to be the Kingdom of *Congo*, the inhabitants whereof were so humane, and docile, that some of them suffered themselves to be brought into *Portugal*, and there, with the Language, they were instructed in the Principles of the Christian Religion, and then Baptized. At their return they perswaded their King and his Subjects also to be Baptized. With this King, and with others of *Ethiopia* JOHN entred into League, and caused in this Countrey to be raised the Cittadel of St. *George*, since called, the *Mine*, from which the Kings his Successors have extracted a good quantity of Gold.

In the beginning of this Voyage the *Portugueses* having arrived at a Cape, which by estimation is the greatest of the World, they conceived so happy success in their enterprise, by the advantage thereof, that they gave it the appellation of, *The Cape of good Hope*, antiently being called the Front of *Affrica*; it opened them the way to the knowledge of the Estate of the *Indian* Princes, and to penetrate further into *Ethiopia*, where they found reigning that Prince, which we vulgarly call *Prester John*; because he is named in his Language, *Belulgian*, which signifieth, *A Precious Stone of incomparable excellence*, a Title and old Sirname usurped by the Antient Emperours of *Ethiopia*, who maintain themselves to be descended from the Blood of *Solomon* by the Queen of *Saba*.

Some time after the same King JOHN II. sent a great Army into *Affrica*, which landed in the Isle of *Gesire*, which is the mouth of the River *Luc*, where the *Portugueses* endeavoured to raise a Fort against the impeachments of the King of *Fez*; but this King, after he had cut off their passage of retreat, forced them to quit their prize, and by composition to return into their own Countrey.

Mariana. lib. 24. C.23.

Viscorcellius.

History of Portugal.

Nun.

Q   In

JOHN II. of the Name,

Vignier.

In the mean time King JOHN being advertised of the Donation made to the King of *Castille*, *Ferdinand*, by Pope *Alexander VI*. of those new Regions which had been discovered by his Subjects, the *Portugal* being interessed therein, as prejudicial to the discovery that for his part he had made upon the Coast of *Ethiopia*, for this reason entred into a difference with the *Castillian*; which caused the Pope on his own accord, to give unto King *Ferdinand* the *Indies* newly found out, and to the King of *Portugal* the Coast of *Affrica*: But to the intent that the one might not attempt any thing upon the other, he caused to be drawn upon the Globe a Line falling from North to South, which passed towards the West, above Four hundred miles distant from the Isles of *Cape-verd*, that it might not touch upon *Affrica*.

Years of CHRIST.

Mariana. Vasconcellius.

This, with other violent Actions of King JOHN, drew upon him the odium of several persons, in such manner, that they were followed with conspiracies against his life; that at last he was found poysoned in the place of *Alvor* in his Kingdom of *Algarve*, the Five and twentieth day of *October*, in the Year, *One thousand four hundred fourscore and fifteen*; after he had lived Forty years, and reigned Fourteen. His body was first inhumed in the Cathedral Church of *Silues*, until that in the Year, *One thousand four hundred fourscore and nineteen*, King *Emanuel* his Cousin and Successor, and his Estates, caused it to be brought to the Abbey of *Battel*.

His Death. 1495.

He was very Pious, and Charitable to the Poor, for whose Retreat, and Relief, he founded and endowed a fair Hospital at *Lisbonne*. His Prudence appeared in the government of his Kingdom, and by the placing his favours upon persons of desert; keeping a most exact Register of the names of those that had faithfully served him, and who were capable, and endued with qualities required, in the administration of his affairs; He had a spirit elated, and ambitious of the greatest things.

Mariana.

About the Year, *One thousand four hundred threescore and ten*, not being above Fifteen years old, he married LEONORA OF PORTUGAL, or OF VISCO, his Cousin, Daughter of his Uncle *Ferdinand* of *Portugal* Duke of *Visco*, and Constable of the Kingdom, by whom he had only one Son, Heir apparent to his Estates, but he had the unhappiness and regret to see him dye before him, contrary to the common course of Nature. Then endeavouring to legitimate his Natural Son *George* Duke of *Aveiro*, with some intention to leave him the Crown; The Queen his Wife opposed this design, not willing that her Brother the Prince *Emanuel* should be deprived of the Right he had to the Kingdom by the decease of his Cousin *Alphonso* the young Prince, and to which he succeeded after decease of King JOHN.

His Marriage. 1470.

Idem. Vasconcellius.

Who took in his Device, a Pelican, a Bird so Natural and affectionate to her young, that she wounds her breast, and feeds them with her own blood, with this Inscription, PRO LEGE ET GREGE; witnessing thereby, how much he both loved, and cherished his people; for whose defence and Religion, he had exposed his life to several hazards; Some have noted, that he was the first among the Kings of *Portugal*, that adorned the Helmet of the *Portugal* Arms with a Sphere for Creast, which he took as a presage of the new Discoveries which were made during his Reign, and of some of the Kings his Successors, under both the Poles.

Children

Children of JOHN II. of the name, King of PORTUGAL, and of LEONOR OF VISCO, his Wife.

13. ALPHONSO Prince OF PORTUGAL. There is remarkable in this young Prince, looked upon as the Hope and Prop of the Royal House of *Portugal*, a notable example of the Inconstancy and frailty of humane things. For after that (in sumpteous apparel, and great magnificence,) he had (in *November*, A° One thousand four hundred fourscore and ten,) espoused the Princess ELIZABETH OF CASTILLE, eldest Daughter of *Ferdinand* V and of *Isabel*, King and Queen of *Castille* and *Arragon*, in the City of *Stremos*, this Marriage, (which it was thought, would be one day the Earnest of a perpetual Concord betwixt the two Neighbouring Crowns) continued not above seven months only, for the young Prince finished his life at *Sanctarem*, by a sad and unhappy accident, being a violent fall from his Horse, (as he was running a Courser;) so that with the bruise thereof he died quickly after, to the great affliction of the Kings and their people, who had the unhappiness to see the Torches of his pompious Funeral set on flame, almost so soon as those of his Nuptials. He was then Sixteen years old. His body was brought and interred in the Monastery of *Battel*. His Widow in second Marriage was espoused to the Great *Emanuel* Successor of *John II.* Father of this ALPHONSO.

Some Authors write, that this death came by the Judgement of God, for his Fathers cruel usage of some Princes of his own Blood.

So the Crown of *Portugal*, that had continued Three hundred and fifty years in a direct Male Line, from Father to Son, or from Brother to Brother, fell into the Collateral of the Dukes of *Visco*.

Margin: His Marriage. 1490. His Death. 1491. PORTUGAL Comme cy devant. PORTUGAL Party de CASTILLE.

A Natural Son of King JOHN II.

13. GEORGE OF PORTUGAL, Duke of *Conimbra*, hath given original to the Dukes of *Aueiro*, who shall be mentioned in the Second Part of this History.

12. EMANUEL

King of PORTUGAL and the ALGARVES, on this and the other side the Sea in *Affrick*; Lord of *Guineé*, and of the Conquest, Navigation, and Commerce of *Ethiopia*, *Arabia*, *Persia*, and *India*.

CHAP. XV.

PORTUGAL
Comme cy devant.

Party de CASTILLE-ARRAGON.

De gueulles au Chasteau d'or, qui est CASTILLE. *Escartele d'argent au lyon de pourpre qui est* LEON.

Party d'or a quatre pals de gueulles qui est ARRAGON.

Contre party de mesme l'escu flinché d'argent à deux Aigles de sable, qui est ARRAGON-SICILIE.

PORTUGAL
Party de CASTILLE-ARRAGON *comme cy dessus.*

He continued success of this Monarch, his heroick Virtues, and so many glorious Conquests and adventures, which he happily atchieved, having vanquished and made tributary several Kings, but chiefly the care he had for the plantation of the Christian Religion in the most remote Regions, have (justly) given him the esteem of one of the greatest, most illustrious, and most happy Princes of the World.

The King of *Portugal* his Grand-father by the Fathers side, had issue a younger Son, who carried the name of *Ferdinand*, and was Duke of *Visco*, who by a Princess of his own Blood (called *Beatrice*, daughter of his Uncle *John* of *Portugal*, Grand Master of the Order of St. *James*, and Constable of the Kingdom,) had among other Children this King EMANUEL, born in the City of *Alcochet* the last day of *May*, in the Year, One thousand four hundred threescore and nine.

1495.

His Birth. 1469.

He

and the ALGARVES, *&c.*

PORTUGAL.
Party D'AUSTRICHE
ou ESPAINE.

Years of CHRIST.

He was first honoured with the Title of Duke of *Beia*; then being in the Six and twentieth year of his age, succeeded to the Crown of *Portugal* after the death of *John II.* his Cosin, dying without Children in the Year, One thousand four hundred thirty and five.

Qui est
Escartelé, Au premier aussy. Escartelé, Au 1. & 4. de CASTILLE; Au 2. & 3. de LEON.
Au 2. grand quartier d'ARRAGON; Party d'ARRAGON-SICILIE.
Au 3. quartier de gueulles a la fasse d'argent qui est AUSTRICHE.
Sousteun de bandé d'or & d'azur de six pieces, a la bordure de gueulles, qui est de BOURGONGNE la primitive Branche.
Au 4. quartier d'azur, a trois Fleurs de Lis d'or, a la bordure composée d'argent & de gueulles, qui est BOURGONGNE de la second Branche.
Sousteun de Sable au Lyon d'or, armé & lampassé de gueulles qui est BRABANT.
Et sur les trois & quatriesme grands quartiers d'or au Lyon de Sable qui est FLANDRES.
Party d'argent a une Aigle esployée de gueulles, becquée & membrée d'or, qui est du Marquisat du Sainct Empire.

1495.
First of all he called a General Council, in which he put the Question, Whether he should prosecute, or decline the designs of the King his Predecessor for the Conquest of new discoveries; after the deliberation, and advice required in a matter of that moment, it was resolved, That he was obliged to prosecute them, as well for the Honour, as the Profit and great advantage, that would thereby accrue to him and his Estate.

Hier. Osorius in Hist. Reg. Emanuel. Mariana.

Then being set on edge by the example of the Kings of *Castille* his Neighbours, who had made discovery of the *West-Indies*, he endeavoured for his part to find out with his Ships, all that Countrey on the further side the Cape of *Good Hope* (at which the Fleet of King *John II.* had before arrived) unto the *East-Indies*, from whence he knew that the precious Stones, Spices, Drouges, Perfumes, Medicinals, and other singular and precious commodities were imported for the accommodation of whole *Europe*.

1499.
So that in the Year, One thousand four hundred fourscore and nineteen, he sent *Vasquez Gama* a *Portugal* Gentleman with four Ships, who in two years Voyage discovered the whole Western Coast of *Ethiopia*, with the Isles of *Quiola*, *Mosambique*, *Monbaze*, *Melinde*, and at last arrived at the Kingdom of *Malabar*, otherwise called *Calecut*, so named from the Capital City so named, which is the place of all the East most frequented by the Merchants, and from whence the greatest quantity of Spices is shipped for this part of the world. Wherefore after that the *Portugueses* had been favourably received by the King of this Countrey, and observed with great danger (which was occasioned by the unfaithfulnesse of the *Moors*) that which they knew their Prince EMANUEL to be most desirous of, they returned to bring the honour to their Countrey of the Discovery of things not known, nor seen; since the Creation of the World, by any Nation of *Europe*, which Antiquity it self thought to be impossible.

Osorius.

1500.
Not long after he sent a second *Caravelle* about the Year, One thousand five hundred, under the Command of *Pedro Alvarez Cupral*, which endeavouring to steer the same course with the former, was by storm driven upon the Coast of *Brasille* (at that time known by the name of St. *Croix*) joyning to *Peru*. By others neverthelesse it's believed, that it was *Americ Vespure* a *Florentine*, who under the Countenance of the same King EMANUEL, discovered the Countrey of *Brazille*: But be it as it will, *Cupral* having informed himself of the state of this Countrey, steered the course that he formerly intended, and passed by the Kingdoms of *Quiola*, *Mosambique*, and *Melinde*, with the Kings whereof he contracted an Alliance in the name of EMANUEL his Master, and there raised several Fortresses,

Idem. Osorius.

Mariana. lib. 16.
Lopez Castagneda in the History of the East-Indies.
John de Barros.

R

tresses. Finally, he arrived at the Port of *Calecut*, the King whereof at his first entrance entertained him with friendship, desiring also to enter into a League with the King of *Portugal*. But the *Moors* and *Sarazens* that held a Commerce in his Kingdom, so wrought upon the King, that they changed his mind, and he became a mortal enemy. This was the ground of a cruel Warre betwixt them, which lasted above Thirteen years, in which time the *Portugals* performing many notable actions of Warre, acquired a grand reputation, and Empire in the East, the experience of their Valour causing the Kings of *Cochan*, *Coulan*, and *Cananor*, Neighbours of *Calecut*, to seek their friendship, by a Peace with their King EMANUEL.

In the mean time the *Portugal* Garisons of *Affrica* under the Government of *John Meneses* the Kings Lieutenant, in the City and Fortress of *Arzille*, and of *Roderick de Castro*, engaged the *Moors* with happy success, and routed the Army of the King of *Fez*, upon his endeavour of the surprise of the Town of *Tangier*. At the same instant a Squadron of three Ships commanded by *John Nuntz*, arrived at the *Indies*, where they engaged the King of *Calecut*, who was shamefully defeated by a number much inferiour to his, in pursuit of which they obtained several other signal Victories.

Sometime after the same King of *Calecut* fell upon the King of *Cochin* with such fury, (because he had given entertainment to the *Portugueses*) that he was forced to forsake his Kingdom; which he chose rather to suffer (like a Noble Prince) than to renounce that League of Amity and Faith which he had promised to the King of *Portugal*, who was so sensible of this Action, that he judged himself obliged to re-establish him, and for that purpose sent ten Ships under the Conduct of the famous Captain *Alphonso d'-Albuquerque*, who chased the *Calecutins* out of the Kingdom of *Cochin*, re-established their King, and built a Fort for his Retreat; then having given some allarums to the King of *Calecut* in his own Countrey, they returned Richly laden with Spices. This Infidel King having raised another Army, consisting of Fifty thousand Souldiers, transported them in an hundred and sixty Gallies, and came before the Pass of *Cochin* to repell the *Portugueses*, but this great Army found so sharp an entertainment, that they returned home, less by the number of Eight thousand, which were there kill'd, without the loss (a Miracle if true) of one Christian.

This happy success gave encouragement to King EMANUEL to send *Francis Almeida* his Viceroy to the *Indies*, to Establish and confirm his Empire, and also to maintain the Kings his Confederates in security against their Enemies. This Viceroy in his Voyage to establish a Lieutenant at *Quiola*, fell upon the King of *Mombaze*, because he would not declare himself subject to the King of *Portugal* his Master, and also upon the King of *Onor*, which is on the Coast of *Arabia*, on whom he gained a famous Victory, and fired the City thereof. At his arrival in the *Indies*, there came an Ambassadour from the King of *Narsingne*, the most considerable of *East-India*, on the other side the River *Ganges*, to Contract a friendship with the *Portugueses*, saying, That *he was incited to search them out, for the wonders that they were reported to have accomplished in those parts.*

At which time the King of *Zophala* in *Ethiopia* came to an engagement with the *Portugueses*, where they not only put his Army to flight, but chased him to the Gates of his own Palace, and for the third time were Victors over the Naval Army of the King of *Calecut*: the like good fortune attended their actions in *Affrica*, where they reduced into their power, the strong

PORTUGAL and the ALGARVES, &c.

Years of Christ. strong Town of *Zafin* situate in the Province of *Morocco*, or *Mauritania Tingitana*, and then raised that Siege which *Mahumet* King of *Fez* had laid to the Citadel of *Arzille*.

About this time *Helen* the Widow of the King of *Ethiopia* (vulgarly called *Prester John*,) who had the Government of the young King *Atani Tingil* her Grand-child, likewise sent her Ambassadour to King EMANUEL, to conclude a Peace with him. In a Letter which she wrote him, she made mention of a Prophesie: That in the later dayes, there should descend from the French Region, a Prince that should extirpate and abolish all the Nations of the *Moors* and *Barbarians*.

1509. The defeat of the Navy of the Souldan of *Babylon*; which was joyned *Osorius. Lib.6.* with those of the Kings of *Cambaye* and *Calecut*, given by the Valiant *Almeida*, constrained also this King to render himself Vassal and Tributary to the *Portugueses*: Who with their new supplies sent to the *Indies*, discovered the Isle of St. *Laurence*, and then delivered from the servitude of the *Arrabes*, the Isle of *Zacocora* inhabited by the Christians.

On the other side *Alphonso d' Albuquerque* Captain of another Army, subdued the Isle of *Ormus*, situate in the mouth of the Gulph of *Persia*, and compelled the King thereof to render himself subject to the King of *Portugal*; being at that time Vassal to the Sophy of *Persia*. The same *Albuquerque* successor of *Almeida*, subjected the City of *Goa* by fine force, which *Thuanus.*
1510. is at present an Arch-bishoprick, and the Chief of this Estate; as also the residence of the Viceroy. The strong City of *Benastarin* also owns him for her Conquerour.

But we cannot without admiration inform you, being a thing which surpasseth almost humane belief, that the Generous *Albuquerque* assisted with a small number, subdued the opulent City of *Malaca* situate in the mouth of the golden *Chersonesus*, a City surrounded with strong Bulwarks, defen- *Vasconcellius;* ded by Thirty thousand Souldiers, and fortified with Eight thousand peeces
1513. of Canon, where he made prise of above Three millions of gold; and then seized the Islands of the *Moluccos*.

In the mean time *Zeiam* Prince of the Puissant City of *Azamor* in *Mau-* *Nonius;* *ritania*, having violated the Faith he had given to the *Portugueses*; EMA- *Osorius,* NUEL to be revenged, sent a Fleet of Two hundred Ships, attacqued *Vignier.* this City with such fury, that the Besieged after they had endured some assaults, were glad to quit the place to the *Portugueses*; who encouraged by the success of so much prosperity, pursued their Conquests, took and sacqued several other Towns and Fortresses; and defeated the Armies of *Cherif* Lord of the Province of *Zela* in *Mauritania*, and also those of *Mahumed* and *Nazec* Kings of *Fez* and of *Mequinesie*.

1515. Not long after, in the Year, *One thousand five hundred and fif-* *Osorius;* *teen*, the Ambassadour of *David* King of *Ethiopia* arrived in *Portugal*, sent to negotiate a Peace with King EMANUEL; so much was the Renown of his Puissance and Authority spread almost over the whole Universe.

But the sweetness of so much Prosperity, was at last somewhat distempered with the bitterness of Adversity; when in the same year, one of the *Portugal* Armies consisting of a considerable number of Ships, was at their return defeated in *Affrica* near unto the River *Mamora*, by that of the Kings of *Fez* and *Morocco*.

For as this great Monarch in all his famous Designs, made the glory, and advancement of the service of God his principal end; so had he a diligent

R 2 care

EMANUEL King of PORTUGAL

care for the establishment of the Christian Religion in *Ethiopia*, *India*, *Affrick*, and divers other Regions. And for other Monuments of his signal Piety, he caused to be built several Temples, which he richly endowed; he did the like in *Portugal*, as the Magnificent Church of *Bethleem* dedicated to the holy Virgin, upon the River *Tagus* near unto *Lisbonne*, and the Monastery of St. *Jerosme* in the same place, another stately Church at *Tomar*, and the Convent of the *Cordeliers* at *Evora*; as also a House at *Lisbonne*, called *De Misericordia*, for the Relief of poor Gentlemen. He also Founded the Royal Palace in the same City, and another at *Conimbra*.

Marians. Lib.26.Cap.17. Vasconcellius.

After so many notable Victories, he sent a stately Ambassade to Pope *Leo X*. with several rich presents, besides a Rinocere, and an Elephant, which was (according to a *Portugal* Historian) the first that *Rome* had ever seen come from the Eastern parts.

1513. *Idem.*

In fine, EMANUEL departed this life at *Lisbonne* the Thirteenth day of *December*, in the Year, *One thousand five hundred twenty and one*, aged Fifty and two years, having Reigned Six and twenty. He was inhumed in the same Church of *Bethleem*, which he left unfinished; But Queen *Katherine* King *John III*. his Sons Wife built the High Altar, and also erected two stately Monuments for this King and Queen, a place since designed for the Mortuary of their Kings.

His Death. 1521. *Marians. Vasconcellius.*

Besides the works of Piety which we have observed in this King, he had also the care to convert unto the Christian faith, a good number of *Jews*, and to exterminate the *Sarazens* his Kingdom. He remitted to the Ecclesiastiques, the tenths which they payed to his Demain for Sales and Acquisitions, caused several profitable Laws to be digested into better Order, and Administred Justice with all Integrity. Also by his Wisdom, and by so many signal Acts, and prosperous Voyages, he rendered his Kingdom, Rich, and Flourishing, abounding in Gold, Silver, Pearl, precious stones, Spices, and other excellent Commodities, so that the *Portugueses* called his Reign, *The Golden Age*. He was furthermore admired for his Sobriety, and to have abstained from Wine the whole course of his life. He was a great Lover of Hunting, Hawlking, and Musick.

Osorius.

His Device was a Sphere, and a terrestial Globe environed with the Sea, with this Circumscription, PRIMUS CIRCUNDEDISTI ME. To signifie, that, His Fleets had compassed the whole Circle of the Earth.

This great King was thrice married; First (*A° One thousand four hundred fourscore and seventeen*, in the Month of *October*, and in the City of *Alcantara*,) to the Princess ISABEL OF CASTILLE, eldest Daughter of *Ferdinand* and *Elizabeth* King and Queen of *Castille* and *Arragon*, and Widow to the Prince of *Portugal Alphonso*, Son of King *John II*. his Cosin and Predecessor. Not long after this Marriage, the young Prince *John* of *Castille*, *Isabels* brother, deceased, so that she became heir apparent to the Kingdoms of her Father and Mother, of which King EMANUEL and she were declared Princes. But a little while after, the Three and twentieth day of *August*, *A° One thousand four hundred fourscore and eighteen*, this young Queen dyed in Child-bed, at *Saragoca* in *Arragon*, her Body was transported to *Toledo*; and interred in the Nunnery of St. *Isabel*, which King *Ferdinand* her Father had founded.

His first Marriage. 1497. *Idem. Marians. Vasconcellius.*

1498. *Idem.*

Two years after, the Thirtieth day of *October*, *A° One thousand five hundred*, King EMANUEL espoused (after Dispensation granted by Pope *Alexander VI.*) his second Wife, at *Setubal*, (not at *Valence* as some write)

His second Marriage. 1500.

and the ALGARVES, *&c.*

Years of CHRIST.	
1517.	write) being the Princess MARY OF CASTILLE, Sister of *Isabel* his first Wife. She also dyed in Child-bed at *Lisbonne*, in the Year, One thousand five hundred and seventeen, aged Five and thirty years, and was buried in the Monastery of our Lady.
His third Marriage. 1519.	The third and last Wife of King EMANUEL, was LEONOR OF AUSTRIA, Sister to the Emperour *Charles V.* and Daughter of *Philip I.* of the name, and of *Joane*, King and Queen of *Castille*. This Marriage was Celebrated in the Year, One thousand five hundred and nineteen, and lasted but two years. *Leonor* espoused for her second Husband *Francis I.* of that name, King of *France*, who had before married Queen *Claude* a former Wife. She deceased at *Validolit*, others say at *Badaios* (where
1558.	she was buried) in *March*, *Anno*, One thousand five hundred eight and fifty, in the Sixtieth year of her age.

The History of King EMANUEL hath been most elegantly written in the Latin Tongue, by *Hierosme Osorio* Bishop of *Silve* in the *Algarvies*, by *Damian Goez* a *Portugal* Knight in his Language, who was employed in several important Voyages and other affairs; His Conquests also have been recorded by *Lopez de Castagneda*, and *Anthony de St. Romain*; in their Histories of *East-India*; by *Alphonso d' Albuquerque* in his Commentaries, *John de Baros* in the History of *Asia*, *Peter de Maris* in his Dialogues, *John-Pedro Maffee* of the Order of *Jesus* in the History of the *Indies* in a most eloquent stile; but incomparably well worded by *John Mariana*, and *Antonio Vasconcellos* of the same Order.

Children of EMANUEL King OF PORTUGAL, and of ISABEL OF CASTILLE his first Wife.

13. His Birth. 1498. His Death. 1500.	MICHAEL Prince OF PORTUGAL, *Castille* and *Gironne*, born in the Year, One thousand four hundred fourscore and eighteen, and in the Month of *August*, was acknowledged for the Prince, and Heir apparent of the Kingdoms of *Castille* and *Arragon*, but he lived only two years, and dyed, *Anno*; One thousand five hundred, at *Granada*, where he lieth in the Chappel of the Kings. By his decease the Infanta Donna *Joane* his Aunt by the Mothers side, came to the Succession of the Estates of *Castille*, *Arragon*, *Sicilie*, and several others, which she transmitted to the Emperour *Charles V.* her Son.	PORTUGAL Escartele Au 1. & 4. de PORTUGAL Au 2. & 3. contre-escartele. Au 1. & 4. de CASTILLE. Au 2. & 3. de LEON.

Children of EMANUEL King OF PORTUGAL, and of MARY OF CASTILLE his second Wife.

13.	JOHN III. of the name, King OF PORTUGAL, continued the Succession.	
13.	LEWIS OF PORTUGAL, Duke of BEIA, Seigneur of *Septe*, *Maure*, *Couillan*, and *Almade*, and Constable of *Portugal*, second Son of King EMANUEL by his second Wife MARY OF CASTILLE,	PORTU-GAL-BEIA. Escartele de PORTUGAL & de CASTILLE.

EMANUEL King of CASTILLE, was born in the City of *Abrantes*, the third day of *March*, in the Year, *One thousand five hundred and six*; At what time the Emperour *Charles V*. his Brother-in-law undertook the Voyage of *Affrick* for the Conquest of the City of *Thunes* from the *Moors*, and the protection of *Muleasses*, who had made his application to this great Emperour for assistance; LEWIS accompanied him in that glorious expedition, and had the command of the Ships which King *John III*. his Brother had sent to the Emperours succour.

In this expedition the Duke of *Beia* gave proof of his Valour, and experience in Deeds of War, to which he joyned the knowledge of the Methamaticks, and other liberal Sciences.

He had the choice of two wives offered him; the first was *Mary* afterwards Queen of *England*; the second, the Princess *Barbara* of *Poland*, Daughter of King *Sigismond* first of the name; but he would embrace neither, because (as some Historians write) he had clandestinely espoused a Gentlewoman named YOLAND, whom he took to Wife for her excellent beauty, being much inferiour to this Prince both in Extraction and Riches. It is added, that he would not declare his Marriage, observing King *John* his eldest Brother to have many male-children.

The same Prince LEWIS dyed in the Year, *One thousand five hundred fifty and five*, aged Forty nine years, and Nine Months, and was inhumed in the Abbey of *Bethleem*. By his Will he appointed the Prince *Anthony* his Heir to his whole Estate, not giving him other appellation therein than, His Son, without adding Natural, by which we may believe, he took him for his lawful Son.

Margin: Nonius. Sandoval. Mariana. J. Texera. Years of CHRIST. His Birth, 1506. 1535. His Death, 1555.

A base Son of LEWIS OF PORTUGAL, Duke of BEIA.

14. ANTHONY proclaimed King OF PORTUGAL at St. Arem, whose Story followeth in his place.

---

13. FERDINAND OF PORTUGAL, was born in the City of *Abrantes* the Fifth day of *June*, Anno, *One thousand five hundred and seven*, and was conjoyned in Marriage with *Guiamare Coutinho*, daughter of *Francis Coutinho* Count of *Marialua*, and of *Beatrice Meneses*, by which Wife he had two Children that dyed in their infancy, and being Seven and twenty years old, dyed Anno, *One thousand five hundred four and thirty*, in the same place of *Abrantes*, where he was born, there his body rested, until the Year, *One thousand five hundred fourscore and two*, when *Philip II*. King of *Spain* his Nephew, caused it to be removed, and interred in the Church of the Monastery of *Bethleem* near unto *Lisbonne*.

Margin: PORTUGAL. Escartelé de CASTILLE comme cy dessus. PORTUGAL. Escartelé de CASTILLE. Party de PORTUGAL. His Birth, 1507. His death, 1534.

---

13. ALPHONSO Cardinal OF PORTUGAL, Arch-bishop of *Lisbonne*, Bishop of *Evora*, and Abbot of *Alcobace*, born in the same City of *Evora*, Anno, *One thousand five hundred and nine*. He had attained but the Eighth year of his age, when Pope *Leo X*. associated him to the Colledge of Cardinals, and gave him the Title of St. *Blaise*, in the Year, *One thousand five hundred and seventeen*. He expressed himself to be Magnanimous, Liberal, and Humane, and very diligent in his Episcopal functi-

Margin: PORTUGAL comme cy devant. Nonius. Vasconcellius. His Birth, 1509. 1517.

PORTUGAL and the ALGARVES, &c.   87

Years of CHRIST.

function, administring the Holy Sacraments of the Church in person. To these Virtues he added an extraordinary Piety towards God, Charity in behalf of the Poor, and much affection to those which made profession of Learning.

In fine, having only arrived at the Eight and twentieth year of his age, he deceased *Anno*, *One thousand five hundred seven and thirty*, and was deposited in the Abbey of *Bethleem* near *Lisbonne*. *Onufrius* and *Ciacon* make mention of this Prelate in their Works which treat of the Popes and Cardinals.

His Death. 1537.

13. **HENRY** also Cardinal OF PORTUGAL, then elected King of *Portugal* and the *Algarves*, shall have his Story hereafter.

13. **EDWARD** Prince OF PORTUGAL, Sixth Son of *Emanuel* King of *Portugal*, and of Queen *Mary* of *Castille* his second Wife, was born the Seventh day of *September*, in the Year, *One thousand five hundred and fifteen*, and being but Fifteen years old, finished the course of his life at *Lisbonne* the Twentieth day of *October*, Anno, One thousand five hundred and forty.

He received the honour of Burial in the Monastery of our Lady at *Bethleem*, with several Kings and Princes of the House of *Portugal*, and from this Prince are descended the two last Kings of *Portugal*, viz. *John IV.* and his Son King *Alphonso VI.* who Reigneth at present, 1662.

His Birth. 1515.
His death. 1540.

PORTUGAL Escartelé de CASTILLE. Party de BRAGANCE D'Argent au sautoir de gueulles chargé de cinq Escussons de Portugal.

His Marriage.

The Princess ISABEL OF PORTUGAL his Wife, was Daughter of *James* of *Portugal* fourth Duke of *Braganza*, and of *Eleanor* of *Mendoza* his Wife.

Nonius. Vasconcellius.

Children of EDWARD OF PORTUGAL, and ISABEL OF BRAGANZA his Wife.

14. EDWARD OF PORTUGAL, second of the name, Duke of *Vimerana*, and Constable of *Portugal*, was the only, and posthumus Son of Prince *Edward*, and not being above Fifteen years old, King *John III.* his Uncle (*Anno*, *One thousand five hundred fifty and five*) qualified him with the Dignity of Constable of the Kingdom of *Portugal*, after the decease of his Uncle Prince *Lewis* Duke of *Beia* younger Son of King *Emanuel*. The same King *John* created him also Duke of *Vimerana*.

His Birth. 1540.

PORTUGAL-GUIMARENS. *Nonius. Vasconcellius.*

This Prince EDWARD (which some esteem to be but little favoured by King *Sebastian* his Cosin) was never married. He had attained the Six and thirtieth year of his age, when he departed this world at *Evora*, *Anno*, *One thousand five hundred threescore and sixteen* (not in the Year following, as writeth *Hierosme Heninges* in his Theatre of Kings and Princes) leaving his Cosin *John* of *Portugal* Duke of *Braganza*, his Successor in the Dignity of Constable.

His death. 1576.

14. MARY OF PORTUGAL, Princess of PARMA, was Espoused (in the Year, *One thousand five hundred threescore and six*) to ALEXANDER FARNESE first of the name, Duke

Her Marriage. 1566.

FARNESE; PARMA. D'or a six Fleurs de Lis d'Azure. 3. 2. & 1. Party de PORTUGAL

S 2   OF

68   EMANUEL King of PORTUGAL

Dukes of Parma.

of *Parma* and of *Placentia*, eldest Son of Prince *Octavio*, and of *Margaret* of *Austria* his Wife, and Grand-son of *Peter Lewis* first Duke of *Parma* of the House of *Farnese*.

Her death,
This Princess MARY dyed at *Parma* in *July*, *Anno*, One thousand five hundred threescore and seventeen, and the Prince ALEXANDER her Husband (who carried the reputation of one of the Greatest, and most Renowned Captains of his age) deceased the second day of *December*, in the Year, One thousand five hundred fourscore and twelve. He lieth in the Abbey of St. *Vaast* at *Arras*.

1577.

1592.

From their Marriage issued, among others, two Children, the elder of which was *Rainucio Farnese*, who succeeded to his Fathers Estates, and as being Heir to his Mother, was of the number of those that pretended a right to the Crown of *Portugal*, after the decease of King *Henry*. And notwithstanding that his Dominions were remote, yet besides the Favour of the Church, which it was believed he had sufficiently; it was also thought that it would be agreeable to the *Portugueses* to have a young King (as was *Rainucio*) that they might educate and instruct him after their own fashion, and manners. But King *Philip* of *Spain* having the power in his hand, tendred himself peaceable possessor of this Kingdom.

1580.

Rainucio espoused *Margaret Aldobrandin* Pope *Clement VIII.* his Neece, and had issue *Alexander Farnese* second of the name, Duke of *Parma* and *Placentia*, who after the death of his Father remained under the Tutilage and Government of *Edward Farnese* the Cardinal his Uncle, younger Son of Duke *Alexander* first of the name. *Margaret Farnese* (Sister of *Rainucio*, and *Edward*) was married to *Vincent de Gonzaga* first of that name, Duke of *Mantua*; but they were separated by the Authority of the Church.

14.
PORTU-
GAL-BRA-
GANCE.

D'argent au sautoir de gueulles chargé de cinq Escussons de Portugal.

Partie de PORTUGAL. *H. Franchi Conteaggio.*

KATHERINE OF PORTUGAL, Dutchess of BRA-GANZA, younger Daughter of Prince *Edward*, was married to *John* of *Portugal* her Cosin, sixth Duke of *Braganza*, who was one of those Princes that were Competitors for the Kingdom of *Portugal*, in the right of this *Katherine* his Wife, alledging that she ought to precede the King of *Spain Philip II.* Son of the Empress *Isabel* of *Portugal*, as being Daughter of *Edward*, this *Isabels* Brother, whom she did represent. And caused to be written in the University of *Conimbra*, divers reasons in her favour, which they sent to several Kings, and forrein Princes. *Katherine* grounded principally upon these reasons, That in all Successions of Crowns, the last possessor was to be succeeded *jure hereditatis*, which allowed the benefit of representation, that she representing the Infante *Don Edward* her Father, Brother of *Henry*, ought to precede all the other pretendants, the Catholique King because issued from a Daughter, the Prince *Anthony* for being Illegitimate; *Raynucio Farnese*, as being farther removed from *Henry* by the decease of *Mary* of *Portugal* his Mother (the Law never allowing a Grand-child that benefit) But especially by the prime and fundamental Laws of the Kingdom (put in execution against *Beatrix* Daughter of *Ferdinand* King of *Portugal*, who having married out of the Kingdom to the King of *Castille* (as you may note *page* 35.) her right of succeeding was utterly lost, and King *John* chosen in her stead) she was to be preferred before all Claimers or Competitors whomsoever, in regard of her being both born, and married within the Kingdom.

Her Marriage!

See also a clause of the Law of Lamego, Fol. 6.

They had issue *Theodosius II.* of the name, seventh Duke of *Braganza*,

Father

and the ALGARVES, *&c.*

Years of Father of *John II.* of that name, eighth Duke of *Braganza*, Crowned
CHRIST. King of *Portugal*, by the name of *John IV.* who by this just Title left
the Kingdom to his Son King *Alphonso VI.* Reigning at present. 1662.

Here are continued Children of King EMANUEL, by MARY OF CASTILLE his second Wife.

13. **ANTHONY OF PORTUGAL**, dyed not long after his Birth, in the Year, *One thousand five hundred and seventeen*.

13. **ISABEL OF PORTUGAL**, Empress and Queen of SPAIN, born at *Lisbonne* in the Year, *One thousand five hundred and three*, the
Her Birth. Fourth day of *October*, and having arrived at the Three and twentieth year
1503. of her age, was (in the Year, *One thousand five hundred twenty and six*)
Her espoused at *Seville*, to **CHARLES OF AUSTRIA**, fifth of that
Marriage. name, Emperour and King of *Spain*, eldest Son of *Philip* of *Austria* first
1526. of the name, and of *Joane* Queen of *Castille* and *Arragon* his Wife. This
Empress **ISABEL** brought to her Husband the Summe of Nine hundred thousand Ducates in Dower. They were married by the Cardinal
Salviati Pope *Clement V.* his Legate.
Her death. She dyed in the City of *Toledo* the first day of *May*, in the Year, *One*
1539. *thousand five hundred nine and thirty*, aged only Six and thirty years, and
her body was transported to *Granada*.
The Emperour her Husband deceased the One and twentieth day of
1558. *September*, A° *One thousand five hundred eight and fifty*, having carried
the honour and reputation of one of the greatest and most virtuous Monarchs
that have commanded since *Charles* the Great. Having gained several
signal Victories upon the *Turks* and *Infidels*, he most of all shewed the
grandure of his Courage in this, that he, which had so many times vanquished others, remained now Victorious upon himself, in quitting the Empire, with
the other Estates and Kingdoms which he possessed, and all worldly pomp,
to retire into a place of Solitude, and there to pass the remainder of his
life, that he might the better apply himself to the service of God, which
he did after he had held his Empire Six and thirty years, and his Hereditary
Kingdoms Forty. He left one Son, *Philip II.* King of *Spain*, who in the right
of his Mother, was of the number of the pretenders to the Kingdom of
Portugal, and rendred himself Master thereof, as you have heard before.
Charles V. had also two Daughters, the elder of which, *Mary* of *Austria*
was espoused to the Emperour *Maximilian II.* and the younger was married to *John* Prince of *Portugal*, Son of King *John III.* and had issue King
Sebastian.

13. **BEATRICE OF PORTUGAL**, Duchess of SAVOYE,
Her Birth. born at *Lisbonne* the last day of *December*, in the Year, *One thousand*
1504. *five hundred and four*, was conjoyned by Marriage (in *March*, Anno, *One*
Her *thousand five hundred twenty and one*) with *Charles III.* Duke of *Savoye*,
Marriage. Son of *Philip* Duke of *Savoye*, and of *Claude* of *Bretagne* his Wife. This
1521.
Her death. Duchess dyed at *Nice*, in the Year, *One thousand five hundred seven and*
1537. *thirty*, the Eighth day of *January*, at the same age with the Empress her Sister,

AUS-
TRICHE-
ESPAGNE.
Escartele
Au premier
quartier aussi
Escartele.
An 1. & 4.
de CAS-
TILLE.
Au 2. & 3.
de LEON.
Au 1. quartier
D' ARRA-
GON.
Party de
ARRA-
GON-SI-
CILIE.
Au 3. de
gueulles à la
Fasse d'argent
qui est AU-
STRICHE
Soustenu de
l'ancienne
BOUR-
GONGNE.
Au 4. quar-
tier de la seconde
branche de
BOUR-
GONGNE.
Soustenu de
BRABANT.
Sur les trois
& quatriesme
quartiers de
FLANDRES.
Party du
Marquisate de
St. *Empire.*
Le tout Party de
PORTUGAL.

SAVOYE
Escartele
Au 1. & 4. de
pourpre au che-
val effrayé
& contourné d'
argent qui est le
HAUTE-
SAXE.
Party de Fasse

T

EMANUEL King of

d'or & d' sable de six pieces, a la couronne de sinople, posie en bande brochant sur le tout, qui est la BASSE-SAXE. Auté en point en forme de t. i. angl', d' avg. n. a trois contr-rolles d' Espee de gueul. 1. 2. & 1. qui est AN-GRIE. Au 2. quartier d'argent au Lyon de sable, l' Escu s né de billettes de mesme qui est du Duché de CHABLAIS. Au 3. de sable, au Lyon d' argent armé & lampassé de gueulles, qui est d'Aouste. Sur le tout de gueulles a la Croix plain: d'argent, qui est l'Escu de SAVOYE moderne. Party de PORTUGAL.

Sister, which was Three and thirty years. As for Duke *Charles* her Husband, he departed this life at *Verceil, Anno,* One thousand five hundred fifty and three, the Seventeenth day of *August,* being aged Threescore and seven years.

From this his Marriage with the Princess BEATRICE OF PORTUGAL, came the Duke *Emanuel-Philibert* his Successor, who by *Margaret* of *France,* had his only Son *Charles-Emanuel* Duke of *Savoye.*

This Duke *Emanuel* was of the number of those Princes Competitors for the Kingdom of *Portugal,* although he was Son of the younger Daughter of King *Emanuel.* An Historian writes, that among the pretenders that were strangers, the *Portugueses* were more inclined to him, than to any other; and this inclination proceeded from the opinion they had, that in regard of the quality of his person, he was fitter than any other to defend them from their enemies, and if need were, he might vigorously resist King *Philip* if he should stirre, both by reason of his Valour, and for the means he had to molest him in his Dutchy of *Millain*, joyning unto *Piedmont,* using chiefly the Alliance and Neighbourhood he had with the *French,* who laid claim to that Dukedom. But his pretentions succeeded not according to his desire, for he dyed immediately after this overture was made.

Years of CHRIST. 1553.

13. **M**ARY OF PORTUGAL the Elder, dyed in her Cradle.

Children of EMANUEL King of PORTUGAL, and of ELEONOR OF AUSTRIA his third Wife.

Nunius.

13. **C**HARLES OF PORTUGAL, born at *Evora,* in the Year, One thousand five hundred and twenty, the Eighteenth day of *February,* and deceased at *Lisbonne* the Fifteenth of *April, Anno,* One thousand five hundred twenty and one.

His Birth. 1520.

Vasconcellius.

13. **M**ARY OF PORTUGAL the younger, came into the world at the end of the Year, *One thousand five hundred twenty and one.* Notwithstanding this Princess was adorned with singular Beauty both of body and soul, and had been courted by several Princes, yet would she never be brought to marry any, but lived with the honour and pudicity required in Princesses of her Quality; then being aged Seven and fifty years, she payed her last debt to Nature at *Lisbonne, Anno,* One thousand five hundred threescore and Eighteen. Her body was inhumed in the Monastery of our Lady of the *Light,* of the Order of the *Warfare of Christ,* which she caused to be built near unto *Lisbonne.*

Her Birth. 1521.

Her death. 1578.

JOHN

PORTUGAL and the ALGARVES, &c.

13. JOHN III.

Of the Name, KING of PORTUGAL and the ALGARVES, on this, and the other side the *Affrican* Sea, Lord of *Guineé*, &c.

CHAP. XVI.

THIS Prince was the eldest Son of *Emanuel* King of *Portugal*, and of Mary of *Castille* his second Wife. The place of his Birth, *Lisbonne*; The time, the Sixth day of *June*, in the Year, *One thousand five hundred and two*.

At the age of Twenty years he succeeded to the Crown of his Father, and wanted no courage to continue his high designs, as well to maintain himself in those memorable Conquests, that he had so happily accomplished, as for the gaining of other Isles, Kingdoms, Cities, and Countries. To this effect *Nonio Acuna* his Viceroy in the *Indies*, took and ruined the Isle of *Bethleem*, then subjected *Bacin* and *Daman*, two famous *Indian* Cities, slew *Sultan Baduc* the puissant King of *Cambaie*, and subjected the City of *Dium*, where he built a Cittadelle. The success the Christians had in these parts, so perplexed the *Turk*, that he sent a powerful Fleet commanded by the *Bassa* of *Egypt*, to drive the *Portugals* from *Dium* and other places, which they had in that Countrey: This Army joyned with that of *Cambaie*, but at the rencounter they received so sharp a welcome from the Defen-

PORTUGAL
Comme cy devant.

PORTUGAL.
Party de AUTRICHE-ESPAGNE.
Escartelé Au premier quartier aussi escartelé.
Au 1. & 4. de CASTILLE.
Au 2. & 3. de LEON.
Au 2. quartier d'ARRAGON.
Party d'ARRAGON-SICILIE.
Au 3. d'AUSTRICHE.
Soustenu de BOURGONGNE de la premier branch.
Au 4. de BOURGONGNE de la second branche;
soustenu de BRABANT.
Et sur ces deux derniers quartiers est un Escusson de FLANDRES.
Party de L'Escu du Marquisate du St. Empire;

T 2

JOHN III. of the Name, King of

Vasconcellius. Defendants commanded by *Antonio Silueria*, that a great number of them were kill'd upon the place. [Years of CHRIST 1538.]

Andrada. Nine years after this, the second Siege of *Dium*, was with much resolution maintained by *John Mascaregna*, against the Sultan *Mamudin*, not less notorious than the other, being that then also the *Turk* assisted the *Indian* with his Forces. [1547.]

The like success smiled for a time upon the Christians at *Safin* in *Affrica*, where they valiantly endured Six months Siege by the Cheriff Army consisting of an hundred thousand Souldiers, but not long after the Cherif or King of *Suez* worsted the *Portugueses*, which so much cooled their resolutions, that King JOHN deliberated to abandon all his Forts of *Affrica*, the more firmly to settle and establish himself in the *Indies*, *Guineé*, and *Brasille*, but this councel was not followed, for only quitting and dismantling the Inland Forts, he retained, and fortified the Port Towns of *Septe*, *Tangier*, and *Mazagan*, with all things necessary for a resistance.

Vasconcellius. This King JOHN obtained from the Pope, That the City of *Evora* should be erected into an Arch-bishoprick, the Cities of *Portalegre*, *Leiria*, and *Miranda* in *Portugal*, into Bishopricks, as also, of *Cochin* and *Malaca* in *Asia*, of *Baia* in *Brasille*, of Cape *Asinaire* in *Guineé*; and in *Ethiopia* he established *John Bermudes* for first Patriarch of the Latine Church.

Andrada. Following the steps of the King his Father, to him was attributed the honour of having planted the Gospel in the Eastern parts of *Asia*, in *Ethiopia* the Higher, and other remote Provinces; as also in the *Molucco* Islands, and *Japon*, where he sent that famous Jesuite *Francis Xauier*, afterwards Canonized, the fruit of whose labours appeared in the conversion of many Infidels to the faith. Insomuch that it's remarkable, that under the happy Reign of this Prince JOHN, there were twelve *Pagan* Kings baptized, with the greater part of their people. He performed many other profitable works for the advancement of Piety; caused several Monasteries to be reformed according to their Antient Rules, and was one of the first Kings that favoured, and greatly encreased the Order of the Society of *Jesus*, for whom he erected several Colledges in *Portugal*, and his other Dominions.

Nauius. He was a devout Prince, and naturally so benigne and clement, that he even shewed himself slow in Ordering punishment to the Malefactors, and when Judgment was given against such, (which he did in person once a week) he rather inclined to Forgiveness, than Condemnation. A Lover he was of Peace and Tranquility, a favourer of parts of merit, and parts, having given entertainment in his Kingdom to strangers of divers professions. He

Vasconcellius. transferred the University of *Lisbonne* to *Conimbra*, and richly endowed it, augmented the Salaries of the publick Professors, and rendred this Achademy one of the most famous of *Europe*. He raised also several proud Structures at *Evora*, and restored the Aquæduct of this City, which place he so much delighted in, that he made it the most ordinary place of his dwelling.

Mariana. In the Year, *One thousand five hundred twenty and five*, and in the Month of *February*, he espoused *Katherine* of *Austria* at *Salamanca*, she was Sister of the Emperour *Charles V*. and fourth Daughter of *Philip I*. of the name King of *Spain*, and of Queen *Joane* his Wife. She dyed at *Lisbonne*, Anno, *One thousand five hundred threescore and seventeen*, having lived to a very great age. His Grand-son King *Sebastian*, who succeeded this King JOHN, for the respect and reverence which he did bear this Princess his Grand-mother, did for some time bridle the impetuosity of his rash designs. [His Marriage. 1525. 1577.]

King

PORTUGAL and the ALGARVES, &c.

Years of CHRIST.
His Death 1557.

King JOHN III. her Husband, deceased twenty years before her of an Apoplexie, in the City of *Lusbonne*, the Eleventh day of *June*, in the Year, *One thousand five hundred fifty and seven*, after he had lived Fifty and five years, and reigned Five and thirty and an half. His body was interred in the Church of the Monastery of *Bethleem*, which being begun to be built by his Father, was accomplished by him and the Queen his Wife.

The Symbole or Devise of this King, was a Rock composed of five Collumnes, upon which was exalted a Cross, and for the Soul of the Device, IN HOC SIGNO VINCES ; presenting thereby, (in imitation of *Constantine* the great, and of one of his Ancestors) that in this sign of the Redemption of Man-kind, and of the Death of the Saviour of the world, he vanquished the enemies of our Faith.

Children of JOHN III. King OF PORTUGAL, and of KATHERINE OF AUSTRIA his Wife.

14.
1526.

ALPHONSO Prince OF PORTUGAL, born at *Almerin*, the Four and twentieth day of *February*, in the Year, *One thousand five hundred twenty and six*, dyed young.

14.
1531.

EMANUEL OF PORTUGAL, came into this world the first day of *November*, being *All Saints day*, A° *One thousand five hundred thirty and one*, and departed this world three years after.

14.
1533.

PHILIP OF PORTUGAL, first saw the light of day at *Evora*, the Five and twentieth day of *May*, in the Year, *One thousand five hundred thirty and three*, and deceased also in his infancy.

14.
1535.

DIONYSIO or DENIS OF PORTUGAL, born in the same City of *Evora* the Six and twentieth day of *April*, A° *One thousand five hundred thirty and five*, dyed likewise in his youth.

14.
His Birth. 1537.
His Marriage. 1553.
His Death. 1554.

JOHN Prince OF PORTUGAL, out-lived his four Brothers. The place of his Birth was *Evora*, upon the third day of *June*, in the Year, *One thousand five hundred thirty and seven*. About the sixteenth year of his age he espoused JOANE OF AUSTRIA, second daughter of the Emperour *Charles V*. and of *Isabel* of *Portugal* his Wife, who was Aunt by the Fathers side to this Prince. He enjoyed her but seven months, and then dyed the second day of *January*, A° *One thousand five hundred fifty and four*, not having arrived at the Seventeenth year of his age.

PORTUGAL
Comme cy devant.

PORTUGAL
Party d'AUSTRICHE.
Comme cy devant.

1578.

He left this Princess JOANE with child, who after delivery of her posthumus Son King *Sebastian*, returned into *Castille*, and in the absence of her Brother King *Philip II*. who was at that time in the Low-Countreys, governed his Kingdoms with Prince *Charles* his Son, her Nephew, and then departed out of this life into a better, in the Year of Salvation, *One thousand five hundred threescore and eighteen*. She founded a Nunnery for barefooted Sisters at *Madrid*, and had this happiness, not to see the

Mnians.

U

JOHN III. *of the Name*, King of

the loss and miserable death of her only Son, hapning but few Months after her decease.

A Son of JOHN *Prince* OF PORTUGAL, *and* JOANE OF AUSTRIA *his Wife*.

15. SEBASTIAN the last King OF PORTUGAL in descent, of this branch.

14. ANTHONY OF PORTUGAL, sixth Son of King *John III.* born the ninth day of *March*, in the Year, *One thousand five hundred thirty and nine*, finished his dayes in his infancy. 1539.

14. MARY OF PORTUGAL, Princess of SPAIN, eldest Daughter of King *John III.* first saw the light of day at *Conimbra*, the Fifth day of *October, Anno, One thousand five hundred twenty and seven*, and was married at *Salamanca* (in *March, Anno, One thousand five hundred forty and three*) to *Philip II.* at that time Prince, and afterwards King of *Spain*. She was the first of four wives, that he had, and dyed at *Validolit* the Twelfth day of *July*, in the Year, *One thousand five hundred forty and five*, four dayes after she was delivered of her only Son Prince *Charles*, who dyed before the King his Father, and had a sad, and Tragical end. The same King *Philip II.* deceased the Thirteenth day of *September*, in the Year of Grace, *One thousand five hundred fourscore and eighteen*, aged Threescore and eleven years. He reigned Forty years in *Spain*, and Eighteen in *Portugal*. The body of the Princess *Mary* his Wife, was conveyed to *Granada*, and there interred. She never carried the Title of Queen, for her Husband came to the Crown a long time after her decease.

AUTRICHE
ou ES-
PAGNE.

Escartelé
Au premier
quartier aussi
escartelé.
Au 1. & 4.
de CAS-
TILLE.
Au 2. & 3.
de LEON.
Au 2. quartier d'ARRA-
GON.
Party d'AR-
RAGON-
SICILIE.

Her Birth.
1517.
Her
Marriage.
1543.
Her death.
1545.

1598.

Sur lesquels deux premiers quartiers est posé l'Escu de Portugal.
Au 3. d'AUSTRICHE, Soustenu de BOURGONGNE *de la premier branche*.
Au 4. de BOURGONGNE *de la second branche*; soustenu de BRABANT.
Et sur ces deux derniers quartiers est un Escusson de FLANDRES. Party du Marquisate du St. Empire.
Le tout Party de PORTUGAL.

14. ISABEL OF PORTUGAL born at *Lisbonne*, the Eight and twentieth day of *April, One thousand five hundred twenty and nine*, was second Daughter of King *John III.* and dyed young. 1529.

14. BEATRIX OF PORTUGAL, brought into this world also at *Lisbonne*, the Fifteenth day of *February*, in the Year of our Redemption, *One thousand five hundred and thirty*, dyed in the Cradle. 1530.

A Natural Son of JOHN III. *King of* PORTUGAL.

14. EDWARD OF PORTUGAL, Arch-bishop of *Bracara*, and Primate of *Spain*, was a Prelate well read in Philosophy, Divinity, and other good Learning; these excellent parts had laid a foundation for higher expectations, when Death surprised him in the flower of his years, to the great affliction of King *John III.* his Father.

Vasconcellus.

SEBASTI-

15. SEBASTIAN

KING of PORTUGAL and the ALGARVES, on this, and the other side the Sea in *Affrica*, Lord of *Guineé*, and of the Conquest, Navigation, and Commerce of *Ethiopia, Arabia, Persia*, and *India*.

CHAP. XVII.

1557.

 HAT Prejudice which yong Princes and their people receive by ill weighed councels, and imprudent deliberations, is apparent in this King, when their hot courage, accompanied with rashness; throws them into the precepice of a deplorable ruine. This was King SEBASTIAN's condition, who being in the first Flower of his age, without experience in Deeds of War, embarqued himself in a dangerous (yet glorious) enterprise, against the Advice of his nearest Friends, and most faithful Councellers, leaving his Kingdom emptyed of Money, naked of Nobility, without a certain Heir, and in the hands of ill-affected Governours; So that in Fine, he miserably perished, and by this unhappy Event gave great advantages to the Infidels, and grief to his Subjects; which was the more increased, for that the Kingdom of *Portugal* having for a long time enjoyed the calm of an happy Peace, and so much Prosperity, was not only agitated with furious Tempests, and intestine Wars; but also fell into the hands of a stranger.

This King SEBASTIAN was only Son of Prince *John* of *Portugal*

PORTUGAL

D'*argent a cinq Escussons d'Azur pris en Croix chacun chargé de cinq besans aussi d'Argent posez en sautoir à la bordure de gueulles chargé de sept Chasteaux d'or, trois en chef deux en fasse & deux en point.*

SEBASTIAN King of.

Nonius.
Vasconcellius.

gal, and of *Joane* of *Austria* his Wife, born a posthumus (in the Year, One thousand five hundred fifty and four) the Twentieth day of *January*, on which day is celebrated the Feast of St. *Sebastian*, in memory of whom he had this name given him.

Years of CHRIST.
His Birth.
1554.

After the death of his Grand-father King *John III.* being but Three years old, he succeeded to the Crown of *Portugal*, and during his minority, was under the Government of Queen *Katherine* of *Austria*. But afterwards this Princess, not being able to undergo so great a charge as that of the Regency, transferred it by the Estates to Cardinal *Henry*, great Uncle by the Fathers side to King SEBASTIAN, who having attained to the Fourteenth year of his age, began to take the Reins of Government into his own hand.

Vasconcellius.

The *Moors* taking advantage by the infirmity of his age, thought it now a fit time to endeavour the reduction of some of his best Garisons in *Africa*. So that *Mahomet* King of *Mauritania*, the Son of *Cherif Abdala*, came with a considerable force, and begirt *Magazon* with a strait Siege, and had it not been by *Roderick de Sosa* nobly defended for the space of Threemonths, they had carried it.

1562.

Touinus.

No better was the Fortune of the Infidels Ten years after, when they undertook the same design upon the Towns of *Goa*, and *Chiaule*. For *Aitaida* and *Mascaregna* so resolutely opposed, that after Six months Siege before the one, and Nine before the other, they were forced to retire with loss and shame.

1572.

Now was King SEBASTIAN in the Twentieth year of his age, who being of an able Body, and of a Couragious, and Martial Soul, not content with those Dominions which he possessed, resolved to make Conquest of new, not considering, that this design was not to be effected, without great hazard, and in the alteration of that repose his Kingdom had so long enjoyed. He had first designed a War against the *Indians*, but that his Kinsmen and Subjects would not consent unto. But as there was some difficulty wholly to withdraw the young Prince (who had a Warlike spirit) from this Enterprise, such as were near him, laboured to divert him by means of another which they laid before him, turning all his Resolution upon *Affrick*, to engage the *Moors* which live in that part called *Mauritania Tingitana*, where the *Portugals* maintained (to their great Charge) upon the Coast of *Barbary*, the three Fortresses of *Septe*, *Tangier*, and *Magazon*, the In-let and Key of *Spain*, by which the *Moors* have heretofore conquered it; But this diversion whereunto they perswaded the King, produced sad effects, principally proceeding for want of Judgment, for although it were difficult wholly to disswade him from the expedition of *India*, and therefore convenient to represent unto him some other Action, yet should they advisedly have foreseen, not to divert him from one mischief, to thrust him into a greater.

Constaggio.

The young King stayed not long to put this design in execution. For in the Year, One thousand five hundred threescore and fourteen, he assembled (against the inclination of his best Friends) certain of his Souldiers, and with four Gallies, and some Ships, and Carvels passed into *Affrica*, under colour of visiting his Forts, although he really desired to effect more than he made shew of; There they came to some Skermishes with the *Moors*, at which he was almost alwayes found in person, where discovering his own weakness, and vexing himself that he could not perform what he desired; He returned back to *Lisbonne*, still devising some new manner of War, which

1574.
King Sebastian's first Voyage into Affrica.

so

PORTUGAL and the ALGARVES, &c.

Years of Christ. so disquieted his conceit, that he neither said nor did any thing to other end; deliberating not as a King, but as a private Souldier, to accustom his body to labour, intending thereby to habituate himself more to the hardships and miseries of War. This inclination (in which the heavens had some part.) was not contradicted by any of his Council; For although these actions of the Kings were rash, yet Ambition, and fear of his displeasure, were of such force, That the Nobility, Magistrates, and other persons (who might have forced him) durst not open their mouths, nor oppose themselves against his Will; and if any did mutter or speak to the contrary, they were men of base Quality, and not admitted.

The Cardinal *Henry* his great Uncle, Brother to *John III.* his Grandfather, and Queen *Katherine*, (in whom Flattery should have found no place) had small credit with the King, neither did they use the Authority they might have had, both fearing they should not prevail; but lose (with the Kings disgrace) that small command was yet remaining in them: So as by a fatal silence, they suffered this young Prince for the second time to return into *Affrica*. *Conestaggio.*

And the more to enflame King SEBASTIAN, it fortuned that *Muley Mahomet* chased out of the Kingdom of *Morocco* by his Uncle *Muley Moluc*, endeavoured his re-establishment by the aide of the Christians; and for this purpose entreated succours from SEBASTIAN, perswading this King, that by the advantage of those Friends that he could make in his own Kingdom, he should be able to defeat *Moluc*, and to open him a way to trace the whole Empire of *Morocco*. *Eytera.*

SEBASTIAN drawn on by this vain hope, embraced the Moors offer, and finding himself not able to perform this expedition without another Confederate, endeavoured to draw into this Action his Uncle by the Mothers side, the King of *Spain*, *Philip II*. to which effect an Interview was appointed at *Guadalupa*; There the Kings met, and proposals were made of a match betwixt King *Philips* Daughter, and King SEBASTIAN, and as to the War of *Affrica*, the Spanish King liked well of it, so that it might be prosecuted by his Lieutenants, but not that he should undertake it in person, excusing himself that he could not assist him with a considerable force, pretending he had occasion for Souldiers to resist the *Turk* in *Italy*; so that from the Catholique King he could expect but small supplies. *Vosconcellim. Nonium.*

1578. King Sebastian's second expedition into Affrica. So that now assisted only with some Regiments of *Italians*, *Germans*, and *Irish* (after he had with great pomp caused the Royal Standerd to be hallowed in the Cathedral Church of *Lisbonne*) SEBASTIAN set Sail for *Affrick* with an Army of Eighteen thousand men, and the assistance of a great number of the Nobility of his Kingdom, among which were several Princes and Lords, descended from the Royal Family. *Mariana in Summario de Hist. Hisp.*

At his arrival, *Muley Moluc*, fearing that the event of this War might fall out to his disadvantage, offered him ten miles Circuit about every one of his Fortresses of *Affrica* for Tillage; But SEBASTIAN would not hearken to any Composition, unless he would yield into his hands the Towns of *Tituan*, *Alarache*, and the Cape of *Aghero*, which the Cherif refused. *Conestaggio.*

In the mean time the *Portugueses* being disswaded from marching by land to lay Siege to *Alarache*, to avoid the iminent danger which the Army would fall into thereby, were so ill councelled, and so unfortunate, as to forsake that by Sea, the far more advantagious, and of less hazard.

The Battel of Alcacer. 1578. The Armies then coming to an engagement the Fourth day of *August*, in the Year, *One thousand five hundred threescore and eighteen*, in the Plain *Thuanus Hist. sui temp.*

SEBASTIAN King of

Livers.
Nonius.
Conestaggio.

of *Alcacer*. King SEBASTIAN's Horse had for sometime the better of the *Moorish* Cavalry, but the grand advantage the *Moors* had of the Christians in number (being ten to one) so much prevailed, that what they could not perform by their valour, they executed with their number, so that the Christians wearied with Conquering, were at last wholly defeated. The King was first wounded in the right Arm with the shot of a Harquebuze, whereof making small account, he went ordering things in all parts of the Army; But being at that time deprived of the greatest Treasure which young Kings ought to have in so important occasions, a person sage and advised, to whom he should give ear; when he began to see his men break, he fell furiously with some Gentlemen that were about him, into the Enemies ranks, valiantly fighting to give incouragement to the Souldiers. Those that saw him, wondred at his Courage, for although they had kill'd three Horses under him without any whit daunting him, yet was he indefatigable in charging, striking, and relieving all parts of the Army where it was most oppressed. But being but a man seconded by few, he cannot resist the Enemies fury, nor make his Friends partakers of his Valour: so that being unhorsed, he was taken and disarmed. And upon a dispute hapning among the *Moors* for this royal Prisoner, was by them most inhumanely butchered in cold blood.

Years of CHRIST.

His Death. 1578.

Vasconcell. iu.

Such was the death of this unfortunate King, wherein did rencounter all things that might make it deplorable; his youth, the expectation of his Virtues, the want of Succession, the violence of his Death, and the prison of his body, remaining in the hands of the *Moors*.

Conestaggio.

He was indued with excellent qualities; which were of no advautage to him, wanting, because of his youth, that Virtue which ought to govern our Actions. For all his designs which carried him to a precipitate end, were built upon his Magnanimity, Liberality, his desire of Military Glory, the Disposition of his body, and the Vigour of his Courage. So that we may well say of this unfortunate young Prince; that which was sometimes spoken of *Alexander* the Great, *That Nature had given him Virtue, and Fortune Vices.* For to say truly, SEBASTIAN had his Virtues from Nature, and his Vices from his Education.

Mariana.

This Battel was the more remarkable, for that the two other Kings, *Moluc* and *Mahumed* dyed there also, the first with the violent access of a natural disease, the other was drowned in passing the River of *Mucazen*, to save himself by flight. There dyed Three thousand *Moors*, and as many Christians, or more; among which were many persons of Honour; For besides the Captains of the strangers, and the Duke of *Aueiro*: there was slain *Alphonso* of *Portugal* Count of *Vimioso*; *Lewis Coutinho* Earl of *Rodondo*; *Vasco de Gama* Count of *Vidiguera*; *Alphonso* of *Norogna* Earl of *Mira*, *John Lobo* Baron of *Alvito*, *Alvara* of *Mello* eldest Son to the Count of *Tentugal*; *James* brother to the Duke of *Braganza*, *John de Silveira* eldest Son to the Earl of *Sorteglia*, *Christopher* of *Tauora*, and many others of account, so as some Noble Families were there wholly extinct; and *Theodosius* Duke of *Barcellos*, and *Anthony* Prior of *Crato*, with many others, were taken Prisoners.

Fayrera.

The Body of King SEBASTIAN pierced with seven wounds, not being known till two dayes after the fight, was brought unto *Alcacer*, and afterwards the King of *Spain* Uncle to the Defunct, by the permission of the Cherif King of *Morocco*, caused it to be conveyed to *Septe*, where it rested, until that in the Year, *One thousand five hundred fourscore and two*,

it

Years of Christ. it was from thence transported into the Kingdom of *Portugal*, and with Magnificent Funeral Pomp (performed in the presence of the same King) interred in the Monastery of *Bethleem*, with the Kings of *Portugal* his Ancestors. *Coteslaggio.*

And here I cannot omit to inform you of that Ceremony used by the *Portugueses* in bewailing their dead Kings, and performed by them upon the news of the death of this King SEBASTIAN. First there parted from the Magistrates house, a Citizen on Horf-back, covered himself and his Horse all in Black, with a great Ensign in his hand likewise of Black, bearing it on his shoulder that it might trail on the ground, after him followed three old men on foot in Mourning weeds, with three Scutchions in their hands, like Shields or Targets, bearing them high upon their heads without any figure upon them, but all Black; Then followed some Citizens of the same Magistrates, and other inferiors in great numbers: All these went through the principal Streets of *Lisbonne*, and coming to the steps of the Cathedral Church, which is near unto the place from whence they parted; those which hold the Scutcheons, mount up certain degrees, and one of them lifting up his Shield, cries with a loud voice, *People of Lisbonne, lament your King SEBASTIAN, who is dead:* Then all the people weep, and cry: Having ended his words, he breaks his Scutchion as a vain thing, striking it on the place where he stands: Then proceed they on; and being come to the New Street, ascending the Stairs of the little Church of our Lady of *Oliuera*, another of them which carried the Scutchions, pronounceth the same words the former had done, and breaks his Shield in the same manner; The like is done by the third upon the stairs of the Hospital: So as all the three Scutchions being broken in those places, they all return home, and thus is the Ceremony ended. *Idem.*

The Ceremony used by the *Portugueses* in bewailing their dead Kings.

The same King was at the time of his death aged Four and twenty years, Seven Months, and Fifteen Dayes, and had Reigned about Two and twenty. *Nonius. Vasconcellim.*

He never married, although there were proposals made of three several wives, *Isabel* of *Austria* Daughter of the King of *Spain*, *Margaret* of *France* Daughter of King *Henry II.* and also another *Isabel* of *Austria* Daughter of the Emperour *Maximilian I.* and Widow of the King of *France*, *Charles IX.*

He had his Piety by inheritance, having made his Religion flourish, and established it in *Brasille* and the *Indies*, where he founded several Churches and Colledges, but more especially those of the Jesuites.

About two and twenty years after his decease, there was a man in *Italy* who reported himself to be the same King SEBASTIAN, and that having escaped from the Battel of *Alcacer*, he had wandred up and down for a long time, without making himself known. Which being represented to the Senate of *Venice* with many Circumstances, some believed it to be a truth, others were doubtful, and also many there were that supposed him to be an Imposter. But certain it was, that having been imprisoned at *Florence*, and from thence conveyed to *Naples*, and put in the Gallies, he there came to a miserable end. *Thuanus.*

The Cardinal *Henry* of *Portugal* being exceeding old, against the common course of Nature succeeded King SEBASTIAN his Nephews Son. Which young Prince in that Warre which he undertook in *Affrick*, endeavouring to deliver a Nation from servitude, by his imprudence rendred the greater part of his Nobility slaves to the *Arabes*, and *V. sconcellius. Mrians.*

Moors,

Coneſtaggio. *Moors*, and of a free Nation, as it was, in a small space of time was reduced under the obedience of the *Caſtillians*, which they for so many years held for their capital Enemies; as writeth *Hierosme Franchi Coneſtaggio*, a Gentleman of *Genoa*, who hath most judiciously discoursed this last Warre of the *Portugueſſes* in *Affrica*, as also the end of this Branch of the House of *Portugal*, the Change of their Government, and the Union of this Kingdom to the Crown of *Caſtille*. The same Subject hath been elegantly Written by *Jaques Auguſtus de Thou*, in the History of his time; and by *Antonio Errera*, Historiographer to the King of *Spain*, *Philip II*.

HENRY

13. HENRY
Cardinal of PORTUGAL, then Elected KING Of PORTUGAL and the ALGARVES, &c.

CHAP. XVIII.

Among the seven Sons issued from the Marriage of *Emanuel* King of *Portugal*, and of *Mary* of *Castille* his second Wife, this HENRY was the fifth: born the last day of *January*, in the Year, *One thousand five hundred and twelve.* He was first of all Archbishop of *Brachara*, and Primate of *Spain*, then of *Lisbonne*, and lastly also first Archbishop of *Evora*, where he founded a fair Colledge for the Jesuites.

 Vasconcellus.

Nonius.

In the Year, *One thousand five hundred forty and six*, Pope *Paul III.* adopted him to the Sacred Colledge of Cardinals. During the Reigns of his Brother, and Nephews Son *John III.* and *Sebastian*, he was Inquisitor Major of the Faith in *Portugal*.

After that *Katherine* of *Austria*, Widow of Prince *John* of *Portugal* his Nephew, Mother of young King *Sebastian*, had quit the Regency of the Kingdom, the Estates conferred it upon this Cardinal HENRY, great Uncle to the young King, in the Year, *One thousand five hundred threescore and two.* He exercised this Charge until the King came to age, who upon his second expedition into *Affrica*, wanting a careful person to whom he might leave the Government of the Kingdom in his absence, went

Y to

to *Evora*, where HENRY at that time lived. And although this Prince was not greatly pleasing to him, yet did he intreat him to take this care in his absence, which the Cardinal would by no means accept, excusing it by reason of his age, and indisposition to Rule; so that the King made choice of four Governours to command in his name, which were *George d' Almeda* Archbishop of *Lisbonne*, *Peter d' Alcasoua*, *Francis de Sada*, and *John Mascaregnas*, to whom he gave a plenipotentiary power.

<small>*Conc[iaggio]*.
Thuanus.
Conestaggio.</small>

After his death in *Affrica*, these Governours committed the management of affairs to the Cardinal, who not long after was Proclaimed, and Sworne King by the *Portugueses*: The Form of the Oath was performed in this manner; The XXV. of *August*, the Hospital Church of *All Saints* was hanged with Silk Tapestry, in the which they erected a Throne, upon which was placed a Seat of Cloth of Gold; thither came the King in the morning, in the habit of a Cardinal; going from the Palace, there marched before him eight Attabales, or Drums on Horf-back, after the *Moresco* manner, and nine Heraulds all on Horf-back, carrying upon their Cloaks their Coats of Arms: after followed on foot, almost all the Officers of the Court, those of the Chamber, and other Magistrates; behind them was the Duke of *Braganza* on Horf-back bareheaded, bearing in his hand a Sword, with a Scabard of Gold, as Constable: a little after came the Cardinal upon a Mule, the which *Alvara de Silva* Count of *Portalegre*, Lord Steward of his Houshold, led by the reins; there followed after many Noblemen and Gentlemen on Horf-back, with a great number of people on foot: The Cardinal invironed with a great multitude, ascended the Stairs of the Hospital, being entred the Church, having heard Service, and ended his Prayers, he seated himself in the Chair of State prepared on the Throne, where presently *Francis de Sada* (one of those that had been Governours) put the Scepter in his hand, and *Michael de Mora* Secretary, standing a little distant, said (reading it with a loud voice) *That King HENRY by the Death of King* Sebastian, *did succeed in the Realm, and therefore they had delivered him the Scepter, and that he was come to take the accustomed Oath, to maintain and observe unto his people, and to any other, all Liberties, Priviledges and Conventions, granted by his Predecessors*: which done, the Secretary kneeling before him with an open Book, the King laid his hand thereon, swearing so to do: Then did the Attabales sound, every man crying, *Reale*, *Reale*, for HENRY King of *Portugal*: This done, he rose, and with the same company, holding still the Scepter in his hand, he returned to the Palace, the Attabales sounding, and the Heraulds crying from time to time as before.

<small>*Conestaggio*.</small>

Now being seated in the Royal Throne, although he was Threescore and seven years of age, and not healthful, yet looked he about him, and (as it were determined from above, that *Portugal* should fall by degrees to its declination) did not provide for the State, according to that opinion that was conceived of him: but the Realm by reason of their miseries past, remained as a body empty and afflicted, which needed a wise Physitian to restore it. For as one mischief comes not alone, the new King did more torment it; for although many supposed, that he being old, a Priest, and of an exemplary life, should lay all passions aside, and be careful to settle the state of the Common-wealth in better order than he had found it; yet notwithstanding he could not temper himself, with such a disposition as was fit for his Quality and years: But as it often falls out in them which have been oppressed, who coming to Rule, seek Revenge upon their enemies,

even

PORTUGAL, *and the* ALGARVES, *&c.* 83

Years of even so did he (not imitating the example of *Lewis XII.* King of *France*,
CHRIST. who disdained to requite the wrongs done to him being Duke of *Orleance*)
who resolved to revenge the injuries done to him being Cardinal, if they may
be justly called injuries, when as Princes be not respected of their inferiours
as they ought: For not being greatly favoured by the King his Predecessor,
the Ministers, and Favourites of his Nephew, did not use him with that
Respect as was required, conceiving (that being so old, and *Sebastian* so
young) that he would never have attained to the Crown: By reason whereof he deprived almost all the Officers of the Court, and some of them that
did manage the Kings Treasure, of their Offices; and advanced his own
Servants.

In the mean time, the Estates of the Kingdom beseeching him to take
care for the declaring of his Successor to the Crown, he Convoked a Solemn
Assembly of the same Estates in the City of *Almerin*, to hear the Claims
of those Princes which pretended to the Kingdom. The number of whom
was many; *viz.* *Antonio* Bastard of *Portugal*, King H E N R Y's Nephew;
the Catholick King *Philip II.* the Duke of *Braganza* in the Right of the
Dutchess his Wife; the Duke of *Savoy*; the Prince of *Parma*; the Queen
of *France*, *Katherine de Medicis*, Mother of King *Henry III.* and Pope
Gregory XIII.

His Death. During this Assembly, King H E N R Y left this World the last day of *Conestaggio.*
1580. *January*, in the Year, *One thousand five hundred and fourscore*; it being
remarkable, That he began to die in the beginning of the Eclipse of the *Thuanus.*
Moon, and finished with it; as if that celestial Sign had wrought that Ef- *Vasconcellius.*
fect in him (being a King of a weak body) which it doth not in stronger; *Mariana.*
or at least, not so suddenly, as *Astrologers* do write. Neither is the houre
to be neglected, being the same wherein he was born, Threescore and eight
years before, having Reigned Seventeen Months, and eight dayes; so that
in him ended the Male Line of the Kings of *Portugal* of that Branch; since
derived from the Collateral of the Dukes of *Braganza*. He was of a thin
Body, small of Stature, and of a lean Face: As for his Judgment, it was
indifferent, indued (besides the Latine Tongue) with some Knowledge.
Alwayes held to be Chaste, and did never blemish this Angelical Virtue, but
with the desire of Marriage in his later dayes. He was acounted sparing, giving rather than denying; for he refused seldom, but he gave sparingly.
Ambitious he was of all Jurisdiction, as well Ecclesiastical, as Civil, zealous
in Religion; yet in the Reformation of religious persons, more strict than
was convenient. He was Bishop, Governour of the Realm, Inquisitor Major, Legate Apostolick, and King: But the more he soared, the more he
discovered his weakness; suffering himself in his most important Affairs to
be governed by his Ministers, not being able to determine the Cause of the *Conestaggio.*
Succession: Opinions were grafted in him with great obstinacy, retaining a
continual remembrance of wrongs; so that Justice was in him, but an unjust execution of his own Passions. In Fine, He was indued with great Virtues, and with fewer, and lesser Vices, yet were they equal in this; for he
had the Virtues of an Ecclesiastical person, and the defects of a Prince:
During his life, he was feared of many, and beloved of few, so as none lamented his death; only such, as were well-affected (desiring the Dispute
of Succession had been determined before his death) had a sensible apprehension of his loss.

His Body rested some time at *Almerin*, until that *Philip II.* King of
Spain, caused it to be brought to the Monastery of our Lady at *Bethleem*,
Y 2 notwith-

84   **ANTHONY** *King of*

notwithstanding that HENRY had Ordered his Sepulture at *Evora*, where he had in his life-time erected a stately Marble Tomb.

His Device was an Anchor, and a Daulphin, with this Inscription, FESTINA LENTE, for to denote, That in the execution of all Actions, Diligence, with Discretion, and a Mediocrity was to be used.

---

14. ANTHONY

The Bastard, Proclaimed King of PORTUGAL, and the ALGARVES, &c.

CHAP. XIX.

THE Prince *Lewis* of *Portugal* Duke of *Beia* his father, whose Natural and only Son he was, educated him in good Learning, but more particularly in the study of Divinity, with intention to make him a Divine; But being come to a riper age, he was made Knight of the Order of St. *John* of *Jerusalem*, and Prior of *Crato*.

He had embraced this Profession against his inclination, so that Pope *Gregory XIII.* was the more willing to dispence with the Vow he had made; which Dispensation was obtained at the instance and pursuit of King *Sebastian* of *Portugal*, who so highly esteemed this Prince ANTHONY his Cosin, that upon his first Voyage into *Affrick*, he made him his Lieutenant General, notwithstanding that Prince *Edward* of *Portugal* the Constable, was present.

Coneslaggio.
Jac. Augustus Thuanus.

At the second expedition that the same King *Sebastian* undertook for *Affrica*, he also accompanied him, and assisted him at the Fatal Battel of *Alcacer*, in which he was made a Prisoner, and reduced to a miserable Captivity for the space of Forty dayes; After which by an especial Providence, he found means to recover his liberty.

Being upon his return, he had intelligence that his Uncle the Cardinal *Henry*, after the Death of King *Sebastian*, was Elected King of *Portugal*.

Coneſtaggio.
Texera.

During whose Reign (as you have read) the Estates having been assembled to advise of a Successor to the Crown, ANTHONY was of the Number of the Competitors, urging, That he ought to be preferred, as only Male-child of the Posterity of King *Emanuel*: In pursuit of which, after the Decease of *Henry*, he was by the consent of the Three Estates, also Elected King the Nineteenth day of *June*, in the Year, *one thousand five hundred and fourscore*, in the City of *Sanctarem*; then afterwards Confirmed in that of *Lisbon*, Metropolis of the Kingdom; then received in the Quality of King at *Setubal*, and acknowledged for such, by all the Towns and Fortresses of *Affrica*, and Isles subject to the Dominion of *Portugal*; as also by the famous University of *Conimbra*.

Years of CHRIST.

1580.

1574.

1578.

1580.

But

PORTUGAL, and the ALGARVES, &c. 85.

Years of Christ.

But the King of *Spain, Philip II.* pretending on the contrary to be lawful Successor to the Crown, in the Right of the Empress, *Isabel* of *Portugal,* his Mother, incontinently raised a considerable Army, under the Conduct of his Martial favourite, that famous Captain, *Ferdinand de Toledo* Duke of *Alva,* who entred the Frontiers, and seized upon divers Towns by accord, which the Populars hearing of, which were with ANTHONY at St. *Arem,* Proclaimed him King, that so they might have a head to their confused body. After which ANTHONY repaired to *Lisbonne,* and there was sworne, sent the Count of *Vimioso* to *Setuval,* whence he expelled the Governours, who there had intended to admit the Spanish Gallies, so that all the places about *Lisbonne* were at his devotion. But *Alva* very much prevailed, as well through his own good Discipline, as the Inconstancy, Headiness, and unskilfulness of his enemies: so that he soon conquered the whole Kingdom of *Algarves*; Notwithstanding the Pope (thinking it not convenient in Reason of State, that the Catholique King, whose power was already so formidable in *Italy,* should grow more potent by the addition of a new Kingdom) had sent his Legate to exhort him to desist from Armes, offering him a Judge to decide the Rights of the Pretendants: but the *Spaniard* being loth to put that to Compromise whereof he was already assured, deceived him with delayes so long, until the Victory was even in his hands; so that the fears of ANTHONY encreased as his hopes decayed: The Duke of *Braganza,* and the greatest part of the Nobility, making their peace with the Enemy to their best advantage, no hope of Relief remaining from other Countries (a foundation built upon succours from the Enemies ill-willers being alwayes unsure, since they will not declare themselves unless their Companions be strong) and his Army which he had levied, being composed either of unwilling minds, or unable bodies, since all were Mechaniques, Mariners, Slaves, or religious persons, whose vaunts before the Fight did more inflame, than their valour in Fight did defend him, whom they had inflamed. Yet such as they were, they banded together under the leading of ANTHONY, at *Alcantara* expecting the Enemy, in the Year, *One thousand five hundred and fourscore,* where they were put to rout, chased to *Lisbonne* Walls, and the Suburbs sacked, a thousand *Portugals* being slain in Fight, partly in their Trenches, and partly at the defence of a Bridge, where they made a valiant resistance, ANTHONY fled to *Viana,* whither he was so sharply pursued by *Zanches d'Avila* Marescal of the Field, that in the habit of a Mariner he hardly escaped in a small Boat, both Captivity from his Pursuers, and drowning through the violence of the wind and waves. The year following, *viz. One thousand five hundred fourscore and one,* he escaped into *France* from *Setuval* in a *Flemmish* Ship which he did hire by the aid of a woman and a Religious person, where he incited the Duke of *Alenzon* to annoy the Catholick King in *Brabant,* and the Queen Mother (who seemed discontented with the *Spaniard,* for interrupting the course of Justice, by the violence of Armes) to assist him with Men and Munition for the recovery of *Portugal,* and the Defence of the *Terceraes,* which stood out in his Cause, and had vanquished *Peter de la Baldes*; with the loss of Four hundred of his men, who had been sent thither to reduce those Islands to the obedience of the King of *Spain.*

Portugal was now peaceably enjoyed by the Catholick King, who had made his Magnificent entry into *Lisbonne,* granted a General Pardon to all ANTHONY's Faction, excepting the Religious, and some few particulars,

H. F. Coneftag: gio.

Thuanus; Texera.

H. F. Coneftag: gio.

ANTHONY's Army defeated near Lisbonne. 1580.

Z

ANTHONY *Proclaimed King of*

culars, and received the Oath of Allegiance to himself and *Dom Diego* his son, from the States of the Kingdom. At this time ANTHONY was armed by the Queen Mother with Sixty Sail, and Seven thousand men for the assurance of the Islands, and the surprising of the *Indian* Fleet under the leading of *Philip Strozzi* Collonel of the French Infantry, and *Monsieur Brisack*, against whom they sent the Marquess of St. *Croix* with a formidable Army, who engaged with the French near the Island of St. *Michael* in a bloody fight, wherein *Strozzi*, and the Count of *Vimioso* were slain, much blood spilt on both sides, but the French received the Foil, and yet not so weakned, but that ANTHONY retained the Island in his hands, from whence he after Sailed into *France*, leaving *Emanuel de Silva* Governour behind. After the Report of this Victory the Catholick King imagining his assurance of *Portugal* to be good, departed into *Castille*, leaving Cardinal *Albert* Arch-duke of *Austria*, Vice-roy in his stead, having first received a new Oath to his Son *Dom Philip*, because *Dom Diego* his eldest Son was deceased.

Conestaggio.

But because he meant to make his Conquest entire, the year following (1583.) he sent the Marquess of St. *Croix*, with a greater Navy than before, to the Islands, where Twelve hundred French, under the Conduct of *Monsieur de Chattes*, being joyned with those *Portugueses* which were under *Emanuel de Silva*, made a valiant resistance, but being oppressed with so great a number of Enemies, being Ten thousand trained Souldiers at least, the French yielded upon Composition, and *Emanuel de Silva* was taken, and beheaded; After which Victory *Faiole* was reduced to obedience, after some small resistance, and thus was the Conquest of the Kingdom of *Portugal* wholly compleated, and subjected to the Catholick King.

ANTHONY being returned into *France*, (the Sanctuary of afflicted Princes,) from thence he writ a long Letter to Pope *Gregory XIII.* representing the Right he had to the Kingdom of *Portugal*; adding, That he had been justly Elected King: That the Marriage of Prince *Lewis* his Father, had been declared lawful, by the Sentence of the Bishop of *Angra*, the Popes Legate: That King *Henry* his Uncle had unjustly Sentenc'd him in his own Defence; for his Legitimation having been proved, the Crown had in Justice fallen upon him the said ANTHONY, before *Henry* himself, as being the Son of his elder Brother, whose Sentence was revoked and annihilated by Pope *Gregory*: To whom, Pope *Sixtus* the Fifth succeeding, the same King ANTHONY writ him also another Letter, as well to Congratulate with him in his Election, offering him the Vowes of an obedient Son; as to implore his help towards his Establishment in his Ancient Possession, and Royal Dignity.

Camdenus.

ANTHONY, not long after, obtained Letters of Recommendation from Queen *Katharine*, to *Elizabeth* Queen of *England*; in which, she forewarned her, and other Princes, to beware of the Spanish Greatness, who now enriched with the Addition of *Portugal*, *East-India*, and many Islands in the Atlantique Sea, might in time over-shadow all his Neighbouring Princes. Queen *Elizabeth*, alwayes Provident of her own, and her Subjects Safety, easily listned to this Councel, and bountifully relieved ANTHONY, which she thought she might do without Offence, considering, that she acknowledged him her Kinsman, descended of the Blood Royal of *England*; nor was there any League made betwixt the *Spaniards* and *English*, that the *Portugals* might not be received into *England*. Here then ANTHONY resided, till that fatal Blow was given to their (as they called

Year of Christ.

Strozzi, and the Count of Vimioso slain.

1583.

Portugal wholly subjected to the Catholick King.

ANTHONY entertained in England.

it)

PORTUGAL, *and the* ALGARVES, *&c.* 87

Years of it) *Invincible Armado*, when Queen *Elizabeth* judged it more Honourable
CHRIST. to attaque her Enemy, than again to be affailed by him; fuffered a Fleet to
be fet forth againſt *Spain*, commanded by Sir *John Norris*, and Sir *Francis
Drake*, and ſome other private Perſons: The *Hollander* likewiſe joined ſome
Ships; ſo that the Fleet confifted of about Eleven thouſand Souldiers, and
Fifteen hundred Mariners.

With this Fleet ANTHONY, with ſome few *Portugueſſes*, ſet Sail
out of *England*, having before aſſured the *Engliſh*, That the *Portugueſſes*
would revolt from the *Spaniard*. and appear for him; and that *Muley Hamet*,
King of *Morocco*, would ſtrengthen him with Twenty thouſand men.

The firſt place the *Engliſh* Fleet put into, was the *Groyne* in *Gallicia*, the
baſe Town they eaſily took; but endeavouring the higher, were repulſed,
and forced to raiſe their Siege, upon Report that the Count of *Andrada* was
coming with Forces to cut off their paſſage to their Ships, which *Norris* re-
ſolving to prevent, marched up to them, defeated them, and had the ſlaugh-
ter of them for Three Miles; after which, having pillaged, and burnt ſome
Villages, they returned to Sea, ſteering their Courſe for *Portugal*.

They had laboured ſome time with contrary Winds, plying to and fro at
Sea, when *Robert* the young Earle of *Eſſex* fell into them, who out of Military Glory, Hate of the *Spaniard*, and Commiſeration of ANTHONY,
had left the Court, without the knowledge or conſent of the Queen, in hope,
by Reaſon of the influence he had upon the Souldiery, to be choſen General
of the Foot. Two dayes after his Conjunction with them, they arrived in
Penicha, where they landed after the loſs of ſome men, and reduced the Ca-
ſtle to ANTHONY'S Obedience.

Sir *John* Hence the Land-forces under the Command of Sir *John Norris*, march-
Norris ed directly, and with all poſſible ſpeed towards *Lisbon*, about Sixty Miles
marcheth diſtant, *Drake* promiſing to follow with the Fleet by the way of the River
directly to *Tagus*. The Army being arrived at *Lisbon*, though they had before at a
Lisbonne. Councel of War determined to encamp on the Eaſt-ſide of the Town, the
better to bar Succours from coming out of *Spain*; now contrary to their
own Reſolutions, ſate down before St. *Katherines* Suburbs on the Weſt-ſide;
whereas at firſt they found no Reſiſtance, ſo they found little help, but what
the prayers of ſome few diſarmed men gave them, who now and then cried
out, *God ſave the King* ANTHONY: And indeed other help they
could not afford him, *Albertus* Arch-duke of *Auſtria* the Vice-Roy having
before diſarmed the *Portugals*.

The next day when the *Engliſh*, weary with their long march, betook
themſelves to their Reſt, the *Spaniſh* Gariſon ſallied out upon them, who
were at firſt reſiſted by *Brett*, and his Companies, till more coming up to
their Aſſiſtance, forced the *Spaniards* to give back, the Valiant Earle of
Eſſex chaſing them to the very Gates; but the *Engliſh* had ſeveral Commanders of Note, and no ſmall quantity of private Souldiers ſlain.

In ſum, when they had now ſtayed two dayes before the Town, and perceived that the *Portugals*, notwithſtanding the great brags and fair-promiſes
of ANTHONY, did not at all incline to a Revolt, and that no Advice
came of any Aſſiſtance from *Muley Hamet* King of *Morocco*; but that inſtead
of them, freſh Forces flocked in great Numbers from the Eaſt-parts into
the City, whilſt their Army was leſſned by a violent Sickneſs, their Proviſi-
on and Ammunition failed, and their great Guns for Battery arrived not, they
raiſed their Siege, and took their way towards *Caſcais*, a ſmall Town at the
mouth of the River, the *Spaniards* following them at a diſtance, but not

Z 2   ever

ANTHONY *Proclaimed King of*

Thuanus.

ever daring to fall in their Rear. The Town of *Cascais* they took, blew up the Castle; and so, notwithstanding all the intreaties of ANTHONY, set Sail for *England*, firing in their way *Vigo*, a Port-town, deserted of its Inhabitants.

So that now after a second Repulse, ANTHONY was forced to retire into *France*, where he was favourably received by King *Henry* the Great, under whose protection he passed the rest of his life; and having lived Threescore and four Years, dyed at *Paris*, the Five and twentieth day of *August*, in the Year, *One thousand five hundred fourscore and fifteen*. His body was deposited in the Church of the *Cordileires* in the same City. There was found in his Cabinet a Latine Paraphrase upon the penitential Psalms, with some Prayers in no Vulgar Stile, which gave Testimony of his Piety, whose Epitaph in Latine Verse, hath been written by *Frederick Morel*, the Kings Greek Professor in the University of *Paris*.

His Death. 1595.

Children of ANTHONY Prior of CRATO, Bastard of PORTUGAL.

15.

PORTUGAL PORTUGAL Party de NASSAU. ORANGES. *Escartele Au 1. quartier d'Azure au Lyon d'or armé & lampassé de gueules, l'Escu semé de billettes d'or, Qui est* NASSAU.
Au 2. d'or au Lyon de gueules, armé & lampassé d'azur.
Au 3. de gueules a la Fasse d'argent.
Au 4. de gueules a deux Leopards d'or armez & lampassez d'argent.
Sur le tout un Escu aussi escartelé; Au 1. & 4. de gueules a la bande d'or.
Au 2. & 3. d'or au Cor d'azur, lié & virolé de gueules; chargé sur le tout de cinq points d'or equippollez a quatre points d'azur.

EMANUEL OF PORTUGAL, eldest Son of ANTHONY, resided for some time with his Father in *France*, and *England*, then retired into the Low-countries unto *Maurice* Count of *Nassau*, afterwards Prince of *Orange*, whose Sister EMILIA of NASSAU Daughter of *William* Prince of ORANGE, and of *Anne* of *Saxony* his second Wife, EMANUEL married in the Year, *One thousand five hundred fourscore and seventeen*; afterwards he travelled unto the Court of the Infanta *Elizabeth* the Arch-dutchess, where he received a favourable entertainment.

His Marriage. 1597.

Children of EMANUEL OF PORTUGAL, and of EMILIA OF NASSAU his Wife.

16. EMANUEL OF PORTUGAL.

16. LEWIS OF PORTUGAL, before named *William*; had for God-father at the time of his Confirmation, *Lewis XIII*. King of *France* and *Navarre*.

16. MARY OF PORTUGAL.

16. LOVISE OF PORTUGAL.

16. ANNE OF PORTUGAL.

16. JULIANE OF PORTUGAL.

16. MAU-

16. **MAURICE OF PORTUGAL.**

16. **SABINE OF PORTUGAL.**

15. **CHRISTOPHER OF PORTUGAL**, after he had been some time with his Father in *France* and *England*, undertook the Voyages of *Affrica* and *Italy*, afterwards returned into *France*, and sheltered himself under the protection of King *Henry* the great, to whom *Anthony* had presented, and recommended him by a Lettter writ to his Majesty not long before his decease. From which time he continued his residence in the Court of that great King, and then in that of King *Lewis* the *Just*, his Son and Successor, the one and the other having honoured him with a particular favour, which upon all occasions they gave him testimony of.

15. **PHILIPPA OF PORTUGAL** a Nun.

15. **LOVISE OF PORTUGAL.**

Although in several places of this History, where I have met with the Persons, I have given you an account of their Pretentions to this Crown of Portugal; yet because they lie scattered in their Stories, and cannot be well compared one with another, (and being it is the Opinion of many, That the Right and Title to that Kingdom resides in the Kings of Spain; An Errour, springing either from their Ignorance in the Descent of those Princes; An apprehension that Sixty years Possession by the Austrian Family could make a Title indubitable, which was never warranted by the Right of Blood, or by the Laws of Portugal: Or, that many being wilfully Ignorant, would have others to be so too) I have therefore thought it necessary to spend this Sheet for the Entrance of the Table of the Competitors, their several pretentions, and to clear the Title of King John IV. to that Crown.

I. *The Pretention of the People.*

The People Claimed, *Jure Regni*, alledging, That the Issue-Male of their Kings failing, the Election belonged unto them, fortifying this Reason by the Example of the Election which was made of their King, *John I.*

But against the People it was answered, That they had no greater Priviledge of Election in this Kingdom, than in the rest of *Spain*, all which Realms fall by Succession, when there is any lawfully descended of the Blood-Royal: And that in *Portugal* they have less Liberty than the rest, growing from the Gifts of the Kings of *Castille*, and from the Conquest of the Kings of *Portugal*. And forasmuch as the People did not give the Realm to their Primative Kings, they could not since be invested with any Power to Choose one. And for that which they alledged concerning the Election of King *John I.* it was answered, That this Reason did so little serve their turn, that it was rather an Argument against them, to prove that the Kingdom in that Case was Successive: having themselves secretly confessed, That they had no Right to Choose, whilst there remained any one lawfully descended of the Royal Issue, Inferring, That *Beatrice* being married to a Stranger; The Realm was in the same estate, wherein according to the Law of *Lamego*, they were to choose the next Prince of the Blood; which Choice proceeded from Duty, rather than any unlimited Power in the People. But to put this Dispute out of doubt, there had been Four several Examples put in Practice against the Peoples Election.

1. *Alphonso III.* Successor to his Brother *Sancto II.* left the Crown to his Son *Dionysio*, by the Right of Inheritance. 2. *Emanuel* in the same Right succeeded *John II.* his Fathers Brothers Son. 3. *Emanuel* upon his journey into *Castille*, declared, That if he deceased without Children, the Succession did belong to *James* Duke of *Braganza* his Sisters Son. 4. And *Henry* the Cardinal in the same manner without Election succeeded *Sebastian*, to whom he was great Uncle. So that Consequently, That Custom was to be observed in the Succession of a Kingdom, which had been ever practised.

II. *Of the POPE.*

THe Popes Title was not forgot, who Challenged to be *Jure divino* Arbitrator (if not Donor) in all Controversies for Crowns, but especially in this, because *Alphonso* the first King to obtain that Title, became Tributary to the See of *Rome*. But this was slighted and disregarded, as not worthy an Answer.

III. *Of Katherine de Medicis.*

KAtherine de Medicis Widow of *Henry* the Second King of *France*, was the Third Competitor for the Crown of *Portugal*, as being descended legitimately from *Alphonso III.* King of *Portugal* (*vide pag.* 22.) charging all that Reigned since to be Usurpers, and that the Kingdom ought to return by direct Line to the Heirs of the Lawful Children of *Alphonso*, and the Countess of *Buillon*, whom they said to be this *Katherine* Daughter of *Lawrence de Medicis*, and of *Magdalene* of *Buillon* and *de la Tour*, the only remainder in Direct Line of that House, and Heir to the County, the which although she did not then possess, being incorporate by the Kings of *France*, as a matter of importance seated upon the Limits of *France* and *England*, yet they gave unto the Queen in Recompence, the Earldom of *Lauregais*, which she enjoyed.

But against the most Christian Queen it was pleaded, That her Pretention was improbable, and prescribed, seeing that the Successors of the Earl of *Buillon*, had never made any mention thereof, neither is it credible, that since this Pretention was incorporate to the Crown of so mighty a Realm, such Wise and Potent Princes as were *Francis I.* and *Henry II.* would have forgotten to call it in question. But the truth was, the Countess *Matilda* left no Children, as it appears in her Testament, in the Publick Registers of *Portugal*, making therein no mention to leave any by King *Alphonso*, nor to have had any. It was likewise proved, That *Matilda* or *Maud* had no Children, by a formal Request found in the same Registers, by the which all the Prelates in the Realm did beseech Pope *Urban*, That it would please him to disannul the Curse which he had laid upon the Realm, and that he would approve the Marriage of *Beatrix* the second Wife of *Alphonso*, that he would make their Children Legitimate, that there might be no hindrance in the Succession of the Kingdom; whereby it was concluded, That if there had been any lawful Children of *Maud*, they could not have perswaded the Pope to preferre the Bastards of *Beatrice*. It was added, That these Reasons were not unknown in *France*, and that of late there had been a Book Printed, of the Genealogie of the Houses of *Medicis* and *Buillon*, continued unto *Katherine* the most Christian Queen, whereby it did clearly appear, That *Maud* left no Children by *Alphonso* her second Husband, having been formerly married to *Philip* Son of *Philip Augustus* King of *France*; by which Marriage she had one Daughter named *Jane*, who did not succeed her Mother in the County, dying before her without Issue: So as *Robert* Son of *Alix* Sister to *Matilda*, came to the Succession,

Claims to the Kingdom of PORTUGAL.

cession, and this is that *Robert* from whom they would draw the descent of Queen *Katherine*, being the Nephew, and not the Son of *Maud*. So as not being at all proved, that *Alphonso III.* had any Children by his first Bed, but the contrary by many Reasons, the Queen had no Reason, they said, to Pretend.

The Interest of the other Pretenders more nearly concerned, this ensuing Table will make clear.

Emanuel Fourteenth King of *Portugal*.
- *Beatrice* Dutchess of *Savoye*, Defunct. — *Emanuel Philibert* D. of *Savoy*, Competitor.
- *Isabel* the Empress, Defunct. — *Philip II.* King of *Castille*, Competitor.
- *John III.* Fifteenth K. of *Portugal*, Def. — *John* Prince of *Portugal*, Defunct. — *Sebastian* 16th King of *Portugal*, Defunct.
- *Lewis* Duke of *Beia*, Defunct. — *Anthony* Prior of *Crato*, Competitor.
- *Henry* Cardinal, and Seventeenth K. of *Portugal*, after whose death these several Princes laid Claim to that Kingdom.
- *Edward* Duke of *Vimerana*, Defunct.
  - *Mary* Dutchess of *Parma*, Defunct. — *Raynusius* Duke of *Parma*, Competit.
  - *Katherine* Dutchess of *Braganza*, Competit.

IV. *Of Emanuel Philebert Duke of Savoye.*

THe Fourth that pretended to this Crown, was *Emanuel Philebert* Duke of *Savoye*, as Son to *Beatrix* younger Daughter to King *Emanuel*, though it is to be supposed, that he laid not his Claim out of any hopes to prevail whil'st he was descended of the younger Daughter, and *Philip II.* King of *Spain* of the Elder; but it is rather to be thought, that he was incited to put in his Claim, by the rest of the Pretenders, who knew, that of the Competitors that were not Natives, he was the fittest Person of all others, to resist and annoy King *Philip*, not only by reason of his Personal Valour, but also because of his Countries bordering upon the Dutchy of *Milan*, which with the assistance of the French his Neighbours on the other side, and Pretenders to that Dukedom, he might with ease at all times invade.

V. *Of Anthony Prior of Crato.*

HE was the Fifth Competitor for the Realm of *Portugal*, who alledged, That his Mother was lawfully wedded to his Father, and endeavoured by all means to Clear the Aspersion of his illegitimation. But *Anthony* was held Directly Unlawful, having always lived in that opinion, and was so held by his Father *Lewis* at his Death (as it appeared by his Testament) That of Four Witnesses that were to prove his Legitimation, Two were convinced to be false, for they recanted, confessing they had been suborned by *Anthony*; and the other Two were suspected, being neer Kinsmen, and disagreeing betwixt themselves: And that although he had demanded his Legitimation at *Rome*, and had obtained it, yet could not any Royal or Pontifical Legitimation serve for the Succession of a Kingdom.

VI. *Of Raynucio Prince of Parma.*

The Sixth who made Claim to this Kingdom, was *Raynucio* the young Prince of *Parma*, who demanded it in the right of his Mother the elder Daughter to the Infante *Edward*, alledging, That *Jure Progenitura*, the Male-line was to be served before the Female; so that until the Line of his Grand-father Prince *Edward* were wholly extinct, neither *Philip II*. nor the Duke of *Savoye* could have any pretence to that Kingdom: And against the Dutchess of *Braganza* he argued, That he ought to precede her, as being descended of the elder Sister. Against the Duke of *Parma* it was not denyed, but that he preceded the Catholique King, and so consequently the Duke of *Savoye*; but as to the Dutchess of *Braganza*, she pleaded, That *Raynucio* could not aid himself with the benefit of Representation, being the Son of her Sister deceased, and therefore out of the degree wherein the Laws allow it.

VII. *Of Katherine Dutchess of Braganza.*

The Seventh Competitor for the Crown of *Portugal*, was *Katherine* Dutchess of *Braganza*, younger Daughter of Prince *Edward*, alledging, That in all Successions whatsoever, these Four Qualities were to be considered, *viz.* The Line, the Degree, the Sex, and the Age; that the better Line ought in Justice first to take place, although others should have advantage in all the other three Qualities, That in all Successions of Crowns, the last Possessor was to be succeeded *Jure hereditatis*, which allowed the Benefit of Representation: That the representing the Infant Don *Edward*, the better Line did by Representation precede *Raynucio* (the Law never allowing a Grand-child that benefit) and that by her better Line she did exclude King *Philip*, who was descended of a Daughter, but especially by the fundamental Laws of the Kingdom (put in execution against *Beatrice* Daughter of *Ferdinand IX*. King of *Portugal*, who having married out of the Kingdom to the King of *Castille*, her Right of succeeding was utterly lost, and King *John I*. chosen in her stead) she was to be preferred before all Claimers whomsoever, in regard of her being both Born and Married within the Kingdom. Nor can it be thought hard measure to the Dukes of *Parma* (being descended from Prince *Edwards* elder Daughter, to be excluded the Succession to the Crown of *Portugal*, and the Dukes of *Braganza* derived from the younger, and Married to a Native of *Portugal*, to have the undoubted Right) if we consider, that by the same Law of *Lamego* the Crown descended to King *Emanuel* himself, which otherwise had belonged unto the same *Beatrice* Queen of *Castille*, only Daughter of King *Ferdinand IX*.

VIII. *Of Philip II. King of Castille.*

Philip II. King of *Castille* was the Eighth and last Pretender; who having employed all the best Wits in *Christendom*, to confute and disprove all other Claims, and to prove and maintain his, Alledged, That the Succession of Crowns was to be decided by the Law of Nations, not of the Empire, upon which only her *Jus representandi Patrem* was grounded; That the nearest male in degree to the last Possessor, ought to succeed; That the Infant Don *Edward* being deceased before his Brother *Henry* was King, could have no right in himself, and therefore could derive none to his Posterity; for *Nemo dat quod in se non habet*, that it was very unreasonable, that *Katherine* should be less prejudiced in her self for her Sex, than King *Philip* should be for his Mother.

PHILIP II, III, IV.
Of that NAME,
KINGS OF SPAIN,
And 19, 20, 21. KINGS of
PORTUGAL.
CHAP. XX.

BUt it was no Arguments could confute, or annul the certain and indubitable right of the Dutchess of *Braganza*, which was clear to the World, both by her Descent, and by the Fundamental Laws of the Nation, and this King PHILIP knew well, and therefore, though he carried on his affairs very candidly to the eyes of men, and seemed unbyassed with proper Interest, by offering to submit his Title to a Disputation, professing, That the Laws of *Portugal* were more favorable to him, than the Law of *Castille*, and openly acknowledging, That if he should chance to die before King *Henry*, his eldest Son being a degree farther off, would come behind some of the Pretenders, of whom himself had the precedence. Though, I say, he carried himself thus fair to the World, yet he clandestinely wrought with Father *Leon Henriques* a Jesuite, and Confessor to King *Henry*, and *Ferdinando Castillo*, a Dominican, and of the Kings bosom Councel, to endeavor by all means possible to divert all Designs in prejudice of his Claims, and especially that *Catherine* Dutchess of *Braganza* might not by *Henry* be declared to be the next Heir apparent; which he, conscious of the justice of the Title, was very willing to have done.

And whilest these two Fathers prosecuted his interest there with the old, and almost doting King *Henry*, the vigilant PHILIP provided an Army in readiness, with which he resolved to enter into *Portugal*, and with his Sword make good his disputable Title, as soon as that old Kings death should give him the Warning-piece to fall on.

Yet when that was given, and PHILIP ready to march with an Army of Twenty thousand men into *Portugal*, he had like to have been prevented; for Pope *Gregory* the Thirteenth pretending still his right to Dispose, or at least to Arbitrate all Difference concerning that Crown, had sent Cardinal *Riario* Legat Apostolique, with Order to dissuade the Catholick King from raising Arms, and that done, to pass into *Portugal*, and in his Holiness name and behalf, to Arbitrate the Right between all Pretenders; which designs of the Popes, this crafty Spanish Fox circumvented, for having pre-advice of it, and resolving to pursue his own intentions of assuring to himself the Kingdom of *Portugal*, and yet approve himself an obedient Son of the Church, he gave Order in all places where the Legat was to pass, he should be moſt Magnificently entertained, ſo that by ſuch ſumptuous Treatments, the time might be dexterouſly protracted, and he poſſeſſed of that Kingdom before the Legat arrived at Court; which was accordingly done, and the Legat returned thanks for his Magnificent Entertainments, though he was diſpleaſed at the ill ſucceſs of his Negotiation.

But to proceed to the manner of his poſſeſſing himſelf of this Kingdom: No ſooner did the News arrive at the Spaniſh Court of the death of King *Henry*, but *Ferdinand de Toledo*, Duke *D' Alva*, was commanded with an Army of Twenty thouſand men to march toward *Lisbonne*, and in the Name and Right of his Catholick Majeſty, to make Conqueſt of the Kingdom, if he found oppoſition.

But all the appearance of oppoſition which he found, was made by *Don Antonio* the Baſtard-ſon of *Lewis* the Infante, who having got into *Lisbonne* in the Head of a tumultuary Rabble, rather than a well-formed Army, endeavored at firſt to make ſome reſiſtance, but was ſoon diſcomfited, and the Suburbs of *Lisbonne* being ſacked to ſatisfie the Souldiers, the City was ſurrendred to him, whither ſoon after the King came, and ſo by a mixt Title of Deſcent and Arms, took poſſeſſion of the Kingdom, A° 1510. *Katherine* Dutcheſs of *Braganza* being enforced to ſurrender to him all her intereſt and pretenſions; which you have read at large in *Anthony*.

The Nobility and People of *Portugal* were, without doubt, extreamly amazed to ſee themſelves ſo ſuddenly ſurprized, and made Subject to a Forein Prince, and eſpecially to a Prince of that Nation, againſt whom they had a natural Antipathy: but finding themſelves in a condition not able to make any reſiſtance, they thought they ſhould gain more by ſubmitting freely to that King, than by being forced to it; and therefore they made their humble ſubmiſſion, which PHILIP met as it were half way, and condeſcended in the General Aſſembly of Eſtates, to be ſworn to theſe Articles or Capitulations following.

I. *That the ſaid* PHILIP *King of* Spain, &c. *ſhould obſerve all the Laws, Liberties, Priviledges, and Cuſtoms granted to the People by the former Kings of* Portugal.

II. *That the Vice-King, or Governor, ſhould be alwayes the Son, Brother, Uncle, or Nephew of the King, or elſe a Native of* Portugal.

III. *That all chief Offices of the Church or State, ſhould be beſtowed upon the Natives of* Portugal, *and not upon Strangers; likewiſe the Governments of all Towns and Places.*

IV. *That all Countries now belonging to the* Portugal, *ſhould ſo continue, to the commodity and benefit of the Nation.*

V. *That the* Portugal *Nation ſhould be admitted to all Offices in the Kings Houſe, as well as the* Caſtillians.

VI. *That becauſe the King could not conveniently be alwayes in* Portugal, *he ſhould ſend the Prince to be bred up amongſt them.*

Theſe Articles were ſhut up, or concluded, with a Bleſſing upon ſuch Kings as ſhould obſerve and keep them, and a Curſe on thoſe who ſhould break or violate them. And ſome Authors likewiſe affirm, that there was another Clauſe added to them, ſignifying, *That in caſe* (which God forbid) *that the King which then was, or his Succeſſors, ſhould not obſerve this Agreement, or ſhould procure a Diſpenſation*

spensation for this Oath, the Three States of the Kingdom might freely deny Subjection and Obedience to the King, without being guilty either of Perjury or Treason.

Though these Articles were thus sworn to, and the Cardinal *Albertus* Archduke of *Austria*, Son to the Emperour, and Nephew to the King of *Spain*, appointed Vice-King of *Portugal*, PHILIP the Second durst not in Person yet leave the Kingdom; for he perceived by their Murmurs and visible Discontents, that their Submission to him, proceeded more out of Fear, than Love; and that as he had in a moment gained that Kingdom, so he should as soon lose it, if he should but give them the least opportunity.

For that the People were highly discontented, might easily appear by their attentive listning after old Prophesies, among which, was one of an old Hermit, who told *Alphonso* the first King of *Portugal*, *Of the great Victory that he should obtain over the Five Kings of the Moors; that he and his Posterity should Reign happily Kings of* Portugal, *but that in the Sixteenth Generation his Line should fail, but that God at length should have mercy again upon them, and restore them.*

Others had respect to a Letter written by St. *Bernard* to the same King *Alphonso* (the Original of which is reported to have been given to the *Portugal* Embassadours, by *Lewis* the Thirteenth King of *France*, *A° One thousand six hundred and forty one*) the substance of which was to this effect: *That he rendred thanks to him for the Lands bestowed upon him, that in recompence thereof, God had declared unto him, That there should not fail a Native of* Portugal *to sit upon that Throne, unless for the greatness of their sins God would chastise them for a time; but that this time of Chastisement should not last above Sixty Years.*

Other Prophesies there were of this Nature, and to this Effect, which put the People in hopes of a Deliverance, and many of them flattered themselves, That *Don Sebastian* was yet alive, and would come and deliver them; nay, so foolish were some of them, that though they believed him slain at the Battel of *Alcacer* in *Barbary*; yet they thought he should live again, and miraculously come to redeem them.

But that which most of all expressed the Peoples Discontents, was, what was publickly spoken by the mouths of their Oratours, the Priests in their Pulpits, who would ordinarily in their Sermons utter Speeches much in prejudice of the Spaniards Title, and in Favour of the Dutchess of *Braganza*; nor were they sparing to do so in the presence of the King himself, who would therefore often say, *That the Portuguez Clergy had made the sharpest War with him.*

Father *Lewis Alvarez* a Jesuite, preaching one day before the Vice-Roy, took his Text, *Surge, tolle Grabatum tuum, & ambula*; and turning himself to the Duke, said, Sir, the meaning of that is, *Arise, Take up your Pack, and be gone home.* But above all this, might the Discontents be perceived in the Noblemens Chappels, especially in the Duke of *Braganza*'s, where they were wont to sing the *Lamentations of Jeremy*, applying all the scorn and reproach of the *Israelites* to themselves; as *Aquam nostram pecunia bibimus*, because of the Excize put by the *Spaniards* upon Wine, and other Necessaries: And that, *Servi Dominati sunt in nos*; and that, *Cecidit Corona Capitis nostri*; most commonly ending with this Invocation, *Recordare Domine, Quid acciderit nobis Intuere & respice opprobrium nostrum: Hæreditas nostra versa est ad alienos.*

Yet did King PHILIP bear all these Affronts with an incomparable Patience, dissembling with an admirable Prudence his Passion (if he had any) for these Discontents; for he knew, the only way to win this Nation to an Obedience and Compliance, must be Lenity at first, whatever he intended to practise afterwards; and that he had by his exact keeping of his Word and Oath, won much upon this People, appears, in that during his whole Reign, and the Reign of his Successor, PHILIP the Third, who followed his Fathers foot-steps, though not with that Craft and Dissimulation, they made no Attempts, nor were inclinable to a Revolt.

Those Attempts made by *Anthony* (which you may read in his story) and some small bustles with one or two Counterfeit *Sebastians* not worth mentioning, were the only storms, that hapned in this Kingdom during the reigns of PHILIP the second, and third; for they keeping their words in most things, though some of their priviledges they infringed, had almost brought the people to a willingnesse to be their slaves, whereas PHILIP the fourth committing the whole charge of the Government to Count *Olivarez*, (who though without doubt an able Statesman, yet would seem to have a way in policy by himself, which no body else could understand the reason of) lost the whole Kingdom, and all its Territories.

For such was the new rigorous ways which he would prescribe in the Government of *Catalonia* and *Portugal*, both people very tender of their Priviledges, the least breach of which should have been seconded by a potent Force to have suppressed them, in case they should attempt an Insurrection, when instead of having such power in readiness, the *Catalonians* had rather opportunity given them to rebel, and spurs to provoke them to make use of the opportunity; for some Souldiers being scatteringly quartered among them, but too few to curb them, they looked upon that as a greater intrenchment upon their Liberties than any before, and a design utterly to enslave them : wherefore converting their patience into fury, they took Arms, massacred those Souldiers, slew their Viceroy, and put themselves under the *French* Protection.

This Revolt of the *Catalonians* was a president to the *Portugals*, who had extreamly suffered under the breach of their Priviledges: for contrary to the second Article sworn to by King PHILIP the Second, which said, *That the Viceroy or Governor, should be either Son, Brother, Uncle, or Nephew to the King of* Spain : The Infanta *Margarita di Mantoua*, who had no relation at all to the Kings of *Castille*, was made Governess, which they might, and perhaps would have born, had they not been incensed by a more feeling injury *Anno* 1636. when the Tax of a fifth part was imposed upon all the Subjects of that Kingdom; an intollerable grievance, and thought so insufferable by the Southern parts of the Nation, that they rose in Arms to oppose it, and had set the whole Kingdom in a combustion, had it not been timely quenched by the timely care and industry of the then Governess, the *Infanta Margarita of Mantoua*.

Yet this small stir gave an *Item* to the Court of *Spain*, of the readiness of the people to revolt, which made *Olivarez* endeavor by all ways possible to cut off the means of their being able to do, but whilest he endeavored to prevent them, he gave them the means to do it, though he failed not to make use of those courses which in probability might ensure that Kingdom; the chief of which was, the endeavoring to allure from thence the Duke of *Braganza*, whom the people of *Portugal* looked upon as the person who of right ought to be their King, and who was the only Native of the Kingdom who might restore again the Line of *Alphonso*; besides, he was a Prince, who for Power, Riches, and Number of Tenants, not only exceeded all the Nobles of *Portugal*, but even of *Spain* it self.

And indeed the Duke of *Braganza* was one of the most glorious Subjects in *Europe*, being allied to most Kings in Christendom; which made the Kings of *Spain*, though they were Competitors for the Crown of *Portugal*, treat this Family with more honor than any other of his Grandees, receiving them almost with as much respect, as if they were Soveraign Princes; which appeared in PHILIP the Second, who most of all desired to abase this Family, yet would always when the Duke of *Braganza* came to visit him; meet him in the middle of the room, and not permitting him to kiss his hand, seat him with himself under the Canopy of Estate.

To draw him therefore out of that Kingdom, *Olivarez* first politickly offered him the Government of *Milan*, a place of great trust and honor, but he modestly refused it, as not in a condition at that present to undertake so great a Command, and indeed expressing an unwillingness to go out of *Portugal*.

But his unwillingnesse to go from thence, made the King of *Spain*, and Count *Olivarez* the more willing to draw him from thence, it was therefore given out; That the King himself was resolved to go in person to reduce the revolted *Catalonians*, and that therefore all the Nobility should be in a readiness in four months time to attend his Majesty in that Expedition. But the Duke of *Braganza* being suspitious of the *Spaniards*, because he knew himself suspected by them, and likely to be, whil'st the *Portuguesses* so much affected him; to assure himself of the ones Love, and to avoid (if possible) the others Suspect, retires himself to his Countrey-house at *Villa-Viciosa*, and there follows his Sports of Hunting, &c. not at all regarding matters of State, withal sending an Excuse to Count *Olivarez*, That his Affairs at present were in so low and mean a Condition, that he could not appear to attend his Majesty in that Pomp and Splendor that became a Person of his Quality; and that therefore he should do his Majesty more Service in staying at Home, when the other Nobles were abroad, than he could possibly do by attending him.

This Plot thus failing, made the Court of *Spain* more suspitious of the Duke than ever before; Count *Olivarez* therefore resolves to employ his utmost Art of Dissimulation to entrap him, which he sets upon by a Fetch so far about, that to the eye of Reason, it might put the Duke into ambitious Thoughts of endeavouring to assume his Throne, and in a way to accomplish those Thoughts, rather than any way prejudice him; but it appeared afterwards that *Olivarez* Design in so far trusting the Duke, was only because the Duke should trust him.

In Answer to *Braganza*'s Letter of Excuse, the Count assures him that his Majesty was very well satisfied with his Reasons of not attending him in the intended Expedition against *Catalonia*, and that he was very sensible of his good Inclinations to his Service: That for his own part, he was very sorry that his Affairs were in so low a Condition; for he could not but Commiserate his Interest as his own. That his Majesty, to let him know how great Confidence he reposed in his Fidelity, had appointed him General of the Militia of that Kingdom, and had for his present Supply, sent him Sixty thousand Crowns, leaving it to his Choice to reside in what place near *Lisbon* he pleased.

This strange Confidence put in the Duke by the King of *Spain*, much amazed the greatest Politicians, who thought it reasonable, That the *Spaniard* should have permitted the Duke still to have kept retired in the Countrey, rather than to have given him such a Command, and called him to *Lisbon* into the continual View of the People, who looking upon him as the Heir of that House which had ever been represented to have the only Right to the Crown, might easily be inflamed with a Desire to have a King of their own.

And these things was the Princess of *Mantoua* very sensible of, and therefore continually sollicited the King to know his Reason, or to desire him to remove those apparent Opportunities which he had given the Duke of *Braganza* to effect a Revolt: But she not only received intricate and enigmatical Answers from the King, and Duke *D' Olivarez*; but likewise had the former Actions seconded with one, which made her of Opinion that his Catholick Majesty had a mind to toss the Kingdom into *Braganza*'s hands whether he would or no; for on a sudden, without any notice given to her, all the *Spanish* Garison in St. *Johns* Castle, which commanded the City of *Lisbon*; and indeed upon the strength of which, the whole safety and security of the Kingdom depended, were suddenly drawn forth, and the Castle left to the disposure of Don *John* of *Braganza*.

But

But this was the laſt Act of Count *Olivarez* Confidence in the Duke; for by truſting him ſo much, he now thought that he could not but reciprocally repoſe Confidence in him; and therefore next Summer, *A° One thouſand ſix hundred and forty:* He again by Letters ſollicites him to leave *Portugal*, and come to *Madrid*, firſt telling him, That his Catholick Majeſty gave him many Thanks, and greatly applauded his Loyalty in the Exerciſe of the Office of General, and was very ſenſible of the good Effects which his Authority had wrought over the *Portugals*. Next he repreſented unto him the preſent declining Condition of the *Spaniſh* Monarchy; not only by Reaſon of the Diſorders in *Flanders* and *Italy*, and the preparations of the *Turk*; but more eſpecially, for that their moſt potent Enemies the *French*, were now in Aſſiſtance of the Revolted *Catalonians*, entred into *Spain:* That it highly concerned his Catholick Majeſty to drive theſe out of his Territories, which could not be effected, but by a very powerful Force; that he being one of the prime Grandees of the Kingdom, might by his preſence in the Head of a good number of his Tenants, encourage others to a ſutable Aſſiſtance; that to that purpoſe his Catholick Majeſty expected him every Moment, having deſigned for him great Honours, Priviledges and Dignities ſutable to his Merit.

But as cunning an Angler as *Olivarez* was, yet he failed of his Mark, the Bait would not yet hook in the Fiſh; for though the Duke of *Braganza* was accounted no very great Polititian, yet his own Safety taught him to know that all theſe Truſts, and fair Promiſes, were but gilded Allurements to draw him to his Deſtruction; having therefore ſupplied the King with a conſiderable number of his Tenants and Friends, he found Excuſes for his own not going in Perſon; and to take off all ſuſpition of Jealouſie or Thoughts, that he had any Deſign againſt the State, he retired again to his Countrey-houſe. Thus did theſe two great Perſonages by Craft and Diſſimulation, endeavour to ſupplant each other, only the one ſtrove the others Deſtruction, the other only ſtudied his own Safety and Preſervation.

During all theſe paſſages, the Vice-Queen *Margarita* of *Mantoua*, was very vigilant in her Government, and foreſeeing what in Reaſon might be the iſſue of theſe proceedings, wrote very importunately to the King, aſſuring him; That if it were not ſuddenly prevented, the Kingdom would infallibly be loſt. To which, his Majeſty returned her no Anſwer; and *Olivarez* in his ſlighting her judgment (as fitter to Govern a private Houſe, than a Kingdom) deſired her, That if her Capacity would not reach to the height and drift of thoſe Myſteries of State, yet that her Wiſdom would prompt her not to diſcover them.

Yet without doubt *Olivarez* was inwardly perplexed to ſee all his Plots thus fail, and foul means he durſt not openly attempt, ſuch was the Dukes Potency, and the great Love the People bore him; he therefore at laſt has Recourſe to Treachery, and to that intent gives ſecret Advice to *Don Lopez D' Oſſis*, and *Don Antonie D' Oquendo*, That when they had relieved *Flanders* with Men and money, they ſhould with the whole Fleet put into *Portugal*, and then as ſoon as the Duke ſhould according to the Duty of his new Place and Office come aboard, they ſhould immediately ſet Sail, and bring him away to *Cales*: But this Plot was by a ſtrange Divine Providence prevented; for that Fleet was totally Routed by the *Hollanders* upon the Coaſt of *England*, in the Year, *One thouſand ſix hundred thirty and nine.*

JOHN

17. JOHN IV.

Of the Name, KING of PORTUGAL, *Algarvia, Affrick, Arabia, Persia, India, and Brasil,* &c.

CHAP. XXI.

PORTUGAL.
PORTUGAL
D'argent a cinq Escussons d'Azure peris en Croix chacun charge de cinq besans aussi d'argent posez en sautoir, a la Bordure de gueulles charge de sept Chasteaux d'or.

Party de MEDINA-SIDONIA.

Now was the time come, wherein, according to St. *Bernards* Prophecy, the Kingdom of *Portugal* was to be released from the Tyranny of Strangers, and restored again to the Government of a Native King, to which all things seemed so well to quadrate, that we cannot imagine there was less than a Divine Hand in it; for though (all Plots failing against the Duke of *Braganza,*) the *Spaniards* beginning to fear somewhat, drew out as many of the Native Souldiers out of the Kingdom as conveniently they could, thinking thereby to lessen the ill humours which began now to appear; yet they did thereby only the more stir up and enflame those discontents which were taken at *Vasconsellos* managing all Affairs of State.

For although the most Illustrious Infanta *Margarita* of *Mantona* was a Princess of great judgment and knowledge in State-affairs, yet she permitted her self to be so much over-ruled by *Vasconsellos* Secretary of State, or at least was so much over-ruled by him, - whether she would or no, that he either by some secret consent of his Catholick Majesty, or led on by his own ambitious spirit, confiding in the great favour he had at Court, never permitted the *Infanta* to enjoy other than the title of Vice-Queen.

And insufferable was the Government of *Vasconcellos* to the *Portugueses*, who as much hated his obscure Birth, as they did his evil Customs: He was a man wholly composed of Pride, Cruelty, and Avarice, that knew no moderation but in excesses: small lapses were by him made capital crimes, chastising with all severity those whom he did but suppose dissatisfied with his Government; And exercising with

JOHN IV. *of the Name*,

all rigor the *Spanish Inquisition*, punished not only the actions, but the very thoughts of men. The infringing of the greatest Priviledges of the *Portugal* Nation seemed to him but a trifle; which continued oppressions, in the end so exasperated the whole People, that animated by the knowledge of their own strength, by the many diversions of the Spanish Nation, by the late example of the *Catalonians*, and incited by the absolute ruine which they saw hung over their heads, whil'st Six thousand of them were yearly listed and forced to serve the *Spaniard* in his forreign Wars, they resolved to loose his Yoke from off their Necks, and to disclaim his obedience, by the election of a King of their own.

Some have been of opinion, That this Conspiracy was at least of Ten years standing, agreed and assented to by most of the Grandees of *Portugal*: I dare not affirm it, nor deny it; for such great actions of State do resemble Lightning, which once past, leave but the greater darkness: the Air of State-mysteries is not to be flown in by less than Eagles; I shall therefore omit to search into so great a Privacy, and only recount the Publick Action.

On *Saturday* the First of *February*, *Anno*, *One thousand six hundred and forty*, (and *Saturdayes* have been often observed to be propitious to the *Portugal* Nation,) all the Nobility of the Kingdom, led on by the Marquesses of *Ferreira*, and the Count of *Vimioso*, took Arms, and accompanied with a great multitude of the Inhabitants of *Lisbonne*, and some *Portuguese* Souldiers came to the Castle, which scituate in the middest of *Lisbonne*, serves both for a Palace and a Castle: this was the residence of the Vice-Queen, and hither assembled all the Magistrates for Governing of the Kingdom, the Guards which were two Companies of *Spaniards*, and two of *High Dutch*, either before gained by secret intelligence, or frighted with the great numbers of the *Portugals*, or desire of Novelty, or else perhaps unwilling to make resistance against those to whom they were most of them joyned by friendship or Marriage, without the least opposition, abandoning their Post, gave them free admittance.

Whilest these things had hapned, the Secretary *Vasconsellos* was in the Chambers of his Office (upon some reasons he had by the Discontents of the People, to suspect an Insurrection) at that instant writing into *Spain*, of the Alienation of the minds of the Nobility from the Spanish Government, and ernestly pressing that some rigorous Resolution might be taken to prevent it; which Letters afterwards taken, did sufficiently demonstrate his ill will to the *Portuguese* Nation.

Whil'st he was thus busied, the confused noise of the Souldiers pierced his ears, at which wondring not so much at the tumult, as at what should be the cause of it, being accompanied only with a *Dutch*-man, and another of the Guard, he would have gone down, but was hindred by the *Portugals*, who came running up, crying, *Kill the Traytor*, *Kill the Enemy of our Blood*; whereupon not knowing where to save himself, he fled, with those two accompanying him, into an inner Chamber, and there with his Sword in his hand, accompanied and assisted by those two that were with him, disposed himself to sell his Life at the dearest rate he could: but his Valour stood him in no stead, for those two who endeavored to defend him, being slain with two Musquet-shot, he seeing it vain to defend himself there longer, leapt desperately out of the Window, rather to seek his Death, than out of any hopes to save his life; for no sooner was he down, but numberless Swords were embrued in his Blood, the very women and children running to tear in pieces his dead body, with the same alacrity as he used to torment them, when alive.

In the mean time the Marquess of *Ferreira* was gone to secure the Vice-Queen, whom having committed to the Guard of Two hundred Musquetteers, he calls a Council, and in a short Discourse sets forth the miseries the Kingdom had endured whilest it lay subject to the Spanish Government, who had sought no other end but their

their destruction: Then putting them in mind of the Valor and Merits of their Nation, he exhorts them to condescend to the Election of a New King, nominating to them the Duke of *Braganza*, as the most worthy of the Crown, not so much for his Power, Riches, or the Greatness of his House, as because the Kingdom was his indubitable Right; he being the only Person left of that Stock, which for so many years had gloriously governed *Portugal*.

A long Discourse was superfluous to those who were before perswaded. A publick shout interrupted the Marquesses Speech, all of them crying with a loud voice, *That they would have* JOHN *Duke of* Braganza *for their King*. In the whole multitude there was not a face, much less a voice that did gainsay this general Vote, either because they did all really rejoyce to see that they should again have a King of their own Nation, or because none could without danger oppose themselves to the torrent of so a Publick Will.

The Duke was at this time at his Countrey-house at *Villa-Vitiosa*, whether by accident, or because he would always have had occasion to excuse himself, if the business should not have succeeded, I cannot guess: but by reason of his absence they thought fit to make choice of two Governors, whom, to avoid the pretences of others, they nominated to be the Archbishops of *Lisbon* and *Braganza*.

These began immediately to exercise their Command, and were obeyed with so much quiet, that in all that great and populous City of *Lisbon* there was none slain, but only those before-mentioned; the prisons were opened, nor was there any that suffered any wrong, either in their goods or life: All the Shops were opened as if there had not happened any Change of Government.

Only the house of *Vasconcellos* was sackt, with so much anger and despite, that they did not pardon the very Doors and Windows; nay, such was the fury of the people, that had they not been hindred by the Souldiers of the Guard, they had levelled it with the ground. As for his carcase, it suffered all those disgraces which a people wronged both in their liberties and estates, could inflict: they ran like mad men to express living sentiments of Revenge upon his dead and senseless Corps, vaunting who could invent the newest ways of disgrace and scorn, till at length almost wearied with their inhumane sport, they left it in the street so mangled, that it did not seem to have the least resemblance of a man; from whence it was the next day carried by the Fraternity *della misericordia*, and thrown into the Burying-place of the Moors.

The Marquess of *Alemquer*, after he had by command from the Governor assured the strongest posts of the City, sent several Souldiers into the streets, crying, *Long live King* JOHN *the Fourth*; which the people hearing, distracted as it were with very joy, leaving their Trades, ran up and down proclaiming him with voices of *Jubilee*, the greatest part through excess of passion, not being able to refrain from tears.

The Messengers did not run, but flie to the Duke of *Braganza*, to give him notice of his promotion to the Crown: The first arrived on *Sunday* morning before day; he feigned a great alteration at this Advice; whereupon some have presumed to say, That he had not any knowledge of the Design. He seemed at first not to believe it, but told the Messengers, that though he might have desert, and a spirit fit for the Crown of *Portugal*, yet he had neither will nor ambition to desire. That his enemies wronged him, by tempting him with Stratagems as far from his Genius, as his Faith. But at the arrival of the Count of *Monte Santo*, who came to accompany him to *Lisbon*, he seemed of another mind; and having been with him in private discourse for the space of about two hours, without any further delay, then what the relating the business to his Wife, and to the Prince his

his son, made, he departed with the Count from *Villa Vizosa*, accompanied with about five hundred persons.

Yet others there be that affirm, That he was not only acquainted with the design of the Revolt, but of Council about it, and that some time before the Nobility having had a private Meeting at *Lisbon*, it was at first propounded; That they should reduce the Kingdom into the form of a Common-wealth; but that not being approved of by the major part, the Arch-bishop of *Lisbon* stood up, and in a most eloquent Speech, having laid before them the miseries they had endured under the Spanish yoke, recommended unto them JOHN Duke of *Braganza*, as the indubitable Heir of the Crown, and their rightful Soveraign.

This Motion needed not to be seconded with many Arguments to induce a general Consent, they all most willingly assented to it, and concluded to send *Gaston Cotigno*, a man of a fluent and voluble tongue, to acquaint the Duke with their intentions, and to perswade him to accept the Crown, and free his Countrey.

Gaston being arrived, with many well-coucht words acquaints him, That there was now a pregnant opportunity offered to recover the indubitable right of his Ancestors to the Crown of *Portugal*: That the Nobility and Clergy were wholly inclined to redeem themselves from the Tyranny of the *Castillians*, by securing the Crown upon his head: That the universal *Odium* of the whole People to the Spanish Government, the present low Condition of the House of *Austria*, distracted on every side with War; the assured Assistance that *France* and other Nations, emulating the greatness of *Spain*, would lend, were as so many Motives to perswade them not to let slip so fair an opportunity to regain their liberty: That if he by Refusal, should be the sole Enemy to his Countries Freedom, they would effect it themselves, and reduce it into a Common-wealth, with many other Arguments used he, which his Love to the House of *Braganza*, his hatred to the *Castillians*, or his own Ingenuity prompted to him.

The Duke's amazement permitted him not to return a sudden Answer: but after a little pause, he replied, That he was highly obliged both to him and all the Nobility, for their affections to him, but that this was a Business required great deliberation: That there was no *Medium* between a Throne and a Chair of Execution, that therefore he would first advise with himself, and not rashly attempt so hazardous a business.

He therefore communicates the whole business to his Dutchess *Donna Lucia*, Sister to the Duke of *Medina Sidonia*, a woman of a Noble, Heroick, and Masculine Spirit, with her he consults whether he were best accept of the Propositions of the Nobility, or to prevent all hazards go to *Madrid*: and being anxious what course to take, his Wife nobly told him: *My friend, if thou goest to* Madrid *, thou do'st incurre the danger of losing thy life; and if thou acceptest the Crown, thou do'st no more: consider then whether it be not better to dye Nobly at home, than basely abroad.*

These words of his Ladies (say some) animated him to a resolution to accept the Crown; so he returned *Gaston* in answer, That he would conform himself to the councels of the Nobility, resolving to live and run all hazards whatever with them, for the regaining of his Countries Liberty.

In the mean time the Marquess of *Ferreira* used his utmost endeavors for the reducing of those Castles which still held out for his Catholick Majesty. The first day the Castle of *Colline* was rendred, which for its situation was judged inexpugnable, yet the Captain of it no sooner saw it besieged, but moved either with Gold, or Fear, he delivered it up on Articles. The Tower of *Belem*, and that *De la Cabera* were suddenly surprized before they within had any notice of what was done; The strong Fortress of St. *Giuliano*, a modern Fortification, and built to defend the Mouth of the River, was ready to surrender, when a *Castellane*, who was there

there a Prisoner, and under Sentence of Death for the Surrendry of a Fort in *Brazil*, shut out the Captain, who was gone to Parlie with the *Portugueses*, and resolved to defend it many dayes: he might have held it out the Siege, but finding neither Ammunition nor Provision, consumed, as was believed, on purpose by the Captain, who unwilling to have the Blot of a Traytor cast upon him for so sudden a delivery, thought it fitter to be forced by necessity to open the Gates to the Marquesse.

After the Surrendry of Fort *San Giuliano*, the Marquess of *Ferreira* in the name of the King, gave the Sacrament of Fidelity, or an Oath of Allegiance to all the Orders, to wit, to the Clergy, Nobility and Commons, which was received with so much readiness, that had not the Marquess seen the necessary Orders observed, the People had run into certain inconveniencies, so much they strived to prevent one another in willingness to perform this duty.

On *Thursday* the Sixth of *February*, His Majesty made his entrance into *Lisbonne*, with all these applauses that a beloved King can expect from his most loving Subjects. The rich Liveries given by the Nobles, the Triumphal Arches, the Streets hung with Tapestry, the multitudes of the People flocking to see him, and the excellent Fire-works, (which were so many, that a *Spaniard* cryed out, *Es possible que se quita un Reyno a el Rey D Felippe, cun solas Luminarias & vivas sinmas exercito in Poder, Gran senal y efeto sin Duda del Brazo de dios todo Poderoso!* Is it possible that King *Philip* should be deprived of a Kingdom, with only Lights and Fire-works, without a powerful Army! certainly this is an evident Token that 'tis the Almighty hand of God,) were the least demonstrations of that Cities love and joy: so great was the concourse of those that flocked to see their new King, that though his Majesty entred into the City by Noon, he could not through the Throng arrive at the Palace till Two hours after Sun-set: curiosity and love which usually have the force to stir up all affections, made this People flock so fast to the sight of their Prince. And because it is prudence in a Publick joy, to accommodate ones self to the will of the most, even those who either for envy, or some other cause, hated the House of *Braganza*, did not cease to make some demonstration of reverence and mirth, and by how much the more they thought themselves observed, by so much the more they strove to seem other than they were.

His Majesty being arrived at the Palace, instead of reposing himself, addicted himself wholly to consult about carrying on the War; knowing well that onely labour produces true rest. The first consultations were concerning the expugnation of the Tower of *St. John*, which of all the Forts in the Kingdom only held out for the Catholick King. To reduce this Cittadel, the Marquess of *Ferreira* was sent in person with a numerous Army, though for the most part tumultuary, and ill ordered; but what they wanted in discipline, they supplyed in affection; not refusing to engage themselves in the extreamest dangers: for two days the Marquess found strong resistance, but on the third day it yielded, as it is supposed, forced rather by bullets of Gold, than of Iron. *Don Antonio de Mascarendas*, with a *Portuguess* Garison was appointed commander of this Fortress, which he very diligently repaired, not only of the damages now received by Battery, but with other necessary fortifications, to bring it to greater perfection.

The Kingdom thus suddenly reduced to the devotion of King J O H N the fourth, the several Governors were commanded to their Countries to levy Forces, who listed the inhabitants indifferently from the age of Eighteen to Sixty; in whom they found so much disposition, that many offered their estates, and their lives, and would follow the colours, although they had licence to depart.

On the 25. of the same Month, followed the Coronation of his Majesty, accompanied with all those applauses and demonstrations of joy, which could proceed from a people of infinite Riches, who weary of the Command of strangers, were consequently ambitious of a King of their own Nation.

In the publique Place before the Palace upon a most sumptuous Theatre, was erected a great Stage, and upon that a less, upon the top of which but three steps higher, stood a Chair of State under a Canopy, all covered over with Cloth of Gold. About noon His Majesty came forth of his Palace Royal in a Suit of Chesnut coloured Velvet embroidered with Gold, and buttons richly set with Diamonds: about his neck was a Collar of great value, whereunto hung the badge of the chief Order of Knight-hood, called *El Ordine di Christo*. He was girded with a gilt Sword, his Robe was Cloth of God lined with white, wrought with Gold and flowers, the Sword was born before him by *Don Francisco De Alello* Marquess of *Ferreira*, High Constable of the Kingdom, and before him was the Kings Banner displayed by *Ferdinando Telles de Meneses* Earl Marshal, before him went *D. Manrique De Silva*, Marquess of *Govea*, Steward of the Kings Houshold, and so in order his Nobles and Grandees of the Realm one before another, before all went *Portugal* King at Arms, with the Heralds Pursuivants, *&c.*

His Majesty being ascended the Stage, and having placed himself in the Chair of Estate, had the Crown set upon His Head, and the Scepter delivered to him, with the accustomed Ceremonies by the Archbishop of *Lisbon*; which done, he spoke to His Majesty to this effect.

Behold, O most Sacred Majesty, these your Subjects who do more rejoyce to see this day, than of all the days of their lives: They rejoyce to see the Crown of Portugal, *returned into its Antient stock, they rejoyce to have found a Father who will govern them like Children, not Tyrannize over them like slaves. They here, Great* SIR, *offer their estates, their lives, and oblige themselves to run through all the accidents of fortunes, to establish that Crown upon your Head, which now with so much devotion, with so much readiness they have placed upon it. They cannot sufficiently express their affections to Your Majesty; could they bring their hearts, and lay them down at your Majesties feet, they would not refuse to do it, so sure are they that they have found a King all goodness, all love, who will not let slip any means for the Establishing of the Crown, for the quiet of his Subjects, for augmenting his Dominions, and for the conservation of those priviledges which have been written with the blood of our progenitors: Be your Majesty graciously pleased to accept this common resentment expressed by my mouth, there being nothing that more comforts the minds of good Subjects, than the pleasing of their Prince.*

The good old Prelate spoke these words with so much feeling, that the tears of his eyes testified the affection of his heart.

To this speech of the Archbishops, His Majesty returned answer, in expressions equal to his love and greatness: That the weight of the Scepter, and subjection to the Crown, were things always dissonant to his Genius; That he had of late years given them sufficient testimony of it, whilst they were not more affectionate in offering, than he was ready to deny the taking upon him the weight of the Kingdom. That his now condescending to their desires, was only to provide for the Kingdom, which had been acquisted, and agrandized with the blood of his Predecessors, and to take it from the hands of those, who besides their unjustly possessing it, had rendred themselves unworthy of it, by endeavouring by all means to ruine it: in sum, he concluded with thanks for their love, offering himself ready to adventure his health, and life, for their preservation; the redeeming them from slavery, and maintaining of their priviledges.

This short discourse ended, His Majesty went to the great Church in the same order as before, where being set in a Chair of Estate, raised upon a Stage for that purpose, with a Christal Scepter in his right hand, at which stood the Lord Constable,

stable, and behind him the Lord *Chamberlain*, there was placed before him a Table Covered with Cloth of Gold, and a Cushion thereon, upon the Cushion lay a Gold Crucifix and a Messal. Here the Archbishops of *Lisbon* and *Braga*, administred the ensuing Oath to the King.

WE *swear and promise by the grace of God, to rule and govern you well, and justly, and to administer justice as far as humane frailty will permit, to maintain unto you your Customs, Priviledges and liberties, granted unto you by the Kings our Predecessors. So God help us God, and this his holy Gospel.*

This Oath being administred, the three Estates, to wit, the *Clergy*, *Nobility*, and *Commons*, took the following Oath of Allegiance to his Majesty, one for every one of the Estates, pronouncing these words.

I *Swear by this holy Gospel of God; touching corporally with my hand, That I receive for our King and lawful Soveraign, the High and Mighty King* DON JOHN *the fourth, our Soveraign, and do homage unto him, according to the use and custome of his Kingdoms.*

This, and the Ceremonies attendant ended, his Majesty, accompanied with all his Nobles, returned to his Palace, whether notwithstanding it was a very great rain, all the *Grandees* went bare-headed, where there was a most sumptuous Banquet prepared, but his Majesty gave himself wholly to consult of preparations for the Warre, shewing thereby that Kings in their greatest felicity and delights, should not forget affairs of State, and taking care for the preservation of their Subjects.

But amongst debates of the War abroad, there happened one of an affair near home, concerning the placing or displacing Officers of State; and because His Majesty knew that the charge of such Officers, must needs be with the resentment of many, and that there is nothing more alienates the minds of men, than to see themselves undeservedly deprived of their honours, he took away only the places of two, to wit, that of the *Providitore* of the Custom-house, because he was Son-in-Law to *Diego Soarez*, and Brother-in-Law to *Vasconsellos* the late deservedly-slain Secretary; and that of the Count of *Castanhie*, who was President of the *Tribunal*, or Court of Conscience, because he was too much interessed with His Catholick Majesty.

As for the Infanta *Margarita di Mantoua*, late Vice-Queen, and the Marquess *Della Puebla* Kinsman to *Olivarez*, the Castle called *Pasos de Angiobregas*, was assigned them, with Fourteen thousand Crowns a year for maintenance. An honorable Prison it was, nor could they desire any thing but liberty, which show'd a great Nobleness of mind in King JOHN: but Princes alwayes do like Princes, and much it demonstrates the Magnanimity of the mind, to honour our Enemies, though they be our Prisoners.

Nor must we here forget the Magnanimous and Couragious Carriage of the Dutchess of *Mantoua* late Vice-Queen, during these confusions and distractions; for King JOHN sending to ascertain her, That she should want none of those Civilities that were suitable to a Princess of her high Birth, Provided she would forbear all Discourse and Practises which might infuse into any an ill opinion of his present Government. She returned Thanks to the Duke, (for she would not stile him King) for his Complement: but withal fell into a grave Exhortation to those Nobles that carried the Message, telling them, *That they should lay aside all vain hopes, and not cozen themselves, but return to their old Allegiance, according as they were obliged by Oath, which if they did, she doubted not to find them all pardon.*

The rest of the *Castillians* of Authority were confined in the Castle, and all the Souldiers

JOHN IV. of the Name,

Souldiers took the *Portuguese* Pay, either because they believed doing so, to be most for their interest, or else because being most of them linkt in Parentage with the *Portugueses*, they believed the *Portugal* interest to be their own.

Shortly after, *Lucia* now Queen of *Portugal*, Sister to the Duke of *Medina Sidonia*, with her Son the Prince *Theodosio* arrived at *Lisbonne*, who were received with all imaginable expressions of joy: the Queen was soon after Solemnly Crowned, and the Prince installed, at whose Installation, the Nobles and Grandees of the Realm, took to him the following Oath.

WE acknowledge, and receive for our true and natural Prince, the high and excellent Prince D. Theodosio, *as Sonne, Heir, and Successor of our Soveraign Lord the King; and as his true and natural Subjects, we do him homage in the hands of the King, and after the death of our true and natural King and Soveraign of these Kingdoms of* Portugal *and* Algarve, *and beyond Sea in* Affrica, *Lord of* Guiana; *of the Conquests, Navigations, and commerce in* Ethiopia, Arabia, Persia, India, *&c. we will obey his Commands and Decrees in all, and through all, both high and low: we will make War and maintain Peace with all those that His Highness shall Command us: And all this we swear to God upon the holy Cross, and the holy Gospel.*

These Ceremonies performed with all fitting Solemnity, the King, to show that the good of his Subjects was his only care, called an Assembly of the Three Estates of the Kingdom, who being Convened, and the King seated in His Royal Throne, *Don Emanuel D' Acugna* Bishop of *Elvas* made a Speech to them, to the following purpose.

THat one of the first Laws of Nature, was, *The uniting of men together, from whence Cities and Kingdoms had their Original, and by which they after defended themselves in War, and maintained themselves in Peace; That for that cause His Majesty had called this Assembly to Consult for the better service of God, Defence in War, and Government in Peace: That there could be no Service of God without Union of Religion, no Defence without Union amongst men, no Regular Government without Union of Councils: That His Majesty did expect to be informed by his loyal Subjects what was for the good of the State; That they were to render thanks to the Almighty, who had given them a King that would govern them by known Laws; That His Majesty did not esteem those Tributes lawful that were paid with tears, and therefore did from that present, take off from His Subjects all Tributes that had been imposed by the Kings of* Castille, *because His Majesty would not Reign over their Goods, nor over their Heads, nor over their Priviledges, but over their Hearts, hoping that they would find out a sweet expedient to defend their Countrey against their Potent enemy, who threatned to make them all slaves, and to destroy, and to annihilate their Nation. That they would therefore, considering His Majesties Goodness, and their own Honor, manifest at once unto the world, That as never Subjects had such a Gracious King, so never King had such Loyal Subjects.*

The Bishop having ended his Speech, the most antient Officer of the Chamber of *Lisbonne*, stood up, and in the name of all the three Estates, (who stood up likewise,) returned humble thanks to His Majesty, for this gracious bounty, heartily professing, That they did not only offer up their Goods, but their Lives to His Majesties service, earnestly intreating His Majesty to dispose both of the one and the other, as he pleased. And to manifest that their hearts and their mouths concorded in this free offer of themselves to His Majesty, they presently Voted, That Two Millions should be immediately raised by the Kingdom: but His Majesty wisely and politickly declined the imposing of a Tax upon his Subjects, chusing rather to accept

cept of their Benevolence; which made every one strive who should offer most; so instead of the Two Millions, there was in short time brought into the Treasury Four Millions of Gold.

Nor was this Money intended by them, nor employed to any other use than to maintain the *Grandezza* and Splendour of the King and Kingdom, there being no need of Money for the payment of Souldiers, every one offering to serve freely, and at their own Charge, against their Vow'd Enemies the *Castillians*.

But let us for some time leave the Assembly sitting, and give an account how this Action was resented into the Spanish Court: Most mens minds were struck with consternation, but *Olivarez* came smiling to the King, saying; *Sir, I pray give me* las Albricias *to hansel the good news, for now you are more absolute King of* Portugal *than ever, for the People have forfeited all their Priviledges by this Rebellion, besides the Estate of the Duke of* Braganza*, with all his Complices, are yours by right of Confiscation, so that you have enough to distribute among your Loyal Subjects by way of reward.* But however *Olivarez* seemed thus to dissemble his passion; it was believed, that this news struck deeper into him than any.

The King of *Spain* upon the first news of the Proclamation of King JOHN, sent a Letter to him to this purpose:

Cousin and Duke: *Some odd news are brought me lately, which I esteem but folly, considering the proof I have had of the fidelity of your House, give me advertisement accordingly, because I ought to expect it from you, and hazard not the esteem I make of your self to the fury of a mutinous Rabble, but let your Wisdom comport you so, that your Person may escape the danger, my Council will advise you farther; so God guard you.*

Your Cousin and King.

To this Letter His Majesty of Portugal returned answer:

MY Cousin: *My Kingdom desiring its Natural King, and my Subjects being oppressed with Taxes, and new Impositions, have executed, without opposition, that which they had often designed, by giving me possession of a Kingdom which appertains to me; wherefore if any will go about to take it from me, I will seek Justice in my Arms: God preserve your Majesty.*

DON JOHN IV.
King of Portugal.

Thus was this Kingdom utterly lost to the Spanish Monarchy, and not only it, but with it all that they enjoyed by that Kingdom in the *East-Indies*, the *Tercera* Islands, and other Islands in the *Atlantick* Sea, the Kingdom of *Algarve*, *Brasil*, together with all they had in *Affrica*, except the Town of *Cexta*, which was the whole remained to the Spanish Nation of all those great Dominions.

But that all men might know the greatness of their loss, and what the Crown of *Portugal* enjoys abroad, take here a brief narration:

First, Those Islands of the *Tercera*, *Madera*, and St. *Michael*, so long time possessed by the *Portugal* Nation, which though inconsiderable to their other Dominions, yet deserve to be mentioned; next those many strong places of which they have made themselves Masters in *Affrica*, as in *Guiana*, in the Kingdoms of *Congo* and *Angola*, the great Island of St. *Laurence*, of *Soffola* and *Mozambique*: on the Continent thence passing the Mouth of the Red-Sea, they have setled a Trade with *Socatra* and *Calaite*; thence passing the Bay of *Persia*, to the Mouth of the River *Indus*, they subdued *Calecut*, *Coetium*, &c. the Island of *Goa*, *Ciaul*, *Daman*, &c.

&c. thence toward the River *Ganges*, they possessed *Ceilam, Malacca, Sumatra, Solon, Larantuca*, &c. Thence farther they were entred into the Kingdom of *Pegu*, into *Java-major*, and *Minor*, into the Kingdom of *China* where they fortified *Macca*: In sum, the Kingdoms, Provinces, Islands, and Cities, that the *Portugal* Nation had Conquered, and were possessed of abroad, may in some measure be compared to the Antient *Roman* Empire; nor was their Valour much inferior to the *Romans*; if we consider the War they made with the King of *Cambaia*, who for Puissance and Military Courage, or numbers of Men of War, did exceed *Xerxes, Darius*, or *Pyrrhus*; the Battels they had with *Ismalucco*, and *Idaliam* in the Kingdom of *Decam*, both equal to mighty Kings and their Armies, consisting of the best Warriors of the East; the War they have waged with the *Moors* of *Malacca, Sumatra*, and *Molucco*, as also with the Kings of *Bengala*, *Peug*, and *Siam*, &c. with many other formidable powers. Many of those places most certain it is, were lost while the Catholique King had possession of *Portugal*; but with it he likewise lost, and King JOHN IV. had possession of above Fifty Towns and Forts accounted impregnable, such were, *Mozambique, Cuama, Monomotasca, Mombaza, Masiala, Dui, Damam, Bazaine, Chiaul, Onor, Barcelor, Mangalor, Cananor, Cranganor, Cochim Conlan, Negapatan, Meliapor*, the Isle of *Ceilam*, the Kingdom of *Jasanapalan*, the Cities of *Manac*, and *Nombrede Jesu*; then more Northward, *Azarim, Danue Agazim, Maim Trapor*, and many other places, in all which were maintained Governours and Souldiers, and a Vice-Roy, residing at *Goa*, with Courts of Justice, &c. Hither many Kings of the East used to send Ambassadors to maintain Amity with the King of *Portugal*, and to bring Tribute to him. Thus the *Portugal* Trade in the East extendeth it self no less than Four thousand Leagues, by which Trade all the Garisons are maintained, and all the Ships (whereof they are oftentimes Two or three Fleets) and much Wealth sent home every Year; besides those aforementioned, the Crown of *Portugal* has several Towns on the Coast of *Affrica*, so strongly fortified, That the Moors of the Countrey could never yet recover them, such as *Tangier*, &c.

In *America* they possess the famous Countrey of *Brazile*, which stretcheth it self One thousand four hundred Leagues upon the Sea-Coast, containing Fourteen Governments, and many principal Cities, St. *Salvador, Pernambuco*, &c.

Thus great a loss did the Spanish Monarchy suffer by the Revolt of *Portugal*, which the Catholick King *Philip* the Fourth was very solicitous to recover, and to that end and purpose did not only consult with the greatest States-men at home, but likewise with those abroad, from one of whom he to that effect received the ensuing Letter.

'BY the Letter which your Majesty was pleased to write to me on the 6th. of
' *March* past, I am commanded to deliver my Advice touching the best Expe-
' dient for the Recovery of *Portugal*: Sir, the Clemency used by King *Philip* the
' Second, your Majesties Grandfather, towards the Kingdom of *Portugal*, was a fatal
' presage of the present Calamities, and future Destruction, not only of *Spain*, but
' the whole *Spanish* Monarchy, because that Kingdom was only in name, but never
' really Conquered, remaining Rich, and abundant with the same, if not greater Pri-
' viledges than before; the Grandees and Nobles at Home, the People not at all
' Crushed, and (which is more than all) the Government in the hands of Na-
' tives, and all his Majesties other Subjects excluded from all places of Power, Ho-
' nour, or Profit. Sir, The Holy Scripture, which is the Mirrour and Rule of our
' Actions, teacheth, That when *Salmanazar* conquered the Kingdom of *Israel*, he
' did carry away, not only the Royal Family, but transported all the Nobility and Peo-
' ple into divers Provinces of his Kingdoms, and into the new Conquests sent new
' Inhabitants; yet the *Israelites* were never such inveterate Enemies to the *Assyrians*,

' as

'as the *Portugals* with devilish madness have shewed themselves against the Interest
'and Conveniencies of this Monarchy.

'Moreover in the same Scripture it is read, That *Nebuchadonosor* having Con-
'quered *Jerusalem*, transplanted all that he found in that Kingdom, leaving only a
'few miserable inconsiderable people to remain there.

'So *Athalia* Queen of *Judah* saw no other way to preserve a Kingdom newly
'Conquered, but by extinguishing all the Generation, upon whom the *Jews* could
'cast their eyes in hopes of Revolt.

'And *Jehu*, King elected by God, extinguished all the Family of *Ahab*, together
'with all his dependants, friends, and acquaintance, not sparing so much as the Priests.

'These, Sir, are the Rules that the Holy Scripture teacheth to be practised upon
'the Families and People that abhor the Dominion of their own Soveraigns.

'It was, Sir, very fatal to stand expecting and hoping for better times and oppor-
'tunities for the securing of *Portugal*.

'In the Yeer, *One thousand six hundred and thirty nine*, observing the ill affection
'of that Nation, my Advice was, That without any delay that Kingdom was to be
'secured by Force of Arms; others were of the same Judgments, but Fate would
'have it that (for fear of new troubles) by delayes way should be made for Rebelli-
'on, than which there could not have been a greater, although that Form of Go-
'vernment, which was expedient for the Spanish Monarchy, and was alwayes held
'necessary for the preserving that Crown, had been put in execution with the greatest
'violence imaginable.

'But when a Jewel is gone, the main enquiry should be, By what means it may be
'found again, not How it came to be lost.

'The first means of recovering that Crown, may be (what your Majesties
'Grand-father made use of) to buy your Rights of your own Subjects by Gifts and
'Promises, wherein your Majesty is to be as Prodigal, as the *Portugals* are insolent
'in expecting or demanding, and indeed experience teacheth; That that Nation is
'so addicted to their own Interest, that more may be effected this way, than by a pow-
'erful Army: to him will they be subject who will give most, or from whom most
'can be expected herein, Prodigality will be good Husbandry; for when *Portugal*
'shall be returned to the obedience of your Majesty, all that Wealth which hath
'been bestowed amongst them, will return likewise.

'The second means is by course of Arms, but this will be difficult at present, by
'Reason of the several Engagements of this Monarchy elsewhere: I suppose Sir,
'That in case *Portugal* should be Conquered by Force, all their Conquests in the
'*East-Indies*, &c. will remain in their hands; for thither will they all flie, and from
'thence will they be alwayes ready to assist our Enemies; wherefore it would be very
'expedient for your Majesties service, that a Truce were first made with the *Hol-
'landers*, upon condition that they make War upon the *Portugal* in the *Indies*, and
'have whatever they can Conquer, whence will arise this Commodity that they will
'want the Wealth of their Conquests, your Majesty being disengaged with the
'*Hollander*, will sooner Conquer them at home, and the *Hollander* will only come to
'receive to day at the hand of your Majesty, what to morrow the *Portugal* must deli-
'ver up to them: At the same time the *Hollanders* and *Flemings* may scour the
'Coast of *Portugal*, and the English may be invited to a more frequent Navigation
'in the *East-Indies* and *China*, whereby the *Portugal* Trade may easily be ruined.

'The third way is, that the Pope be perswaded to thunder his Excommunicati-
'ons against the House of *Braganza*, and against the whole Kingdom, as Perjured and
'Perturbators of the publick Peace, animating all Christian Princes to assist in the
'regaining that Kingdom, upon pretence of advancing the Catholick Faith.

'Moreover, diffidencies and jealousies between the Duke of *Braganza*, and other

F f
'people,

'people, may easily be fomented by means of Merchants, Strangers, and by *Flemings*
'and *Burgundians*, under the name of *French*. And to effect these diffidencies the
'better, a Treaty may really be begun with the Duke, which being discovered by
'the People (though it be before the Duke could know thereof) they will destroy
'him and all his Family, and in such case the Civil dissentions will open a way for
'your Majesty to recover your Rights: desperate evils must have desperate reme-
'dies, the Kingdom of *Portugal* is the Cancer of the Spanish Monarchy; therefore,

Ense recidendum: ne pars symera trahatur.

'Let not your Majesty defer the right Remedy, the greatest Rigor is here the great-
'est Charity; and to have no Charity, is to have much Prudence; to Bury this
'*Hydra* in its own ashes, will be Triumph enough; to live without this arm, will be
'better than to have it employed against ones own head: Let your Majesty never be-
'lieve, or hope better of that Nation, than you have seen these Sixty years past;
'never think to keep that Countrey, if not planted with other People; the detesta-
'tion against your Majesties Government, is hereditary.

'The Interest of the King, Sir, is very ample, and hath no bounds against Rebels,
'every action is just and honourable that tends to the recovery of the Kings right.

'Moreover, a Truce is to be made with the *Catalonians*, whereby they being fre-
'ed from the tumultuous courses of War, will have time to take notice of the
'French insolencies, and growing weary of that Yoke, will at length easily embrace
'the next opportunity to return to their obedience, which once effected, will make
'the People of *Portugal* waver betwixt hopes and fears, and beget variety of opini-
'ons amongst them, which for the Conquering of Kingdoms (the Emperour *Juli-
'an* used to say) was much more advantageous than the force of an Army, as the
'Grand-father of your Majesty found in the Succession of *Portugal*: To this may be
'added, That it will be very expedient that your Majesty name Bishops to dispose
'of all Governments, and Offices of the Crown, to the most confiding Persons in
'that Kingdom, for this will beget distrust amongst them all, and the ignorant peo-
'ple not knowing whom to trust, will put all into Confusion, whereby your Majesties
'service will be more easily advanced.

'This in obedience to your Majesties Commands, I have imparted my weak ad-
'vice, wherein if I have erred, your Majesties goodness will attribute it to my want of
'abilities, not of affection: God preserve the Catholick and Royal Person of your
'Majesty, as the Christian World, and we your Majesties Subjects have need.

But notwithstanding all these endeavors, and these proposed Artifices, nothing prevailed towards the King of *Spain*'s recovery of this Kingdom, not was it probable that any of these Deceits ever should, whil'st is considered the extraordinary love and affection which the whole Nation of the *Portugueses* bore to the Family of their present King, and the inveterate hatred which they did, and always have born to the *Castillians*, which was so exceeding great, that it is believed they would rather have suffered themselves to be extirpated and routed out, than again submit their Necks to the Spanish Yoke.

And that ever the *Spaniard* should again recover it *per* force, is incredible, if we either consider the Union and Unanimity of the *Portugal* Nation, and their Resolutions to undergo the greatest miseries of War can inflict, or the Interest of all the other Princes of Christendom, who may justly suspect the encroaching greatness of the *Spaniard*, and therefore endeavor rather to Lop off more Limbs from that great Body, than suffer this to be rejoyned.

But it is now high time to return to a Review of the Actions of the Grand Assembly of the Estates of *Portugal*, who next Resolved to Dispatch Ambassadors to all States of Christendom, to enter into Confederacies, for the better defence and establishment of the Kingdom, and for the Glory and Reputation of the King.

In the first place, the Father *Ignatius Mascarenas* a Jesuite, with another Father of the same Order, was sent into *Catalonia*, to offer them all assistance and supplies for their maintenance, and defence against the Catholique King, for very well did the King of *Portugal* know that it highly did import his Interest to correspond with them, that so they might joyntly, not onely defend, but also offend the King of *Spain*, whose Country lying betwixt them both, they might at pleasure invade, or molest it, either by Sea or Land.

This Embassie of King JOHN'S so rejoyced and encouraged the *Catalonians*, that the very next day after the Ambassadors had Audience, they obtained a most signal Victory in their own defence against the *Spaniards*, who had assaulted them with an Army of twenty five thousand men under the Command of the Marquiss *De los veles*.

Shortly after that the Father *Ignatius Mascarenas* was dispatched to the *Catalonians D. Francisco de Mello*, and *Don Antonia Caelle Carravallio*, (persons both of excellent and admired abilities, the one for his great experience and judgment in State-affairs, and the other for his noble Spirit, and eminent knowledge in the Civil Law) to go on a solemn Embassie to the most Christian King *Lewis* the thirteenth of *France*.

These attended with a Stately and most Magnificent Train, landed soon after at *Rochel* and on the fifteenth of *March* 1641. made a solemn Entrance into *Paris*, being met and conducted in by a great number of Coaches, filled with the Grandees of the Kingdom, besides numbers of the French Nobility, who came to attend them on horse-back.

Thus accompanied, they were conducted to the Palace appointed for the Entertainment of the Extraordinary Ambassadors, where they were in a sumptuous and magnificent manner feasted at the Kings Charges.

From thence they were by the Duke of *Chevereux*, and the Count *de Brulon*, conducted in the Kings Coaches unto his Majesty then at St. *Germains*, to receive the first Audience; which was performed with extraordinary shews of love and respect: for upon the entrance of the Ambassadors into the place appointed for their Audience, the King rose out of his Chair of Estate: and went forward three steps to receive them, nor would he permit them to deliver their Embassie with their Hats off, or to descend so low, as to kiss his hands at their departure, but in stead of that Ceremony, he affectionately imbraced them in his Arms, promising them the greatest Assistance his Power was able to give.

They were from the Kings presence conducted to a sumptuous Dinner provided for them, and after that brought to the Queens Lodging, who was set to expect their coming; at their entrance she likewise rose, and advanced three steps to meet them, receiving them with a cheerful and courteous countenance, and not permitting them to be uncovered.

Amongst other Discourses which they had with her, *D. Francisco de Mello* told her, That he feared his Embassie might not be acceptable, because the King his Master had deprived her Brother of one of his Kingdoms. Whereunto she readily replyed, *That though she was sister to the King of Spain, yet she was wife to the King of France.*

After some Discourse in *French*, her Majesty began to speak to them in *Spanish*, which they observing, desired to know wherefore her Majesty had not vouchsafed them that favor sooner, it being a Language by them better understood; To which the Queen jestingly answered, For fear they should be frighted to hear her speak *Spanish*, and the Embassador to improve the jest, replyed, *Como a tam Grand Signora*

Signora sì, pero coma a Castiliano no, that it was true considering her Greatness, but not her Country: The Queen smiling, went on, promising them all assistance possible, and wishing all prosperity to King JOHN and his Queen; and so they having delivered her Majesty a Letter from the Queen of *Portugal*, took their leave.

From her Majesty they went to visit his Eminence the Cardinal *Richlieu*, who being advertised of their coming, came forward to the third Chamber to meet them, where he received them with expressions of great affection, and promises and proffers of services, and from thence conducted them to his own Chamber.

Being all three sate, the Cardinal (who was the most experienced and greatest Statesman of his time) discoursed with them of divers affairs of great importance, and they endeavored to explain to his Eminence what was before his sentiment, that it very much imported the two Crowns of *France* and *Portugal* to be united by an indissoluble League, considering that it was the Chief and Principal end and aim of the House of *Austria*, (whose Branches were spread over almost all *Europe*) not only to be the greatest, but to be the sole and only Monarch of *Christendom*: That to effect those ambitious desires, he had never made scruple to usurp and seize upon Kingdoms and States upon the least pretences imaginable, as had appeared in the Kingdoms of *Naples*, *Sicily*, *Navarre*, the Dutchy of *Millan*, and lately several States in *Germany*, seizing upon the *Valtoline*, whereby they had a passage open to lead an Army of *Germans* into *Italy* at pleasure.

That considering the vast power and interest that this Family had, not only in *Europe*, but also in *America*, it could not but be confessed, That they had a large foundation of their imaginary Universal Monarchy; but that nothing gave them so great hopes, as the possession of *Portugal*.

For by the addition of that Kingdom to the Crown of *Castille*, they became absolute Masters, not only of all *Spain*, but of all the *East-Indies*, of all the Eastern Trade of *Ethiopia*, *Persia*, *Arabia*, *China*, *Japan*, and all that incredible wealth that was raised out of the *Portugal* Traffick, whereby the *Austrian* Greatness (if not their Monarchy) was principally sustained, that therefore it concerned all States whatsoever, not only to put a stop to the raving Tyranny of this devouring Monster, but to suppress and lessen his Power by all means possible.

That to do this, none was more concerned, or more able, than the Kingdom of *France* united with that of *Portugal*: That this having been called the Right Arm (as *Catalonia* the Left) of that great *Austrian Colossus*, now both being separated from it, and united to *France*, will be able to do greater service against it, than they were ever forced to do for it, not only by assaulting the *Spaniard* within his own doors, but by intercepting the *Plate-Fleet*; which in its return from the *West-Indies*, it being necessarily forced to pass by the *Tercera* Islands, must run in danger of the *Portuguez* Fleet, or be forced to be at the Charge of an extraordinary Convoy.

These were the sum of the Ambassadors Discourses to the Cardinal: In answer to which, his Eminence made offer, not only of all the Assistance of the most Christian King his Master, but that he would disburse himself for the service of the King of *Portugal*, promising that he would presently send thither a Fleet of Twenty Sail with his Nephew, Admiral and Ambassador Extraordinary.

This Treatment thus ended, the Ambassadors took their leaves, his Eminence waiting upon them as far as the Stairs; which when they endeavored to hinder, he replied, That the Ambassadors of the King of *Portugal*, were to be Treated with as much Respect as those of the *Emperor* or *Pope*.

Few dayes after, a *Juncto* of the King of *France* his Council, were appointed to Treat with the Ambassadors in the House of the Lord High Chancellor of the Kingdom, where a Peace was fully concluded between the two Kingdoms of *France* and *Portugal*. Other

King of PORTUGAL, &c.

Other Ambassadors were (about the same time that the afore-mentioned were sent into *France*) dispatched into *England*; for it very much concerned the Kingdom of *Portugal* to maintain a good Correspondence with the Crown of *England*, both in regard of the Navigation and Commerce of both States, and also the better to break that Amity and good Understanding which was now held between the Crown of *Spain* and that State. Hither therefore were sent Don *Antonio D'Almado*, and Don *Francisco D'Averado Leilon*, both persons of exquisite parts; who, notwithstanding that the Dunkirkers Chased them, arrived safe in *England*.

And for all the sturdy endeavors of the Spanish Ambassadors, they were received on shore with abundance of Respect; yet His Majesty of *England* would not give them Audience, or accept of the Ambassage from the King of *Portugal*, so tender was He of His Honor and Conscience, till Don *Antonia de Sofa* their Secretary, had drawn up a Paper, to satisfie Him of the Right and Title of the Duke of *Braganza* to the Crown of *Portugal*. The sum of which was:

Upon the Death of King Henry the Cardinal, without Issue, many pretended (together with the Infanta Donna Catherina *Dutchess of* Braganza, *and Grand-mother to this present King) to the Crown of* Portugal; *but all their pretences wanting foundation, soon fell, except that of* Philip *the Second, King of* Spain, *who propt up his with force.*

King Henry *was Uncle, equally near to both, but with this difference;* Catherine *was the Daughter of a Son named* Edward, *and* Philip *was the Son of a Daughter named* Isabella, *Brother and Sister to King* Henry.

King Philip *pleaded, That he being in equal degree with* Catherine, *was to be preferred for his Sex.*

Catherine *replyed, That the Constitution of that Kingdom allowing Females to succeed, and withal the benefit of Representation in all Inheritances, she representing* Edward, *must exclude* Philip *by the very same right that her Father (if he were living) would exclude* Philips *Mother.*

This Conclusion is infallible in Jure: *whereto* Philip *answered, That Succession of Kingdoms descending* Jure sanguinis, *there was allowed no Representation.*

Catherine *destroyed that foundation, alledging, That the Succession by the Death of the last King, was derived* Jure hæreditatis, & non sanguinis, *because the Succession of Kingdoms was to be regulated by that Antient way, whereby all things descended by Inheritance; the other way of Succession being not known until later Ages, nor ever practised either in* Spain *or* Portugal *in such Cases.*

Briefly in behalf of Catherine *it was urged, (which by the* Castillians *can never be denied, or answered) That she was no stranger, but a Native of the Kingdom, to whom alone (according to the Laws of* Lamego) *the Crown of* Portugal *can appertain.*

The King having perused and deliberated upon this Paper, gave immediately Order they should be presently conducted to *London*, which was done with all convenient Solemnity, and they lodged in a Palace ready prepared for them: soon after with great Ceremony they received Audience of His Majesty, in a fair and Stately Hall prepared for that purpose, where His Majesty sate upon a Throne raised two steps, and at the entrance of the Ambassador pulled off His Hat, nor would be covered till they were so too.

To the Propositions made in the Speech of D. *Antonia D'Almoda*, concerning a Peace between *Portugal* and *England*, His Majesty replied, That he should be very glad if an expedient might be found out to renew the Antient Leagues of Friendship between the two Crowns, without the breaking with *Spain*.

Some few dayes after, the Ambassadors were conducted to give a Visit to *Mary*

Queen of *England*, who sate in a Chair of Estate ready to entertain them: when they came into the Presence, She rose out of the Chair, and came as far as the Carpetting, making low reverence as the Ambassadors bowed; when they came near, Her Majesty made them be covered, but afterwards they spoke with their Hats off. In conclusion the Queen told them, That she much desired to hold Correspondence with Her Majesty of *Portugal*.

In fine, on the Thirteenth of *June*, *One thousand six hundred and forty one*, a Peace was absolutely concluded with the *Portugal*, notwithstanding the earnest endeavors of Don *Alonza Cardenas*, Leiger Ambassador for *Spain*, who by Gifts and Promises, even as far as the restitution of the *Palatinate*, endeavored to hinder it.

The Ambassadors that were sent to the King of *Denmark* (notwithstanding the great Traffick and Commerce that had formerly bin held between that Kingdom and *Portugal*) were not (by reason of the great interest the House of *Austria* had with those Kings) received; yet the King gave all possible Respect otherwise to them. From thence they passed into *Sweden*, and were Magnificently entertained at the young Queens Court at *Stockholm*, where a League was soon concluded, and the Ambassadors dismissed, according to the Custom of that Nation, with Gold Chains, and the Queens Portraicture in a Meddal of Gold.

The Ambassador D. *Tristano De Mendoza Hurtada*, that was sent to the States of the *United Provinces*, was received with the like Magnificence and seeming affection, and a Truce concluded with the Kingdom of *Portugal* for Ten years; for a Peace the States would not assent to, because they having Conquered many places in *Brasil*, *Angola*, &c which belonged to the Crown and Kingdom of *Portugal*, could not make restitution of them, by reason they now belonged to the *West-India* Company; nor could the King of *Portugal* allow the Conquest, as things of right belonging to his Crown, and depending on it.

But now we come to treat of a more solemn Embassie, to wit, that to the Pope: Long was it debated in the Assembly of Estates, whether an Ambassador should be sent to *Rome* immediately, or a more opportune conjuncture of time be expected. Some were of opinion that the sending an Ambassador without further delay, would be a testification of their duty, and incline the Popes Holiness to acknowledge DON JOHN the lawful Heir, and rightful King of *Portugal*, which would extreamly further and advance the Affairs of the Kingdom.

But others there were who conceived those things rather desirable than feasable, and were of the opinion they should rather stay till a fitter opportunity, alledging, that the King of *Spain*'s present power at *Rome*, might probably oppose the Reception of their Ambassador: that although the Pope never was in his heart a *Spaniard*, yet he would never yield to show himself an enemy to the Catholick King: That the *Spaniards* cunningly fomenting the opinion which all the world had entertainted, that his Holiness did in all things favor the *French* interest, would from such a Reception, draw as much as ever they could ask or desire. That for this cause the Pope (that he might not seem their enemy) had alwayes granted them whatever they desired; That therefore they thought it convenient first to sound his Holiness, before they run the hazard of the disgrace and affront which might fall upon his Majesty, and the whole Kingdom; That in case the Pope should decline the reception of the Ambassador, to whom could they repair or appeal to vindicate the injury done to the Crown? That many Popes had been so fascinated to the interest of their own family, that the world had very great occasion to believe, that their designs tended rather to what was best for themselves, than to what was best indeed: That the *Portugal* Nation, had as much reason to distrust the See of *Rome* as any, whilst they had to their cost had examples how they onely pursued their own ends. As particularly *Gregory* the thirteenth, who at

King of PORTUGAL, &c.

first seemed so affectionate to the Kingdom of *Portugal*, that he imployed the utmost of his Power for the Interest of his own Family, approved of all that King had done; that there was none who had more to give, or at least who had more to promise, than the Catholick King; so that in any business of Competition he must necessarily gain the better.

But notwithstanding all these Arguments to the contrary, upon the promises of the King of *France*, to be a Mediator at the See of *Rome*, for the Reception of their Ambassadors, by the suffrage of some few Voices, to make the *major* part, it was concluded, That Ambassadors should immediately be sent to *Rome*.

And in pursuance of this Vote, the King immediately made choice of two Reverend and able Persons, to wit, *Michael De Portogallo*, Son to the Count *Vimioso* of the Blood *Royal*, Bishop of *Lamego*, and D. *Petableone Rodriguiz*, Bishop of *Elvas*: No sooner was the news arrived at *Rome* of their being landed in *Italy*, but the *Spaniards* in *Rome* mustred themselves together, with resolution either to oppose their entrance, or at least hinder their reception; whil'st on the other side the *French*, *Portugal*, and *Catalonians* assembled themselves together, resolving to hazard their dearest Blood in their Cause.

His Holiness seeing these preparations on both sides, feared lest his Countrey should be made the Seat of a petty War, and considering that in any case the dishonour would accrue to him, if whil'st under his Command and Protection, the Person of an Ambassador should be violated, strictly Commanded all his Guards to take special care to prevent the Violencies intended.

The *Spaniards* by this Order hindred from what they purposed, their Ambassadors openly protested, That if his Holiness did receive the *Portugal* Ambassador, they would immediately leave *Rome*. But notwithstanding these protestations, and all other opposition they could possibly make, in *November*, One thousand six hundred and forty one, the two *Portugal* Ambassadors being met by divers Cardinals, Princes, and Cavaliers, well armed, entred into *Rome*, and were conducted to the Palace of the French Ambassador, who received them with all Respect possible, still giving them the precedence.

Hereupon several Manifesto's are scattered abroad by the two Spanish Ambassadors, the Marquess *De los Veles*, and D. *John Chiumarrero*, labouring to prove that his Holiness ought not to receive the Ambassadors of the Duke of *Braganza*, as they stiled him. First, because he was a Tyrant, and Usurper of that Kingdom, which had been in the quiet possession of the Catholick King these Sixty years. Secondly, Because he was a Rebel, and a Perjured Person, having sworn Allegiance to the Catholick King. Thirdly, That the Reception of these Ambassadors would animate other Subjects of the Catholick King to Rebellion.

But whil'st the Spanish Ambassadors are violently shooting such Paper-Bullets, the *Portugueses* used all their endeavors, both by themselves, and the French Ambassadors, (who had express Order from the most Christian King his Master to that purpose,) to prevail with the Pope, to give them Audience, and admit their Embassie: but his Holiness was so fearful to displease the *Spaniard*, lest he should afterwards take occasion to revenge himself upon his Nephews, that he utterly declined their Reception, yet not out of any of the *Spaniards* Allegations, but upon pretence that certain of the Church Rites had been violated in *Portugal*; the Arch-bishop of *Braga*, and other Ecclesiastical Persons, being kept in durance, though it was for very good reasons, as hereafter shall appear.

Yet the *Spaniards* were not content with this Resolution of his Holiness, but (whil'st the *Portugals* were endeavoring to prove their Cause, by both Political and Legal Declarations, Allegations, and Arguments,) fearing lest the Pope might chance to alter his mind, resolved to make a quick dispatch of the Business, and to that purpose Two hundred *Banditi* were hired to seize upon the Bishop of *Lamego*, and carry him to *Naples*, as the Prince of *Sans* had been before served by them, and there put to Death.

But this Design, themselves at length could not agree upon, for the Marquess *De Los Velos*, thought it would be better and less dangerous to give the *Portugals* a Publick Affront in the City, which was concluded to be put in effect, and to that purpose it was communicated to the rest of the Nation, (whereof upon several occasions there are alwayes many in *Rome*) who assembled together well Armed at the Ambassadors Palace: and so great is the Power of Revenge: that to the end they might the better effect their design, and yet not appear as Souldiers, though there were many Gentlemen of quality amongst them, they condescended to go under the name of Foot-men to the Marquess.

The Popes Holiness hearing of the great preparations of the *Spaniard*, sent to them to let them know, that he could not but be very much distasted to see such disorders attempted in a peaceable City, and therefore desiring them for his Honors sake to desist, and withal sent a Messenger to the Bishop of *Lamego*, to assure him that he need not fear any thing, for upon the Word of his Holiness, he should walk the Streets undisturbed.

But do the Pope what he could, either by threats, desires, or perswasions, the *Spaniards* were resolved to prosecute their design, which they put in execution to their own cost, on the twenty of *August*, One thousand six hundred forty two. On which day the Bishop of *Lamego* going to visit the *French* Ambassador, one of his retinue observed, that he was dog'd by a *Spanish* Spie; whereupon a Counter-Spie was sent to the Marquesses to bring intelligence what they were doing there, who brought word to the *French* Ambassadors, that there was great preparations of Coaches and Men: whereupon the *French*, *Portugals*, and *Catalonians*, assembled, and armed themselves with Pistols and Fire-locks, to convoy home the Bishop.

By the way they were met by the *Spanish* Ambassador, accompanied with about eight Coaches full of Captains and Officers come from *Naples*, and guarded with about sixty Foot men, besides divers others of that Nation. No sooner came they in sight of the Bishops Coach, but they cried aloud, *Che si fermassero all' Ambasciatore di Spagna*; that they should stop for the Ambassador of *Spain*: but the *Portugals* driving on, answered, *Che si fermassero Lavo*, that they should stop.

Hereupon both sides with their Swords drawn leapt out of the Coaches, and making a stand, one Gun was first fired by the *Spaniards* side, and immediately seconded with a brave volley on both sides; when they fell into Swords point, the Bishops side soon getting the better of it, yet there was slain a Knight of *Malta*, an *Italian*, and a *French* and *Portugal* page, but on the *Spanish* Marquesses side, there were eight killed upon the place, and above twenty wounded, the Marquess leaving his Coach-horses dead, escaped out of the back of the Coach, which stood upon the place till next day, and got into the next shop without his hat, and trembling for fear, from whence he was carried to the *Spanish* Cardinal *Albornoz* Palace. The *Portuguesse* Ambassador returned first to the *French* Palace, and from thence went safely home.

His Holiness the Pope was extreamly perplexed at these disturbances, and therefore to prevent the like for the future, Commanded a guard of Souldiers to be put upon the houses, both of the Bishop and the Marquess. But shortly after, when the Bishop of *Lamego* had again pressed the Pope, by a large memorial of the reasons why he should be received, and was absolutely refused, he was by his Master the King of *Portugal* called home.

Whilst these things were acting abroad, the *Castillians* begun to make continual in-roads into the borders of *Portugal*, which made King JOHN look more narrowly into the defence of his Kingdom, fortifie all the Frontiers, and train up his Subjects to military exercises.

The *Spaniards* in one in-road which they made into *Portugal*, laid waste all before them, sparing neither Sex nor Age wheresoever they came, which made the *Portugals* in revenge, commit the like out-rages in an in-road they made into *Gallicia*.

But these were publick enmities, and therefore more easie to be opposed; but there was a private Serpent that lay Lurking at home, which was so much the likelier to do mischief, by how much it was more secretly hidden. Some few there were who thought themselves so highly obliged to the Catholick King, as to endeavour the re-uniting of the Crown of *Portugal* to his vast Dominions, and again inslave their Countrey to Forreigners.

The principal of these was the Arch-bishop of *Braga*, always a great Creature and Favourite of the Count *Olivarez*, who had at the beginning of the Revolt, show'd himself so opposite to the Freedom of his Countrey, that many Gentlemen were once resolved to make him suffer the same fate with *Vasconcellos* the Secretary; Nor had he ceased ever since to show visible signs of his discontentment at the Government.

In this Arch-bishops head was the whole Conspiracy first hatch't, and by him communicated to *D. Lewis de Meneses* Marquess of *Villa-real*, and the Duke of *Camigna* his Son, two Persons sufficiently Ambitious, and both discontented, as not thinking themselves sufficiently rewarded according to their Merit: These the Arch-bishop tampered with, perswading them, That it was a low and unworthy thing, much beneath their Birth and Greatness, to suffer themselves to be subject to a fellow-Subject: That it would be much more Noble and Generous in them, to return their Allegiance to the King of *Spain* their Antient Soveraign, who was able to bestow more upon a Person deserving in one day, than the Duke of *Braganza* could in an hundred years. These and few other Arguments were sufficient to draw those, who before out of their envy to the House of *Braganza*, were inclinable to a change.

These made sure, the Arch-bishop next draws into this Plot a Gentleman of a Noble Blood, named, *D. Augustine Emanuel*, a man of excellent parts, but somewhat necessitated, nor had ever been looked upon, or put into any employment, which without any other incentives, were motives sufficient to move a man to any desperate design. Next him was added to this Conspiracy, *Pietro Baeza*, a lately converted *Jew*, whom the *Portugueses* call Upstart Christians; he was Famous for nothing, but his vast Riches; being a great *Criado* of the Count *Olivarez*, whose Favour, he used often to say, would one day advance him to high Honor, or to a high pair of Gallows, which last proved very true.

Many private Meetings had these, and some few other Conspirators; where they debated to bring their Designs to effect; some were of opinion, that before they could bring it to perfection, more should be acquainted with it, for it was impossible that so few should ever be able to compass it: But in this course there arose many fears and doubts, lest too many being acquainted with it, some should discover it, as had often hapned in Designs of that high Nature: yet at length it was found necessary to draw more into the Plot, for whil'st they were so few, the Business only rested in imagination, but could never be put in execution.

Having therefore added some more to the number, their next debates were of the manner how to bring it to effect; some advised that a Power of the Catholick Kings was to be got in a readiness, but they then thought that the King of *Portugal* would raise as great a force, and so prevent a sudden Invasion: Yet in answer to that Objection, it was by some alledged, That the *Spaniard* by way of Intelligence might be let in, which again seemed as difficult, the *Militia* being in the hands of Persons most Loyal and Trusty to the King: Others proposed, That the only way to effect it, was by a sudden and violent making away of the King; but this advice was opposed by most, who inclined to a mediocrity, and would rather have found out a way to make his Majesty renounce his own Right and Title to the Crown, and retire himself from the dangers which should be presented unto him.

But whilst they thus wavered in opinions, and inclined to that moderation, which is the ruine of all Designs of this Nature, they gave the King time and occasion to search out their Plots; for his Majesty having alwayes had a suspitious eye upon the Arch-bishop of *Braga*, and the Marquess of *Villa-Real*, and having received now private notice, that they had had sundry Meetings, and were observed daily to converse with Persons as discontented as themselves, endeavored by all means possible to know the depth of their Counsel, and at length intercepts some of their Letters to *Madrid*, which discovered not only the whole Plot, but even the names of all the Conspirators.

The Act of Holding Correspondence with the *Spaniard*, was Treason in it self, sufficient to take away their lives, being contrary to his Majesties express command, its being to this intent, made it but so much the more hainous: His Majesty therefore not knowing how far it might have proceeded, made no delayes, but presently by the sound of Drum and Trumpet (as the Custom is) caused to be Proclaimed, That he intended to go forth of the City; upon which all the Nobles and Gentry, according to the usual manner, assembled at the Palace to accompany his Majesty, who when he saw them all ready, commanded first that a Council of Estate should be called, which was done, many of the Conspirators being assistant in it, who being sate, his Majesty without any noise caused them to be arrested one by one, which without the taking of this course, he could never have effected; for if the Conspiracy had been detected, before their Persons had been seized, they had either been torn in pieces by the fury of the People, or else had some of them escaped.

It was very strange that of all the Plotters in this Conspiracy, not one should, either by accident, or otherwise, escape, for the Persons of these now taken, were no sooner imprisoned, but his Majesty published a Proclamation, declaring a Free Pardon to all the Complices in this Conspiracy, that should within Four dayes come and acknowledge their fault, and beg it; but the Kings diligence had been such before, that there was not one left to accept of this Grace.

Shortly after those who had been taken, were Arraigned according to Law, found Guilty of High Treason, and in manner following executed.

On the last day of *August*, One thousand six hundred and forty one, the Marquess of *Villa-Real*, the Duke of *Camigna*, his Son, the *Count de Armamac*, and *D. Augustine Manuele*, were led along a Gallery to a Scaffold erected for the purpose, with two stories, on the uppermost of which stood two Chairs, on the next one, and on the Scaffold it self the fourth.

The first that was conducted forth to Execution, was the Marquess of *Villa-Real*, who was clothed in a long black Bayes Cloak, and his servants attending him in mourning, being mounted to the uppermost part of the Scaffold, he prayed for a good space upon his knees, and then rising up, asked, If there were no hopes of Pardon? which made the people with one voice cry out, *No, let him die, let him die for a Traytor*.

The next funebrious Ceremony of his Execution, was the Proclamation, which according to the usual manner was made by the Executioner, in these words; *This is the Justice that the King our Soveraign Lord, commands to be executed upon the person of* Don Lewis de Meneses, *sometimes Marquess of* Villa-Real, *that his throat be cut as a Traytor to his Majesty, Nobility and People of this Kingdom, that for his Crime his goods be confiscated, and his memory banished out of the World*. Whereat all the people cryed out, *Justice, Justice*.

The Marquess thereupon seeing no hopes of any Repreive, with a sober and becoming gravity demanded Pardon of all the Spectators, desiring them to

assist

assist him with their prayers to God for the Pardon of this, and all his other sins; then turning to a Father-Jesuite his Confessor, he prayed him in his behalf to present himself at his Majesties feet, and beseech him out of his wonted goodness, to forgive him that hainous offence committed against him and the whole Kingdom.

Having ended this Speech, he very patiently sate down in the Chair, and the Executioner having tied his arms and legs, to the arms and legs of the Chair; he leaned his neck over the back of the Chair, and the Executioner with his knife cut his throat, covering him afterwards with a black Scarf.

In the same maner his son the Duke of *Camigna* came to the Scaffold, his servants all attending him in mourning; as he came to his fathers Corps he kneeled down, and several times kissed his feet, begged of the people the suffrage of one *Pater noster* for his fathers soul; then after some prayers, and Proclamation made by the Executioner, he received the same punishment.

Next that suffered was the Count of *Armamac*, in the Chair seated upon the lower story; and after him *Don Augustin Manuel* upon the Scaffold it self; the Judges would have had all their necks cut behind, but his Majesty would not consent thereto, as a punishment too ignominious for persons of their quality.

The same day *Pietro de Baeza*, and *Melchior Correa de Franca*, were drawn at a horse-tail to an extraordinary high gallows, and there hanged, whilest *Diego de Brito Nabo*, and *Antonio Valente*, were executed upon a lower; the Quarters of these four were set up at the Gates of the City, and their Heads placed upon several Frontier Towns.

In the Month of *September* following, for the same offence *Antonia Cogamigne*, and *Antonio Correa*, were likewise executed; the first of which during the whole time of his Imprisonment, was an example of Penitence, feeding only upon Bread and Water, and whipping himself very often, with continual prayers to God for Pardon of that, and all his other sins.

As for the Arch-Bishop of *Braga*, and the Bishops of *Martiria* and *Malacca*, and Fryer *Emannel de Macedo*, though they were the persons that had the greatest hand in the Conspiracy; yet in regard they were Ecclesiastical persons, they suffered not death, according to their deserts, but were kept in prison, till the Popes pleasure were known concerning them.

Here must not be forgot a great example of humility and repentance in the Arch-Bishop of *Braga*, not only in his life time (when he often writ to the King, that he might suffer, and others be spared, who were rather drawn in, in complyance and obedience to him, than out of any ill-will to the King and Kingdom (but also at his death (which hapned about Three years after his Imprisonment) when he gave Order, That as soon as he was dead, his Last Will and Testament should be carried to the King, wherein he humbly intreated his Majesty to Pardon the Treason committed against him, and his Native Countrey, and that he would permit his body to be buried without the Church of any Parish of *Lisbonne*, and that without any Inscription or Tomb-stone, that there might remain no memory of a man who had been a Traytor to his King and Countrey.

This exemplary punishment, and rigorous execution of Justice upon the forementioned trayterous Delinquents, established the King in his Kingdom, struck a terror into his enemies, and increased his Subjects love and care of him more diligently to Watch his Royal Families, and the Kingdoms safety.

But in the mean time daily incursions were made upon the Frontiers between the *Castillians* and *Portugueses*, with the same Violence, Cruelty and Animosity, as formerly.

About the beginning of the year, One thousand six hundred and forty two (notwithstanding

JOHN IV. *of the Name*,

standing the Truce that had been concluded between *Portugal* and *Holland*, and that a great Fleet of *Hollanders* had been sent to assist the *Portugal* against the *Spaniard*) there passed very high Acts of Hostility between the two Nations in *Affrica* and *America*, beyond the Line; for the *Hollanders* seeing the disunion of *Portugal* from *Castille*, made all speed possible to perfect the Conquest of those parts before a perfect Peace should be concluded with *Portugal*, that so in the Treaty they might pretend Reason, that all things should continue in the state they were then found.

To this purpose, that is, the expediting their Conquest, the *Hollanders* treacherously (whilest there was all quiet and peacable Commerce held between the two Nations in the Kingdom of *Angola*) surprized the *Portugals* that were Governors of the place, Killed divers, and Robbed all of the great Wealth they there found; of which Perfidiousness, as also of the Barbarous Usage of the Prisoners there taken, Complaints were made to the *States General* at the *Hague*, but no Redress was granted; nor was the King of *Portugal* of Ability to force it.

In the mean time the Affairs in *Portugal* were a little discomposed by the general Discontent and Distaste taken at the Secretary of State, *Don Francisco de Lucena*: This man had lived a long time in the Court of *Spain*, till he was by *Olivarez* made Under-Secretary to *Vasconcellos*; his Readiness to Proclaim King JOHN, and his Abilities in the place, made the King continue him in it, reposing in him so great a Confidence, That though some had Advertized his Majesty that he kept Correspondence with the Court at *Madrid*, yet the King would not suspect him, nor permit him to be brought to a Trial.

But about the middle of the Year, *One thousand six hundred and forty three*; the urgent Affairs of the Kingdom requiring a Convention of the Three Estates, they openly refused all Acts that should pass the hands of Secretary *Lucena*, positively telling his Majesty, That until he were brought to Trial, no Acts should Pass in the Assembly of Estates, nor any farther Proceedings be made.

His Majesty was very much Grieved hereat, yet prudently Resolved to give his Subjects Satisfaction, by delivering up his Secretary to Justice; yet Resolving he should have a fair Trial, and to that purpose sitting himself to hear the Witnesses examined. Whilest Process was framed against the Secretary, some secret Advice came to his Majesty, which caused the Imprisonment of the Brother, and Three Servants of the Secretary, together with an English Monck, and a Cavalier of the Habit; not long after, the Secretary was Arraigned and Condemned for betraying his Truth, in holding Correspondence with the Enemy, and in neglecting timely to Advertise the Infanta *Edward* to retire out of *Germany*, &c. and according to his Sentence, executed in a Publick place in *Lisbon*, where at his Death, he protested his Innocency touching any Treachery towards his Majesty.

The Death of the Secretary both pleased the People, and satisfied the Assembly of Estates, who now, according to his Majesties Command, met on *September* 18. *One thousand six hundred and forty three*; and being all sate, and his Majesty seated in his Throne, *D. Emanuel D' Acugna*, Dean of his Majesties Chappel, rose up, and after Reverence made to the King, spake to the Effect following.

'THat in the space of Sixty Years, that that Kingdom was under the Power of
' the Kings of *Castille*, there had been but Two Assemblies of States; the
' first to Inslave, the next to Abuse them. But that since they were under the
' present King, within the space of Two Years, they had Two Assemblies, the for-
' mer to settle their Liberties, the present to beget a right Understanding between the
' King and his People, wherein they had all Freedom to demand whatever was neces-
' sary, That the World might see they are now no longer Slaves, but Children; no
' longer

longer Strangers, but Natives; and that they are under rather a Loving Father, than a Severe Soveraign.

'In the former Assembly, said he, His Majesty took all the Customs, and left the Defence of the Kingdom to your hands, you Ordered what seemed good unto your selves, you made Choice of a General Assistance by way of Contribution; but in the leaving thereof, the first Payment was found ineffectual, the second unequal, the third insufficient; whence arose some Complaints, some imagining that the fault proceeded from the unequal Division of the Contribution; others from the Change of Value in Money and Commodities, and others from the disorderly Gathering and Disbursing the whole. I may easily say, That if there were any errour committed, yet it might be excusable for that; *Never had any weighty affair its Conception and Perfection at once: Then shall Errours cease to be in Government, when Men shall cease to be in the World.* These things are to be endured with the same Patience that Droughts, Dearths, Inundations, and such other Disorders in Nature, for the Wit of Man cannot hold forth a Remedy for all Diseases. But certainly they will be no ground of Reprehension, (though much of Admiration) to him that shall Consider how His Majesty entred upon a Kingdom, exhausted by the *Castillians* of Money and other Necessaries, for Offence or Defence, and yet how in less than a Year and an half, we should want neither Shipping, nor Artillery, nor Horse, nor Arms, nor Fortification, nor Armies upon the Frontiers, three Powerful Fleets put to Sea, divers Honorable, and Extraordinary Ambassages, besides many Secret (yet Necessary) Expences; all which will astonish any Understanding Man. Now to the end that the People may have full satisfaction, His Majesty hath Commanded, That (before further Proceeding) it be made appear Particularly how all the Money Received hath been laid out, and then it is Expected, and the present state of Affairs Requireth, That we all Contribute Liberally, Considering that these Charges are but for a time; but our Liberties are for ever: That we shall never have a better opportunity to Destroy our Enemy. That Nature teacheth, To Hazard an Arm, to Save the whole Body: The Merchants at Sea cast away some part of their Goods sometimes, to save the rest; we are now on Ship-board in a Storm, our Goods, our Lives, our Liberties, our Honour, our Countrey, are all in Danger.

'Moreover, the Barbarous Usage of the King of *Castille* towards the Infante *Don Edward*, calls upon this Assembly for Revenge, that we spend not only our Money, but our Blood in Affection to Him, and that we make our Enemies spend theirs in Satisfaction for Him, &c.'

This Speech of the Deans was spoken with so much Affection, that it stirred up and encouraged the States readily to give all Assistance imaginable, both for Redressing of Grievances, and for the Levying Arms, so that within a small time after, the King was in the Head of Twenty thousand Foot, and Three thousand Horse, marching towards the Frontiers of *Castille*.

Whil'st these great preparations for Hostility were made, the Queen brought forth into the World a second Son to His Majesty, but first Child after he came to the Crown, which added to the Magnificence of his Christning, he was named *Alphonso*, and his Brother *Theodosio* dying before his Father, succeeded in the Kingdom and is at present King of *Portugal*.

Many Skirmishes had passed between the *Castillians* and *Portugueses*, many town, had been surprized, many lands wasted, but never happened a set-battel between them till in the year, *One thousand six hundred and forty four*, when both Armies met upon the Border of *Portugal* in a field called *Campo Major*. The *Spanish* Army which for the most part consisted of strangers, was under the Command of the

I i   Marquess

Marquess of *Forrecusa*, and the *Portugal* Army consisting of Natives, and some few *Hollanders*, were commanded by *Macchias de Albuquerque*. This fight was maintained with all possible courage and resolution on both sides; but the *Spaniards* being more numerous, especially in horse, at length put the whole *Portuguese* Army in Disorder, seized on their whole Artillery, and Baggage, and slew *Albuquerques* Horse under him, took many Prisoners, and assured themselves of an absolute Victory. But Fortune which had thus favourably smiled upon them in the begining of the Day, frowned as harshly upon them in the Conclusion; for *Albuquerque* being re-mounted, Rallied again his scattered Forces, re-charged the pursuing *Spaniards*, put them to a total Rout, and pursued the Chase for above three Miles.

In this Battel the *Castillians* lost One thousand six hundred men upon the place, amongst which were the Lieutenant General, the General of the Horse, the General of the Artillery, the Count *de Montixo*, five Camp-masters, two Adjutants of Horse, three Serjeant Majors, three and twenty Cornets, together with many Knights of the Order of St. *James Calatrava* and *Alcantara*: there were taken about Four thousand Arms, and a thousand Horse.

On the *Portuguese* side there were not above Three hundred slain, among which were two Camp-masters, one Serjeant Major, a Captain of Horse, and eight of Foot, but many Noblemen, Commanders, and Officers taken Prisoners in the first encounter, were carried away by the *Spaniards* in their flight.

It was not long after this Battel, that the Marquess *De Montalban*, D. *George Mascaneras* Lord Treasurer, President of the Council of the *Indies*, and Councellor of Estate, with some others, were imprisoned upon suspition of a Conspiracy against the King of *Portugal*: but it being upon Examination found, that the suspition was by the *Spaniards* cunningly raised, to deprive King JOHN of his most able Ministers, and to make the World believe the *Portuguese* Nobility were discontented with their King; they were set at Liberty, and their Honours fully repaired by a Proclamation of the Kings.

For the *Spaniards* ceased not by all means and devices, which the Will and Policy of the most wicked States-men could invent, not only to weaken the *Portuguess* Nation within it self, by breeding discontents (if possible) between the King and the three Estates, but likewise to undervalue them, and make their credit be slighted and disregarded by other Kingdoms and States, their Confederates and Allies.

Yet besides these subtile Ambages, the King of *Castille* did not desist the endeavoring to oppress this Kingdom by force of Arms; but not only the resolved and immutable unity of the *Portuguess* Nation, was a strong Tower and invincible Fortress against the *Spanish* Power, but so extreamly was the House of *Austria* involved in Wars and Disasters on every side, that that vast Body was rather in a condition to crave help and assistance from others, than indeed to oppress them. For besides the Wars in *Catalonia*, which had put itself under the protection of the most potent King of *France*, in the *Low-countreys*, which had proved so tedious and so chargeable a War to *Spain*; in *Italy*, in this Kingdom, and in *Germany*, there happened several Commotions and popular Tumults in some of the King of *Spain's* Dominions, which not only robbed the King of a present supply of Treasure, but were otherwise retardments to the prosecution of his Wars in other places.

The first of these Commotions began in the Island of *Sicily*, where the people gathering together in a tumultuous manner, forced the Vice-roy to take off all new Imposts and Taxes which the Kings present necessities had enforced him to lay upon them. This encouraged their neighbours on the adjacent Continent, the

Inhabitants of the Famous City of *Naples*, in hopes to rid themselves of their oppressions, to rise in like manner in Arms; which they did, encouraged and commanded by one *Thomas Aniello*, or vulgarly *Masaniello*, who though of so mean and obscure a birth as a poor Fisher-boy; yet to the wonder of the World for ten dayes Commanded this mighty City, and freed it from all Gabels, so that ever since these two Kingdoms of *Naples* and *Sicily* have rather been a great charge, than any benefit to the Spanish Monarch.

These Troubles, and the *Austrian* Families being every where encompassed and embroiled in Wars, together with the earnest desire of the King of *Castille* to prosecute a vigorous War against *Catalonia*, and *Portugal*, were I suppose the motives which perswaded the Catholique King to end those Wars, which had lasted in the low Countreys for above ninety years, by owning now at last (what he had so long refused) the united Provinces free States, so an obsolute peace was concluded on, and proclaimed at all the chief towns in the *Netherlands*, on the 5. of *June*, *One thousand six hundred and forty eight*, a Peace no less advantagious to the *Spaniards*, than disadvantagious to the *Portugals*, by reason of the pretences the *Dutch* had to *Brazil*, and other places in the *West-Indies*. King JOHN of *Portugal* about the beginning of the year, *One thousand six hundred and forty nine*, thought his Son the Prince *Theodosio* arrived at an age fitting to keep a Court of himself; Lodgings were therefore appointed for him, divided from the Royal Palace, and Officers of his Houshold nominated and appointed by the King, amongst whom the Earls of *Villa nova*, of *Miranda*, of *Valdereis* & *Fernando*, *Telles de Monezez*, (who had formerly been Governour of the City of *Port*,) were entrusted as the principal Gentlemen of his Chamber.

The King likewise thought fit to adde a third to the two former Superintendants of his Revenue, whom he nominated to be *D. Rey de Moure Tellez*, whose former Office of Steward to the Queen, was at the same time conferred on *D. Antonio de Silva* Lord of *Billas*.

Notwithstanding the Truce, the *Hollanders* still continued their outrages on the other side the Line, but principally in *Brazil*, where they seized upon many of the *Portugal* forts, impeded the Traffick, abused and murthered the Subjects, which made His Majesty resolve to call the Earl of *Castle Melhor* from his charge of being General of the *Portugal* Forces upon the Frontiers of *Gallicia*, and committing that to the young *Viscount de Villanova de Servera* that the Earl might be imployed as Viceroy to *Brazil* to curb the *Flemmings* insolencies, and to secure the *Portuguess* Merchants Ships from their Pyracies, the King appointed a Fleet of forty Ships of War, and six thousand Men to attend that service as Convoys.

His Holiness the Popes anger as yet continued towards the Kingdom of *Portugal*, for he had not only hitherto refused to receive Ambassadors from thence, but to supply those Archbishopricks, Bishopricks, and other Ecclesiastical Offices of the Kingdom, which by the death of the former possessors were vacant: this the King found a great inconveniency in, and therefore thought fit once more to attempt his Holiness; and to present him the names of such of his own Subjects, whose piety, learning, or other sufficiencies he thought might make them capable of such dignities; As first, for the Archbishoprick of *Braga*, (formerly acknowledged to be the primacy of all *Spain*, notwithstanding the pretensions of *Toledo*) he nominated *Don Pedro de Lancastro*, President of the Justice of the Palace of the House of *Ameiro*, and descended from JOHN the second King of *Portugal*. For the Archbishoprick of *Evora*, His Majesty nominated *D. Francisco Borrez* Bishop of the *Algarez*, Bishoprick he bestowed upon the Father *Dennis Des Anges* an Augustine Monk, and Confessor to His Majesty: for the Bishoprick of *Guarda* was appointed *D. Antonio Pobo*, great Prior of the Military Order of St. *James*: for the Bishoprick

rick of *Lamego*, *D. Antonio de Mendosa* Commiſſary of the *Bula de la Croiſaida:* for the Biſhoprick of *Lerida*, *D. Deigo de Souza* Inquiſitor of the holy Office: for that of *Conimbra*, *Don Sebaſtian Caſar de Menerez*, who was before nominated for the Biſhoprick of *Porto*, but that was given by his Majeſty to *D. Pedro de Menerez*, once named Biſhop of *Miranda*, of which laſt place *D. Pedro de Porros* Tutor of the Prince *D. Theodoſio* was now named Biſhop. Theſe choices of his Majeſty, the Pope after ſome time Confirmed *D. Franciſco de Souza*, who was ſent as extraordinary Ambaſſador, notwithſtanding the oppoſition of the *Spaniards* received, not unlikely out of a fear that they would Officiate without his Confirmation, and ſo in a manner Renounce the Power of the See of *Rome*.

But in the middeſt of this ſetling of Eccleſiaſtical affairs, Arms were not ſilent, for upon the Borders there hapned a Skirmiſh between the *Caſtilians* and *Portugueſe* about the latter end of *April*, *One thouſand ſix hundred forty and nine*, Lord of *Themer Court*, Lieutenant General of the *Portugueſe* Horſe, and Monſieur *Du Queſne* the Commiſſary General gained a Victory over a ſmall Army of the *Spaniards*, defeating Seven hundred of the *Spaniards*, and taking divers Priſoners, amongſt whom was the Nephew of the Marqueſs of *Melinguen* Lieutenant General of the *Caſtillian* Army at *Badajox*, who was after exchanged for the Count *Fieſque Lauagna*, who for ſome years paſt had been Priſoner in *Caſtille*: in this Conflict the *Portugueſe* loſt but Twenty five men, the Chief of which was *Sieur de la Touche*, a French Captain, who had behaved himſelf moſt Valorouſly.

The Commotions of the *Periſians* againſt the King of *France*, had given the *Spaniard* great hopes of better ſucceſs than they had many years had, but the middle of the Year, *One thouſand ſix hundred and forty nine*, happily concluding them, the news of their Pacification, and that of a great Victory gained by the *Portugueſſes* againſt the *Hollanders* in *Brazile*, cauſed a general joy over all *Portugal*; for the King appointed Publick Thanks to be given, and *Te Deum* to be Sung in all Churches.

Hopes to revenge the late defeat given by the Lord *Theriміcourt*, and deſire to do ſome Valiant Act before he departed from his Government, made the Marqueſs of *Leganez* Governour of the Spaniſh Forces at *Eſtramadura*, give an Alarum to the *Portugueſe* Frontiers, and enter into the Countrey with Two thouſand Horſe, and Six thouſand Foot, but the Valiant Count of St. *Laurence* aſſaulting him, forced him to retire with ſhame, and excuſe himſelf that he marched out only to meet the Marqueſs of *Mortare*, who was appointed to ſucceed him in the Government.

Yet this ſmall and worthleſs Alarum, made the King of *Portugal*, who knew that too much care could not be had of the Safety of his Kingdom, to ſend Orders to the Governors to look more exactly to the Countreys committed to their Charges, than formerly, and ſtrictly to give Charge to *Don Juan de Menezez* Governor of *Porto*. The Viſcount *Ponte de Lima* Governor of the Countreys between *Douro* and *Mimbo*, to the Count of *Arogna* Governor of *Traſmontes*, and *Don Roderigo de Caſtro* Governor of *Beira*, to repair with all expedition to their ſeveral Commands.

Nor was his Majeſty leſs careful of his Dominions abroad, than of thoſe near home, which made him diſpatch the Baron of *Alviro* to be Governor of *Tanger*, and *D. Franciſco de Norogna* to *Mazagan*, both ſtrong Forts in *Affrica*; the laſt of which had been neer ſurprized by the *Moors* of *Barbary*, but the Commander of that Party which aſſaulted it, being ſlain by a Valorous French-man, they were beaten off with loſs, for which ſervice the King beſtowed upon the French-man a Penſion of Six hundred Crowns *per annum*.

And whilſt His Majeſty was diſtributing his Bounties, he could not forget the Lady Dona *Maria Manuel*, Widow to the ſome-time before deceaſed *D. Antonio Coello*, *D. Caravallio*, who had ever ſince His Majeſties coming to the Crown, been one of His Privy-Counſellors, and was one of the Chief Perſons that went Ambaſſadors

bassadors into *France*, to renew the Alliance, and conclude a firm League between the King of *Portugal*, and *Lewis* the Thirteenth King of *France*; His Majesty therefore in consideration of his services, bestowed a valuable Pension on his aforesaid Widow.

There was almost daily in-roads made upon the Frontiers in some places or other, amongst the rest, the Baron of *Themericourt* entred with a strong Party into the Spanish Territories, surprised the Suburbs of the City of *Albuquerque*, and brought away a very rich Booty, without the loss of so much as one Souldier upon the place, and not above Twenty wounded.

The succour of the distressed Subjects of the more distressed King of *England*, about the Year, *One thousand six hundred and fifty*, gave occasion to the King of *Portugal* to manifest his affection to the English Nation, which he did by giving assistance to the Gallant Prince *Rupert*, who being by His Majesty of *England* made Admiral of those few Ships which in the Year, *One thousand six hundred and forty eight*, returned to their Allegiance, had ever since been pursued by the more Potent Fleets of the English Rebels, and was now by them driven to seek the protection of his *Portugal* Majesty, who notwithstanding that the Fleet of the Rebels with threatning *Bravado's*, demanded the said Kings leave, either to assault them in his Port, or to force them to come out bravely, protected them under his Castles.

In Revenge of which, the Rebels of *England*, who stiled themselves a Parliament, Proclaimed an open War with the *Portugal* Nation, which his Majesty, notwithstanding his great Engagement at that present, both against the *Spaniards* at home, and the *Hollanders* on the other side the Line, resolved to endure, rather than deliver up the faithful Subjects of *England* into the hands of Murther, Tyranny, and Treason; and therefore in part to cry quittance with the *English*, who had taken Prize several Ships belonging to this Nation, he made seizure of all the English Ships and Goods within his whole Dominions, but only those he had before Protected.

But at length Prince *Rupert* finding a clear Passage from out his Ports, where he had for many Months been blocked up, the King, by Reason of his other large Expences in defence of his Kingdom, finding himself unable to maintain a War against the *English*; and Nature dictating us to the Preservation of our Selves, Resolved, more moved out of Necessity, than Inclination, to send an Agent into *England* to conclude a Peace.

The Person deputed to go on this unpleasant Employment (*viz.* to Court Rebels) was *D. Suarez de Gimetraines*, who had for his Assistance and Interpreter, Mr. *Miles* an *English* Merchant, these two Embarqued upon a *Hamburgher* hired for that purpose by the King of *Portugal*, arrived in *England*, in *January* 1650. About the beginning of *February*, *D. Suarez* had Audience before a Committee of the pretended Parliament, to whom he made a Speech in Latine to this Effect.

'THE Serenissimo King of *Portugal* my Master, sends me hither to the Parliament of the Common-wealth of *England* that on his behalf, and in his Name, having first most friendly saluted you (as I now do with the greatest Affection of my heart that I am able) I may jointly tender and make known to you the Royal Desire which my Master feels within himself, to conserve, and more and more to knit the knot of that Amity which uninterrupted, hath ever been between the *Serenissimo* Kings of *Portugals* their Ancestors, and this Renowned *English* Nation.

'It being my part to endeavor what lies in me, to remove all obstacles that may hinder the most vigorous effect of this hearty union, and conjunction of minds, so to preserve inviolably the ancient peace between us.

'This I come to continue, hoping and wishing all happy successtherein; this I come to intimate and offer unto the Parliament of the Commonwealth of *England*, with

'with that sincere and pristine affection, which hitherto the experience of many
' ages hath made manifest.

' Nor shall you need to scruple the sincerity of my intention and purpose, by
' reason of the divers past attempts (not to say fights) between your power and ours,
' since they have not been such as have broken or dissolved our amity, nor have had
' their rise or approbation from the King my Master; nor as we believe from the
' Parliament of the Commonwealth of *England*, but more probably carried on ei-
' ther by the impulse of their own private affections, or by the defect of that cir-
' cumspection which in such cases is ever necessary.

' But as I hope particularly and fully to prove (and indeed to demonstrate) this truth
' unto the Parliament of the Republique of *England*, so I am assured they will not
' only rest satisfied therein, but shall also have accruing to them a newer force, and
' sence of mutual friendship between us, since the jars that happen amongst friends,
' are oftentimes justly accounted as certain redintigrations of love.

' And I do admire our enemies have not made this reflection, whilst fed with
' vain hope, they have thought it in their power to sow and foment discords be-
' tween us, upon presumption of this trivial innovation.

' The King my Master sends me to continue and preserve our common and an-
' cient peace, whereof I am to make a tender unto the Parliament of the Common-
' wealth of *England* in His Majesties behalf, as proceeding from a perfect sincerity
' in his Royal breast, and whereunto he is chiefly drawn by the Motive of his sin-
' gular esteem and love, he bears unto this English Nation.

' And this, as the main point I shall recommend unto you, both in regard of
' your greater good and ours, and as a thing of highest concernment, that we re-
' flect how little it can be pleasing to Almighty God, and how derogatory it must
' needs be to our reputation on both sides, to give the least beginning of discord
' between two Christian Nations, so well affected to one another as we are.

' It is manifest unto the Parliament of the Commonwealth of *England*, and to
' all *Europe* besides, in how wonderful a manner (such as was only possible to God,
' the King my Master was restored to his Kingdoms, and how the Divine Majesty
' (whose handy-work this was) doth by his especial care and grace defend and con-
' tinue this Restoration.

' Which as it doth dayly more appear by the victories we have over our enemies
' at home, so again it is seen in our remotest and most distantial dominions in the
' *East-Indies*, where even at a huge distance (His Majesty possessing the hearts of
' his people) enjoyes the greatest peace in the world, and is secure in *Affrica* re-
' lying therein upon his prosperous and happy powers.

' To conclude, the King my Master, lest any thing should be wanting to ren-
' der him compleatly happy, hath (according to the wish of an ancient *Christian*
' Author, for securing the prosperity of the *Roman* Empire) a faithful Senate,
' puissant Armies, and a most obedient people, Fortifications in the judgement
' of wisest politicians, conducing and necessary both to defend and increase Empires
' and Kingdoms.

' Now in this good condition of not only gaining and conserving friends, but al-
' so of vanquishing our enemies, the King my Master loves and embraces peace,
' as the chiefest good amongst humane things, holding it forth to all Kingdoms and
' Commonwealths, but especially to this of *England*, with that exceeding good
' will which he hath hitherto born, and shall ever bear unto the same, standing
' thereunto obliged by such bonds of love and good offices, as shall never be for-
' gotten by His Majesty.

' For the people of this Nation are the most worthy successors of those their He-
' roick Ancestors, who by their just power and Arms came freely to vindicate our

Crowns

'Crowns from the *Mahumetan* oppressions. And are, if not the same persons, at
'least their Children, who inflamed with a fervor and zeal of defending the
'Crown of *Portugal*, justly did disdain to see it in the unjust possession of a forreign
'Prince.

'They are, I say, those who with so mature deliberation and resolution, en-
'deavoured to snatch away this undue possession from the said Usurper, maugre the
'concurrence of some ill-affected *Portugals* with our enemies; and that they might
'atchieve this end glorious to themselves, and to us emolumental, they are those
'who covered these as with their Squadrons and Fleets of Ships, ever formidable
'to their most potent enemies by a new example of an unheard of valour (had our
'unfortunate Stars then given us leave to be happy) come up to the very walls of
'*Lisbon*.

'And this having formerly been between us and them most powerful English-
'men, and our most loving brethren, now that the Crown of *Portugal* (for which
'you have fought so valiantly, when it was unlawfully detained, is happily re-
'stored to the possession of the natural, and lawful King to whom of right it apper-
'tains) who would not admire to see you bend your equal power, (upon no oc-
'casion given) against the true and rightful King of *Portugal* by joyning with, and
'favouring the same Usurper (beaten by us) from whom your selves did heretofore
'by force of your own Arms in our behalfs endeavor to snatch and wrest away that
'Crown he had unjustly seized upon, and whom indeed you have hitherto both in
'desire and effect opposed.

'It would to all the world seem a thing much removed from the innate genero-
'sity and gallantry of this your Nation, and very ill suiting with your Christian
'justice and equality, as also it would be a very unworthy requital of us (who
'have deserved better at your hands) and of that benevolence and affection
'wherewith the whole Kingdom of *Portugal* is passionately carrying on towards
'you, wishing unto you the same happinesse that we our selves desire to en-
'joy.

'Let therefore these imaginary Clouds of discord vanish, and be quite blown
'over from our thoughts, as serving only to Eclipse with darknefs, the clear light
'of our antient amity, which (with what intention God Almighty knows,) the
'importune sagacity of our Common enemy would fain deprive us of.

'Let all obstacles be removed, and thrown quite away, wherewith the true
'serving polititians by their inbred ambition of an universal Monarchy do conspire
'the ruine of us both, aiming at nothing more then to set us together by the ears,
'that overthrowing each other with our own Wars, we may have breasts open
'(when our powers are exhausted) to their swords and wounds, with greater ad-
'vantage against our selves, and less hazard unto them.

'This new Republique is built upon strong and sure foundations, as also our an-
'tient and restored Kingdoms, let us therefore cast our eyes unto the common in-
'terest of our cause, joyning hands, and mutual benevolence to such effect, as
'may render both parties security, the greater forbearing, and bewaring above all
'things, all provocations, or irruptions of War, whereby (besides the incon-
'veniences, and losses which they ever draw after them,) all our own affairs and
'safety may be hazarded extreamly, while their councels and endeavors will be
'promoted, who by hidden and wicked arts, strive to extend their own power
'by the common waste they would make in ours.

'The King of *Portugal* my Master, hath sent me hither furnished with a firm
'ample plenipotentiary power, that discussing, and screwing all the just and con-
'venient means, I may confer about the conservation of Peace, and (removing
'all emergent obstacles and scruples) resolve, and establish with the Parliament of

'the Commonwealth of *England*, whatsoever shall be necessary for composing of
'our present affairs, and maturely to provide with the greatest security that may
'be possible, for their future well-being.

'I therefore beseech the Parliament of the Commonwealth of *England*, that
'weighing and considering these things which I have exhibited, they would please
'to decree whatsoever shall seem to them most convenient and just.

To this large Speech of forced and known flattery, if we respect it in relation to the persons it was spoke to, (though most true in those particulars relating to the *English* Nation whilst monarchical) was answered by the Rebels, with a large Harange of the injuries they supposed done them by the protection of Prince *Ruperts* Fleet, and seizure of the *English* Merchants Ships and Goods, concluding that they must have reparation made them for the publique damage of the Commonwealth, which they would be willing to accept of in any honourable manner, and were willing to that purpose, if the Ambassador had sufficient power to treat with him to that effect.

In summe, after some time the Count *Del Sa* Lord Chamberlain of the Kingdom of *Portugal* arrived in *England*, in the quality of an Ambassador extraordinary, who after many Conferences, Addresses, and large Offers made, obtained a Peace, upon condition to repay great Summes of money towards the satisfaction of the losses of the English Merchants.

During the stay of this Ambassador, his brother *D. Pantaleon Sa*, Knight of *Malta*, led by I know not what frantick madnesse, made a great uproar upon the New Exchange in *London*, where some *English*, were by him and his Followers, murdered; for which several of his retinue were hanged, and himself, notwithstanding the earnest solicitations of his brother, afterwards beheaded on Tower-hill, when the government of *England* was changed from a strange kinde of Commonwealth, to a stranger kind of Monarchy, under a Protector.

But to return back again to the affairs of the Kingdom of *Portugal*. The Earl of *Castle Melhor* who had been sent Vice-Roy into *Brazil*, had so good successe, that with the assistance of those *Portugueses* before in the Kingdom, he expulsed the *Hollanders* out of all their Garrisons there, except the strong Fortress of *Recif*, which was built upon a Rock wholly invironed by the Sea. This animated the United States of the *Netherlands*, to endeavor a revenge and recovery of that country, and to that end and purpose, a Potent Fleet was set out, and notwithstanding the very earnest endeavors, and large offers of the *Portuguess* Ambassador at the *Hague*, set sail to reconquer that Kingdom, but not with that successe which was expected, for the expedition proved wholly fruitless, and after so great an expence, the States were so highly discontented, that the Admiral *Wittison* was arrested at the *Hague*, to answer such things as should be objected against him concerning that voyage.

It much concerns that King who hath to deal with enemies too potent for him, to strengthen himself with such Alliance, as may most advantage him, and endamage his Foe; This consideration made King JOHN of *Portugal*, about the year, *One thousand six hundred and fifty two*, send an Ambassador to the young Duke of *Savoy*, (who by reason of the scituation of his Country, had good and frequent opportunities to annoy the Catholique King,) and divert him from turning his whole Force upon this Kingdom) offering reciprocal Marriage between that Duke and his Daughter, and the young Prince *Theodosia* and *Savoys* Sister. But this his intention, was I suppose diverted, if not wholly hindred by the great power of Cardinal *Mazarine* in *France*, who designed one of his Nieces as a fit match for *Eugenius* young Duke of *Savoy*.

'Tis

'Tis not at all safe nor fit for a subject to grow too rich, at least not to exceed his Soveraign in Treasure, for he thereby layes himself open to the envie and suspition of his Prince, nor is it possible that any who hath managed a publick imployment, can be so without faults, as that somewhat cannot be laid to his charge to render him at a Kings mercy.

Sufficient example of this we have in D. *Phillip de Mascarendas* Vice-Roy of *Goa* in the *East-Indies*, who having for many years officiated in that high imployment, had gathered up an infinite Mass of Riches, and now being called home, thought in peace and quiet to enjoy what with a penurious and industrious hand he had been many years storing up: but the King being informed that he had indeed such a vaste treasure in Gold, Diamonds, Pearls and other Jewels, as he could not with his own honor or safety permit a Subject to enjoy, easily found out them who were ready to form complaints against him, which were as readily listned to by the Kings Council, who presently drawing up a charge against him, for having used an arbitrary power, oppressed, and abused the Subjects, and Merchants trading thither, &c. caused the Ship wherein he came, with all the riches laden on it, to be seized on for the Kings use, and himself for some time imprisoned, nor had it been a wonder if he had made a forfeiture of his life, as well as of the greatest part of his estate.

The strength of the *Hollanders* at Sea, had been the greatest obstacle to the *Portuguese*, not wholly regaining their ancient possession in *Brazile*, but the Wars wherein the *Hollanders* had involved themselves with *England*, proving so powerful a diversion, the *Portuguese* took the advantage to reduce *Recif*, which with several Forts that encompassed it, and some few other, were the only places that held out against them.

Against this therefore with a sufficient Land-force, came *Don Francisco Barreto*, Governor of *Pernambuco*, (whil'st the *Portuguese* Navy consisting of 65 Sayl, blocked it up by sea,) and first by storm took the Fort of *Salines*, and thence coming before that of *Burracco*, found it already abandoned, and blown up by the defendants: he next proceeded to the new Fortress, the next and strongest Fort to that of *Recif*, and well manned and munitioned. Thus having made a sturdy resistance, was at length forced by the *Portugal*, which so amazed the *Hollanders*, that though they had fifteen hundred men, and six months provisions in *Recif*, yet they agreed to yield it upon honorable terms on the 26 of *January* 1654. being twenty four years after they had taken it from the *Portugals*.

THE Conditions upon which this strong Fortress was surrendred up, were to this effect.

1. That D. Francisco Barreto *should forget all Acts of Hostility made by the* Hollanders *against the* Portugals *by Sea and Land.*

2. That *all persons whatsoever, even the* Jewes *in* Recif, *and* Maurice-town, *though Rebels against the King of* Portugal, *should be pardoned.*

3. That all Hollanders *should be free to carry away those Goods they actually possessed.*

4. That *they should have sufficient number of ships able to pass the Equinoctial Line, with Iron-guns for their Transportation.*

5. That the Hollanders *married with* Portugal Women, *or Natives there, should be dealt so withal, as if they had married* Dutch Women, *and should with the consent of the Women, have power to carry them away with them.*

6. That *those who would stay there under the Obedience of the* Portugals, *should be used as well as if they were Native* Portugals, *and as to their Religion, should live as other strangers do in* Portugal.

7. That all Forts about Recif and Maurice town, viz. the Port of St. Bastions, Boa Vista, St. Austines, Convent, the Castle of Maurice-town, that of the three Bastions, the Brum, with it's Redoubt, the Castle of St. George, and all others should be surrendred to

the aforesaid D. Francisco Barreto, *Governour of* Pernambucco, *with all the Ordnance and Ammunition presently after the signing of these Articles.*

8. *That the Hollanders should be free to remain in* Recif *and* Maurice-town *for Three Months, they surrendring their Arms, which should be restored to them when they took shipping, and in the mean while they should have power to buy them necessary provisions of the* Portugals *for the Voyage.*

9. *All Negotiations and Alienations should be made during the said Three Months according to the present Articles.*

10. *That the Governour should quarter his Forces where he pleased, and that the* Hollanders *should be protected during those Three Months, and having Liberty to end their private Differences before their own Judges.*

11. *That they should carry away all their papers whatsoever.*

12. *That if they could not sell their Goods in the said Three Months time, they should leave them with whom they pleased under the Obedience of the* Portugals, *to be disposed of according to their own Order.*

13. *That they should have all the Victuals in the store-houses of* Recif, *and the other Forts for their Voyage.*

14. *That as to their pretensions against the* Portugals, *they might sue them at the King of* Portugals *Court.*

15. *That all their Vessels should be restored unto them, which they might fit for their Voyage.*

16. *That they might have liberty to advise all their ships upon the Coast, to come and lade their Goods at* Recif: *And in the last Article it was expressed, That upon the demand of the* Hollanders, *that this might not prejudice any former Treaty between the King of* Portugal, *and the States General,* D. Francisco Barreto *would not assent thereunto.*

There were other articles likewise granted to the Military Forces, the sum of which were, that all offences and hostages might be forgotten, that all souldiers should go out of *Recif* with their Arms, Match lighted, Bullet in mouth, Flying-colours, but coming near the *Portugal* Army, should put out the Match, and lay their Arms in those Magazines appointed by the governour of *Pernambucco*, to be restored to them at their departure, provided they went to *Nants*, *Rochel*, or to some place in the United Provinces and not to any belonging to the King of *Portugal*; for security whereof they should give three hostages, and all Officers and Souldiers should be shipt together with General *Sigismond Schop*, after the delivery of the Forts of *Riogrando*, *Paraiba*, and *Tamarica*. That the General should have twenty pieces of brass ordnance; from four Pound-Bullet to eighteen, with all their furnitures, besides all necessary Iron-guns, for the defence of the Ships that should be afforded them for their transportation, with convenient supplies of ammunition and provision, according to the thirteenth Article before recited: That General *Sigismond*, and all his Officers of War, should have liberty to carry away or sell all his or their goods or slaves. That sick or wounded persons should have liberty to stay till they recovered, but the Governour would not condescend to release those *Hollanders* which were prisoners before this surrendry: A general pardon was granted to all rebels, chiefly to *Amboyna*, *Mendaz*, and all other Indians and Negroes, but they were not to have the honor to march out with their Arms. In sum, the supream Council at *Recif*, did oblige themselves for the surrendring of these places, upon the signing of these Articles, and for the delivering up the Island of *Farnam*, *Viaca*, *Noroga*, *Riogrand*, *Paraiba*, and *Tamarica*, upon the same conditions for the inhabitants, as had been granted to those of *Recif*.

These articles were signed and delivered on both sides, at the Camp at *Taborda*, on the 18. of *January*, One thousand six hundred and fifty three, and Conditions on both sides

sides punctually observed. Thus did the Hollanders lose all their Acquists in *Brazil*, which so exasperated those high and mighty States, that at the coming into *Holland* of myn Heer *Sigismond Schop*, who had there been General of their *Militia*, they caused him to be imprisoned, and tried for his life by a Council of War, but notwithstanding endeavors of his enemies, he was acquitted.

Nor were the *Portugals* at home less fortunate against their neighbour enemy the *Spaniards*, for to omit many petty skirmishes, in-roads made by them with all success desirable in the summer, *One thousand six hundred and fifty four*, D. *Antonio D' Albuquerque* General of the *Portuguess* horse, taking an advantage upon a party of *Castillians*, which lay upon the Borders neer *Aronches*, under the command of Count *D' Amaranthe*, set upon them, slew their General *Amaranthe*, and took six hundred horse; and farther animated with this success, and the knowledge he had that a vigorous prosecution is the onely mother of a true victory, pursued them with an Army of 3000 Foot and 1500 Horse, eight leagues into their own Country, as far as the old and strong Castle of *D' Oluce*, while encouraging his Soldiers, (made valorous by their former good fortune) he resolved to attacque, and with continued batteries, and storms so wearied out the enemy, that after four days siege they yielded upon composition, and *Albuquerque* looking upon it as a place considerable, both for the countenancing of incursions into the enemies country, and keeping in awe the town of *Xeres*, which is hard by, having repaired it and placed in it a strong Garrison, returned.

About the beginning of the year, *One thousand six hundred and fifty five*, D. *Francisco De Ferrara Rabella* arrived in *England*, with Commission from the King of *Portugal* as Agent, to *Oliver Cromwel*, who then swayed here under the title of Protector, to make a more firm confirmation of the Peace with *England*, and to advise, I suppose, about carrying on the War with *Spain*; which when *Cromwel* had given some reasons to make the world believe he would commence against that Catholick Monarch, and how much such a War was for the Interest of *Portugal*, none will doubt who have read the foregoing story, which made King J O H N Court that English Usurper with more Submissness and Complacency, by both harbouring his Fleets, and sending Presents to his Generals, than otherwise his *Genius* would have permitted him to have done, any way in prejudice of *Englands* lawful KING. In the mean time the death of Pope *Innocentius* the Tenth, made D. *Francisco de Souza*, Ambassadour at *Rome* for the King of *Portugal*, make new Addresses to *Alexander* the Seventh his Successor, for Confirmation of the Church-Officers in that Kingdom; for he never had any full Grant from *Innocent*; but now the Spanish Ambassadors opposed themselves more than ever, and by means of the Queen of *Sweden*, who wholly imployed her interest for the benefit of that Nation, endeavoured to frustrate even the *Portuguesses* Hopes; nay, so desperate was the *Spaniards* Malice, That they laid several Designs to murder the *Portugal* Ambassadour, but all proved ineffectual. In sum, After D. *Francisco de Souza*, had spent some years in the Court of *Rome* to very little purpose, he was, upon the death of King J O H N the Fourth, called home to be Governour of the young King *Alphonso*.

The proffered interchangeable Match with *Savoy*, not taking effect, father *Du Rozaire*, a Dominican, and Arch-bishop of *Goa*, was sent Agent to *France*, to treat about a Marriage between that King, and the Infanta *Donna Catharina*, with Proposals of Three Millions of Gold for Her Portion, and that the King of *Portugal* would for Seven Years maintain Eighteen Men of War at Sea, for the defence and service of the French Crown.

Long was this Business in Negotiation, and by many thought would have taken effect, the Agent being very highly carressed both by the King and Queen-mother of *France*; but whether by reason of Cardinal *Mazarine*'s dislike of it, or other Reasons

JOHN IV. of the Name,

sons of State, it was prolonged by continual demurs, till after the King of Portugal's Death, and then wholly broken off.

His Death. 1656.

For King JOHN being now arrived to about Fifty years of Age, in the Sixteenth year of his Reign, and in the Year of our Lord, *One thousand six-hundred and fifty six*, on the Sixth of *November, S. N.* paid his last debt to Nature, having a long time been troubled with an Obstruction in the Kidneys, occasioned by the Stone and Gravel, which was so sharp all the time of his Sickness, that he seldom urined, and when he did it, was in so little quantity, that it did scarce at all ease him, this violent Pain put him into a Burning-feaver, which in Ten dayes overpressed his Vitals.

Before his Death, he appointed *Donna Lucia* his Queen, to be Regent of the Kingdom during the minority of D. *Alphonso* her Son, recommending to her for Assistants in the management of so great burden as a Crown, the Reverend D. *Emanuel* Arch-bishop of *Lisbon*, Don *Runlio* Marquess of *Nisa*, the Earl of *Canvandake*, and some others, whose abilities, love and fidelity, he had experience of.

His Marriage.

His Queen *Donna Lucia* was eldest Daughter of *John-Emanuel-Perez de Guzman* Duke of *Medina Sidonia*, and of *Jane de Sandoval*, Daughter of the Duke of *Lerme John-Gomez de Sandoval* and *Royas*, by *Katherine de la Cerda*.

He was a Person of a very comely presence, his Countenance pleasant, but inclining to Swarthiness, his Body about a middle stature, yet comely and well proportioned, nor were the lineaments of his mind less becoming, than those of his Body, though if ye believe common fame, he was none of the wisest Kings that ever *Portugal* could boast of: the reason that he left so much of the Reins of the Government to his Wife, a Woman of a Masculine and Politick spirit, from whence perhaps that jesting *Spaniard* might take occasion to say; *That it was not the* Portugal *force, but the* Spanish *policy, that kept that Kingdom from the Catholique King*, alluding to the Queens being a *Spaniard*.

He was buried in the great Church of St. *Vincenza del Foro*, under the High Altar, (a Monastery of *Canons Regular* of the Order of St. *Augustine*) with all accustomed and becoming Ceremonies, lamented by those Kings who had been his Allies, especially by the King of *France*, who honored his memory with a most magnificent Funeral Solemnity, himself (attended by most of the Nobles and Parliament of *France*,) gracing it with his Presence at the Church of *Nostre Dame*, where after the Singing of Mass, the Bishop of *Vance* pronounced a Funeral Oration, suitable to so Royal a Subject and Occasion.

Children of JOHN IV. *of the Name, King of* PORTUGAL, *and of Queen* LUCIA *his Wife.*

18. THEODOSIUS Prince of PORTUGAL, eldest Son of King *John IV.* was born at *Villa-viciosa*, the Eighth day of *February*, in the Year of our Salvation, *One thousand six hundred and thirty four.* After the Duke his Father came to the Crown, the Ceremony of his Installation was performed, when the Nobles and Grandees took an Oath to receive him for their Natural Prince, as Son, Heir and Successor to their Lord the King; but he lived not to give *Portugal* a King of his Name, deceasing in the life-time of his Father, in the Month of *June*, A° *One thousand six hundred and fifty three*, and was interred in the Monastery of *Bethleem*.

His Birth. 1634.

His death. 1653.

ALPHON-

18. **ALPHONSO** second Son of King *John*, was after the Death of his Brother *Theodosius*, also Prince OF PORTUGAL; The City of *Lisbonne* gave him Birth, where he now wears the Royal Diadem of his Father. His Birth. August 21. 1643.

18. **PETER** Infant OF PORTUGAL, third Son, born at *Lisbonne* in the Year of Christ, *One thousand six hundred forty and eight*, is now living, *Anno* 1662.

18. **JANE** Infanta OF PORTUGAL, came into this World at *Villaviciosa* the Eighteenth day of *September*, in the Year of our Lord, *One thousand six hundred thirty and six*: She dyed young, and was inhumed at *Belleil*.

18. **KATHERINE** Infanta OF PORTUGAL, Queen of GREAT BRITAIN, FRANCE and IRELAND, only Daughter (now living) of King *John IV*, took her first breath at *Villa-viciosa*, upon the Five and twentieth day of *November*, being St. *Katharines* day, in the year of our Redemption, *One thousand six hundred thirty and eight*. The Treaties and Articles of this Marriage were concluded in *England* with the Count *Don Francisco de Melo* Ambassador for the King of *Portugal*, who departed hence with the Ratification of the said Treaty of Marriage: Upon his Arrival, I need not acquaint you with what Joy this News affected the King, Queen, Mother, and the whole Court; nor their most Solemn Demonstration thereof, by discharging of their Cannon, making of Bonefires, and other Entertainments; yet were the People unwilling to think of Parting with this their Pious Princess, for whose sake (they were wont to say) *God had given them so Signal and Frequent Victories over their Enemies*.

Not long after, by an Express from *England* from the King to Her, the Infanta KATHERINE was Complemented with the stile of Queen of GREAT BRITAIN; and then, with what possible Speed could be made, was expected for *England*, all things being prepared in a readiness for so great a Princess, and so long a Voyage: Then upon the Thirteenth day of *April*, this present year, *One thousand six hundred threescore and two*, She passed with the King Her Brother, the Queen-Mother, *Don Pedro*, and the whole Court, unto the side of the River *Tagus*, through several Triumphal Arches, and a sumptuous Gallery built upon that Occasion, where Her MAJESTY was received by the Earle of *Sandwich*, who conducted Her on Board a stately *Brigandine*, whence amidst many Tire and Vollies of Cannon, and many more farewel Acclamations in the same Princely Company and Equipage, Her MAJESTY came aboard the ROYAL CHARLES, and was welcomed with the Thunder of the whole Navy.

In the Evening, after a Princely Collation, and many passionate parting Expressions, a Gun from the Admiral gave the Signal of Her MAJESTIES Resolution to depart, when all hands were set on work to weigh Anchor, and let flie their Sails.

The King and Queen-Mother, and their Train, took their Farewel with hearts equally composed of Grief and Joy, and Re-imbarqued for *Lisbon*, returning with the discharge of all the Ordnance; and so immediately with a fair leading Gale, the whole Fleet began their Course, being, as they passed out of the River, saluted by all the Block-houses, Forts and Castles. That Night, and part of the next Day, the Wind stood very propitious; but afterwards proved averse and stormy, so that they were forced to labour to and fro with contrary Winds, it being the Six and twentieth of *April* when they got into the middle of the Bay of *Biscay*. Her MAJESTY, by the continual working and tossing of the Sea, having been sick the most part of the Voyage. About the Fifth of *May*, with unwearied labour

bour and skill, the whole Fleet reached the Iſlands of *Scilly*. Her Arrival had been every day expected a Fortnight before, which cauſed the King to ſend down the Duke of *York*, Lord High Admiral, to attend Her upon the Coaſt, and to Compleſment Her MAJESTY in His Name, whereupon His Highneſs haſted to *Portſmouth*, and on the Tenth of *May*, attended by the Duke of *Ormond*, the Earls of *Suffolk* and *Cheſterfield*, the Lord *Berkley*, and other Perſons of Quality, went aboard the ſtately *YAUGH*, to Coaſt about to meet Her MAJESTY. On *Sunday* morning about Ten of the Clock, they diſcovered the *ROYAL JAMES*; but there was ſo great a Calm, they could not reach the *ROYAL CHARLES* till Six at Evening. The Earl of *Sandwich* having diſcovered His Highneſs *YAUGH*, went out in his Barge to meet Him, the Royal Banner being all the while vailed till He was aboard; when His Highneſs came into the Ship, the Souldiers gave Three ſeveral Shouts, and all the Guns in the *ROYAL CHARLES* (which from the Queens entrance till that time had been ſilent) proclaimed His Welcome; after which, the ſeveral Ships of the Fleet paid Him their Salutes. The Thirteenth of *May* at night, the Royal Fleet came to St. *Helens* Point, the moſt Eaſtern Promontory of the Iſle of *Wight*; and on *Wedneſday* the Fourteenth of *May*, the Queen landed at *Portſmouth* about Four of the Clock in the Afternoon, where She was received by the Nobility, Gentry, and multitudes of *Londoners*; as alſo by the Mayor and Aldermen of that Corporation with all the Expreſſions of Joy.

His MAJESTY having received the Expreſs of His Queens landing, prepared to be gone forthwith to Salute Her upon Her Arrival: But His great Affairs of State, and Bills by Him to be Ratified into Acts of Parliament, which were not fully ready for His Royal Aſſent, delayed him till *Monday* the Nineteenth of *May* (having ſent before Him the Biſhop of *London*, who departed the Seventeenth, in order to the Solemnizing of the Marriage) when He took Coach from the Houſe of Lords at Nine of the Clock in the Evening with His ordinary Guards, and lodged that night at *Gilford*; the next day His MAJESTY poſted with the ſame ſpeed to *Portſmouth*, where He arrived about Noon.

The Queens indiſpoſition which yet held Her in Her Chamber, cauſed the King to ſatiſfie Himſelf only with a Viſit in private that day: Yet it pleaſed God to reſtore Her Majeſty to ſuch a degree of health, that ſhe was ſoon after able to go abroad to conſummate the Marriage-Rites, which were there performed upon *Wedneſday* the 21. of *May*, by *Gilbert* Lord Biſhop of *London*; which being concluded, His Majeſty Bedded His moſt Princely Lady in His Town of *Portſmouth*. The next Week their Majeſties removed to *Wincheſter*, thence to *Farnham*, and then to *Hampton* Court, where They ſpent moſt part of this Summer; as well for the Healthfulneſs, as Majeſty of the Place.

Then on *Saturday* the 23. of *Auguſt*, (being the Eve of St. *Bartholomew*, a Day Remarkable for its Beauty, being the Faireſt of Ten that either came before, or followed it,) after Dinner, the King and Queen took Barge in order to Their entertainment by the City of *London* upon the River of *Thames*, and came to *Putney* about Four of the Clock in the Evening, where They changed Their ſpare Barge, and were by the Lord Chamberlain conducted on Board that Barge which was prepared to bring Them to *Whitehall*, in which They were placed under a Canopy of Cloth of Gold, adorned with Five Plumes of White and Yellow Oſtrich-Feathers; the Barge lined alſo with Cloth of Gold, and Cuſſions of the ſame, the two Gondeloes went on either ſide, before, in which were His Majeſties Trumpets which ſounded continually. At *Chelſey* Their Majeſties were met by the Lord Mayor and Aldermen in their Barge, afterwards by all the Companies in their Barges with loud Muſick, all adorned with their ſeveral Banners and Pennons of Arms: I cannot ſpend time to particularize the ſeveral Pageants and

Re-

Representations of the *Mercers, Drapers, Merchant-Taylors, Goldsmiths*, &c. being neither possible, nor proper for this place; therefore I shall only say (which none but the absent will deny) That the oldest person alive never saw the *Thames* more fully, nor more Nobly covered. Amid'st a Throng of a Thousand Boats, aud more than Ten thousand joyful Subjects, Their Majesties landed at *Whitehall* about 7. of the Clock in the Evening, where the most Excellent Princess the Queen Mother, and the Dutchess of *York*, gave Her Majesty Her Welcome; which was seconded by a Tere of Artillary Planted at *Stangate-Wharf* over against *Whitehall* for that purpose; the same Night, afterwards being made an Artificial Day, by the Number of Bone-fires and Fire-works.

I omit to fix a Character upon the Goodness and Beauty of this our Royal Queen, as deserving a larger Room, and an abler Pen, or to speak of that Portion, store of Money and Jewels, as great as ever any Princess brought a Husband, because I will not presume to meddle with those sublime particulars. As also of those Advantages that the English Merchant receives by the Trade of both the *Indies* where the *Portugueses* over-rule the Dutch; and by the commodious situation of *Tangier* for the checking and curbing the Insolencies of the Pirates of *Algier*, *Tunis*, and *Tripoli*, if at any time they break their League with *England*, it being a place situate upon the mouth of the Streight of *Gibraltar*; so that no Ship can pass that Streight, without Licence first had from the King of Great *Britain*, who upon this Account Commands the whole Trade of the Levant.

May we long enjoy Their Majesties with the Blessings we have received with Them, and from Them a continued Line of Great *Britains* Kings, that we may not want a Soveraign to Reign over us, who derives his Goodness, as well as Greatness, from this our Soveraign Pair.

18. ALPHONSO

18. ALPHONSO VI.

Of the Name, KING of PORTUGAL, *Algarvia, Affrick, Arabia, Persia, India,* and *Brasil,* &c.

CHAP. XXII.

PORTUGAL

D'argent a cinq Escussons en Croix chacun charge de cinq besans aussi d'argent posez en sautoir, a la Bordure de gueulles charge de sept Chasteaux d'or, trois en chef doux en fase & deux en point.

Ing *John* the Fourth being thus deceased, his elder surviving Son ALPHONSO the Sixth of that Name succeeded, being about the Age of Fourteen years, his Mother during his minority administring the affairs of the Kingdom, and causing him to be Crowned on the Fourteenth of *November*, Eight dayes after the death of his Father.

The whole Kingdom of *Portugal* was in a kind of amaze at the so sudden death of Kng *John*, especially considering the youth of their present King, fearing lest their common Enemies should now take advantage of them: but the prudent management of the most important business of State by the Queen Regent, soon banished all those fancied fears.

The Queen being sensible, that upon this occasion of the Kings death, she should have most occasion to use the Souldiery, by the Advice of her Council, Ordered all the Infantry of the Kingdom should have Half a years pay, the better to encourage them, who were of themselves ready enough to fight against their common and inveterate Enemy, the *Castillians*.

And because she knew that the King of *Spain* would lose no opportunity to oppress the Kingdom of *Portugal*, she thought it imprudence to let any slip where an advantage might be gained upon him, and therefore all the Spanish Forces being drawn out of *Andaluzia* to oppose the English, in case they should attempt to land

at

at *Cadiz*, (for they then blocked up that Port with a Potent Fleet,) she commanded Four thousand Horse to make an in-road into that Countrey, who plundered, and laid waste all before them, bringing away between Forty and fifty thousand head of Cattel, and leaving the whole Soil in a manner desolate.

This so exasperated the *Spaniards*, That draining most of the Garisons of his Kingdon, he raised a Potent Army, and with Ten thousand Foot, and Five thousand Horse entred *Portugal*, and laid Siege to the strong City of *Olivenza*, which at length they reduced to that necessity, that the Defendants were willing to Capitulate, and sounded a Parlie, but when they came to treat, the *Spaniards* would not admit the King of *Portugal* any other Title, than that of Duke of *Braganza*, which made the *Portugals* renounce any farther treating.

But at length the *Spaniards* condescending to treat, the Town was delivered upon Articles; but so much did the Queen-Regent and Council of *Portugal* resent it, that they immediately gave Order to Arrest the Person of Don *Mandiol de Saldagna* the Governour, who (with several of his chief Officers,) was by the Count *de St. Lorenze*, General of the *Portuguesse* Forces in those parts, sent Prisoners to *Lisbon*, there to answer their ill-defending of that Town, it appearing, That at the surrendring of it, there marched out Two thousand two hundred well Armed Foot, and One hundred Horse; nor were they reduced to that necessity that was pretended, there remaining in the Stores of Ammunition and Provision, sufficient to have defended the Town a great while longer.

The loss of this Place was a great blow to the *Portuguesses*, it being a strong Frontier Town, and giving the *Spaniard* absolute Command a great way into the Countrey; but this the King of *Spain* resolved should be but a beginning of his Conquest (if possible) of this Kingdom, for he still made all preparations he could to assault it with a greater force, and not only endeavoured this with might and main to oppress it himself, but by his Ambassadors solicited the States General of the United Provinces to send their Vice-Admiral *Opdam*, with the Fleet he then had before *Dantzick*, into *Portugal*, to demand satisfaction for the damage the *Portugals* had done to their *West-India* Company in *Brazil*, and in case the King of *Portugal* should deny to comply with their desires, to force them to a Composition.

The High and Mighty States easily listned to this counsel, and Vice-Admiral *Opdam* with a Potent Fleet was sent to *Lisbon*, carrying with him some Commissioners from the States to make their demands, which the Queen Regent and Council thought so unreasonable, that they could not return any satisfactory answer to them, whereupon the Commissioners departed: But *Opdam* still stayed with his Fleet to wait an opportunity of catching the *Brazil* Fleet in their return home, many of which notwithstanding the care and endeavors of the *Portuguesses* to prevent it, he made prize of, and sent into *Holland*.

By this means was the War, which for many years had been maintained between the *Hollanders* and *Portugals* on the other side the Line, transferred to this side, which the King of *France* endeavoured by all means possible, before its eruption to prevent, and afterwards to compose by his Ambassadours, *Monsieur de Thou* in *Holland*, and the *Sieur de Comings* in *Portugal*, but to no Effect.

Thus assaulted by two potent Nations, both by Sea and by Land were the *Portuguesses*, which yet made them not at all falter in their Courage and Resolution; the generous Queen-Regent causing all possible Levies to be made to oppose the *Castillian*, sending into *Barbary* to buy Horses, and by Leagues abroad endeavouring to strengthen the Interest of the Kingdom, an Ambassadour was sent to that purpose into *England*, to renew and confirm the Amity before concluded on, and many Conferences there were between the Archbishop of *Goa*, who had before been Ambassadour in *France*, and the *Sieur de Comings*; so that many were in hopes that the Match between

'tween the King of *France*, and the *Infanta*, would have gone forward, and an indissoluble League both defensive and offensive, been concluded between the two Nations.

And to join Force to Policy, a gallant Army of about Sixteen thousand Foot, and Three thousand Horse, all *Portugueses*, took the Field, and in Revenge for the loss of *Olivenza*, laid siege to *Mouron*, which in Three or four dayes they took by storm, putting Fifteen hundred *Spaniards* to the Sword, and resolved to proceed to the regaining of *Badajox* and *Olivenza*; and to that purpose marching without opposition by *Caya* (which they left fortified) they came to the Fort of St. *Christopher*, the strongest hold of the City of *Badayox*, which they several dayes battered, and thrice stormed, but were beaten off; yet at the length they took it, and so securely entrenched themselves about the whole City.

The Duke of *Ossima*, General of the *Castillian* Horse, having notice of this strait siege of the City, endeavoured with Sixteen hundred Horse to cut off their Convoyes and Provisions; but the *Count del Prado*, Governour of *Elvas*, receiving Advice of his Design, sallied out of the City with Three Companies of Horse, and all the Foot he had to prevent him, by which means *Ossima* was encompassed on both sides; for at the same time that he was on the other part charged by *Don Andrea D' Albuquerque*, General of the *Portuguesse* Horse, and that with so much Gallantry, that they presently discomfited their Enemies, slew Four hundred upon the place, took Three hundred Prisoners, and forced the Duke of *Ossima* to save himself by swimming.

This happy Success encouraged them to return with more Alacrity to the siege, which they prosecuted with all vigour possible, and on the Three and twentieth of *June* stormed, and took a Redoubt which was palisadosed; but at length when they had spent much time, blood, and treasure, they were enforced by the powerful Army of *Don Lewis de Haro* to raise their siege.

For the King of *Spain* exasperated with the loss of *Mouron*, and fearing likewise to lose *Badayox*, had Rallied a great Army, which he committed to the Care of his Favourite *Don Lewis de Haro*, who not only with it raised the siege from before *Badayox*, but likewise so straitly besieged *Elvas*, one of the *Portugueses* strongest Frontier-towns, the taking of which, might have endangered the whole Kingdom, and reduced it to such Necessity, that it was even upon the point of yielding.

But the *Portugals*, who knew of how much importance it was to them, had ever been anxious for its Relief, and therefore having at length bravely recruited their Army, they advanced with full Resolution to drive the *Spaniards* out of their Trenches, nor did they effect it less bravely than they had resolved it; for they totally Routed their General, *Don Lewis de Haro* very hardly escaping; but in this Battel the *Portuguez* lost the worthy *Albuquerque* General of the Horse.

And to Counterpoise this Victory, the strong Fortress of *Mounson* upon the Borders of *Gallicia*, was surrendred to the *Spaniards*, and a Party of the *Portugals* not having Advice that it was already possessed by the *Castillians*, going to relieve it, were surprized, and forced shamefully to retreat with the loss of some hundreds, and this Success encouraged the *Spaniards* under the Command of the Marquess of *Viana*, to besiege the only City the *Portugals* were possest of 'on the River *Minho*, but it was relieved by the *Portugals*. The *Spaniards* likewise gained a signal Victory over a Party of *Portugal* Horse nigh *Alcantara*; for Advice being brought to the Governour of that Town, That the *Portuguez* with a Party of Four hundred Horse were entring upon the Frontiers in two Bodies; he taking Five hundred Horse, and a select Party of Foot, went to meet them, and so handsomly managed his Business, that he surprized one whole Body, scarce a man escaping a Commissary General, five Captains, and several other Officers being taken Prisoners.

But

But these things were inconsiderable Disadvantages to the interest of *Portugal*, in respect of what it was like to feel by the Peace which was treating of between those two mighty Monarchs of *France* and *Spain*, which the Queen-Regent and Council were sensible of, and therefore dispatch *Don John D' Acosta* Ambassadour Extraordinary to the *French* Court, to represent unto his most Christian Majesty the state of the Kingdom of *Portugal*, and to insist that there might be a due Consideration had of the Interest of his Master in the concluding of the Peace with *Spain*, seeing he had formerly approved himself so good an Ally to the Crown of *France*. But this Embassie could produce no other Effect, than a promise to endeavour a Mediation for them with the King of *Spain* and procure them good terms upon Submission, which by the Magnanimous *Portugueses* was rejected with Indignation.

Nor were they at all Daunted with the great Power of the *Spaniard*, which he intended to employ against them, but Manfully resolved to endure all Hazards; yet would they willingly have concluded a Peace with the *Hollanders*; and to that purpose, *Don Fernando Tellez de Faro*, Duke of *Aveiro*, was sent Ambassadour to the *States-General*; but he like a treacherous Villain, revolted from them to the King of *Spain*, carrying along with him the papers of his Ambassie; for which, according to his Desert, his Effigies was executed at *Lisbon* as a Traytors, his Goods confiscated, his House razed to the ground, and his Children banished, and degraded of Nobility, his Brother, *Don Deigo De Sylva*, who had served the King of *Portugal* in the quality of General at Sea, was likewise upon this Occasion commanded to retire to one of his Houses, and deprived of all publick Employment.

After him was sent *Don Henry de Sousa* Count of *Miranda*, to negotiate an Accomodation with the Netherland States, yet he prevailed little; for the pertinacious *Hollanders* were still resolute in their unreasonable demands, computing their losses in *Brazil* (where they had no right to be) to amount to no less than thirty millions.

The *Spaniards* in the mean time were forced to give the *Portugals* some respite in the summer, *One thousand six hundred and fifty nine*, but preparations were made to assault them; with the whole power of that Monarchy in the Spring, *One thousand six hundred and sixty*, *Don John D' Austria* being called out of *Flanders* to be Generalissimo of the Spanish Forces, and having Orders given him in *April*, *One thousand six hundred and sixty*, to march directly to *Merida*, on the Frontiers of *Portugal*, though he went not that Summer.

But the *Portugueses* resolved not to be behind-hand with their Enemies, and therefore made several in-roads into the Spanish Territories, depopulating all before them, which made the *Spaniards* to be revenged, resolve to do the like to them; Order was therefore given to fall into the Kingdom on all sides, the Marquess of *Viana* Governor of *Gallicis*, marching in that way with Eight thousand Foot, and eight hundred Horse, and the Governor of *Camara* invading that part which was adjacent to his government.

In this condition was the Kingdom of *Portugal*, when His Majesty *Charles* the Second, King of *England*, was restored to his Crowns and Kingdoms, welcomed by his Subjects with all gratulatory and submissive Obedience; the News of which was no sooner by advice from *D. Francisco de Melo*, Ambassador for the King of *Portugal* in *England*, conveyed to the ears of his Master, but he caused all the Guns of the Town, Castle, and Ships in the Road, to be fired, and for three days and nights kept solemn and magnificent Rejoycings; the *Portuguess* Nation as well as by this their joy at the Restoration of King *Charles* the Second, as by their sorrow and general mourning at the Death of King *Charles* the First, expressing their great affection for the English Nation.

But because their joy should be somewhat for their own, as well as our sakes, there at the same time arrived News at *Lisbon*, that Don *Alphonso Turtudo* General of the Horse, on the frontiers of *Alentejo*, meeting with a Brigade of the Enemies Horse nigh to *Bajadox*, had fought and defeated them, killed and took four hundred of them, amongst whom were four Captains of Horse prisoners.

The *Spaniards* still continued their Leavies against *Portugal*, being resolved to employ an Army of four thousand Horse and twelve thousand Foot constantly recruited, about the Frontiers of *Estramadura*, and another of three thousand Horse, and ten thousand Foot about *Gallicia*, and a third of twelve thousand men, to serve as a Reserve to the two former. In this manner were they resolved to assault them by Land, while the Prince of *Montesarchio* with ten men of War, was appointed to coast up and down before their Ports, and do them what mischief he could by Sea.

Thus did this Kingdom struggle with *Spain* for her Liberty, by the prudent management of Affairs, by that sage and industrious Queen-Regent, until this present year, *One thousand six hundred threescore and two*; when upon the Ninteenth of *August* the *Castillian* Army marched towards the Towns of *Barbeisus* and *Chosas*; whereupon the General of the said Province the Earle of *Prado*, and the Earle of St. *John* General of the Horse, with all the Force they could make, did set forth to oppose the Enemy, who being surprized by the Care of the said General, did engage, with the Approbation of the chief Commander *Don Balthasar Pontaju*, who immediately commanded them to fall on; but the Earle of *Prado* did as well receive them, he desiring nothing else but to shew the *Castillians* how little they did value them. The Fight began with a great deal of Resolution on the Enemies side, who for many houres hotly disputed the Quarrel, till wearied by the unwearied Courage of the *Portuguesses*, their whole Army was forced to flie in great Disorder. A considerable number of the Enemies were slain, and many taken Prisoners, by which the said Province was freed from the Enemy, with great Satisfaction to the Crown, and great Honour to the Count of *Prado*, whose Prudence and Valour in the management of this Business was much commended.

In the Province of *Beira* no less Success smiled upon the *Portuguesses*, by the Count of *Villaflor* Governour thereof, and the General of the Horse *Manuel Treire D' Andrada*, who having intelligence that the Duke of *Ossuna* had made himself Master of *Escalas*, and raised a considerable Fort upon it with several Guns, and placed Four hundred men to defend it, went out, and giving Battel to the Duke, put him to Flight, killing about Six hundred men, and taking the greatest part of his Baggage, with all his Ordnance; and then falling upon the said Fort, in few houres took it (at mercy) to the astonishment of the *Castillians*, who fully perceived that they were not able to Act any thing against the same Provinces, being so nobly defended by the same Governour, and the People so unanimous to oppose them.

Nor had the *Castillians* gained those Advantages in *Alentejo*, had it not been for the Civil Dissentions and Animosities amoug the *Portugal* Colonels, which since have been sufficiently provided against by the Care of the Ministers of State, and especially by the Prudence of *Don Antonio De Sousa* of *Macedo*, now principal Secretary of State, heretofore Resident from the King of *Portugal* in *England*.

If that the *Portuguesses* have thus long, and so valiantly defended themselves by their own proper Valour, without a Forreign Assistance, against so potent a Monarch as the King of *Spain*, then how much more now will they be able, since they have renewed the old League with *England*, whose Forces being united, may defie all those that shall oppose them, both Kingdoms being most formidable at Sea, and Masters of a potent Army.

Nor was the King of *Great Britain* unmindful of returning the King of *Portugal* an Acknowledgment for the Happiness His Majesty received from Him, in the Person of His Sister, that Royal Lady the Princess KATHERINE, when He sent Supplies into that

that Kingdom under the Command of that Valiant Lord the Earle of *Inchequeen*; almost as soon as His Majesty had the Assurance of receiving His Beautiful Queen into His own Arms, such was His MAJESTIES Care of the Welfare of that Monarchy, the Knot of a perpetual Alliance being now so firmly tied, That maugre all the Opposition of the most malignant Opposers, They are resolved to link their Concerns together ever hereafter.

Since the Arrival of the *English* Forces in *Portugal*, there hath been little Action, they having been disposed of into Three several Squadrons; so that now in *September* last, the Generals all returned to *Lisbon* to refresh themselves; there being no further Occasion for the Field. *Don John*'s Army had Orders sent them not to march, and the other Two, since the late Defeats given them, have been in no Capacity of doing the least Injury, *Portugal* being now free from the Noise of the *Castillians*, both by Sea and Land. *Don John* was lately at *Badayos*, (having for a while laid all thoughts of farther Action aside) where he mustered all the Forces, and drew them into their Winter-quarters. In the mean time, the King of *Spain* sent Orders to several Places to make great preparation against the next Spring; so that marching in with more Force, they may give a better Account than they have of this years Expedition.

King ALPHONSO VI. entring now upon the Twentieth year of His Age, lately took the Reins of the Government into His own Hand, and hath sate for the Administration of Justice in Criminal Causes, where a Judge, and Secretary of the Court of Orphans, were brought before Him, and Accused for having dealt unjustly in the managery of their Trust. His MAJESTY was pleased with much Patience to attend the whole Tryal, where it being fully proved, That according to the Charge exhibited against them, they had wronged several Orphans, and dealt unjustly in the Disposal of their Goods; Sentence was pronounced upon them both, the Judge to be beheaded, and the Secretary to be hanged. I mention this, only to let the Reader know how much this Action of the Kings hath encreased the Esteem and Affection which His MAJESTIES Subjects had for Him; That at His first sitting in the Administration of Justice, He should so far encourage the Causes of His weaker People, as not to spare Offenders, though of the greatest Quality; but to see Sentence of Condemnation passed against those that injure them.

Thus have you an Account of the Lives and Issues of the KINGS of PORTUGAL, from the Foundation of that Monarchy, to the Sixth year of the Reign of KING ALPHONSO VI. being this present year, 1662. leaving that KINGDOM in an assured Confidence, That ENGLAND will prove (as it hath ever been) a better Bulwark to them, than any other their Confederates.

AN ALPHABETICAL TABLE,

Containing the Principal NAMES in this HISTORY.

A.

ALPHONSO I. *King of Portugal.* Chap. II.
ALPHONSO II. *King of Portugal.* IV.
ALPHONSO III. *King of Portugal.* VI.
ALPHONSO IV. *King of Portugal.* VIII.
ALPHONSO V. *King of Portugal.* XIII.
ANTHONY *Prior of Crato, proclaimed King of Portugal.* XIX.
ALPHONSO VI. *King of Portugal.* XXII.

Alphonso of Portugal, Knight of the Order of St. John of Jerusalem. Pag. 8
Alphonso of Portugal, Lord of Portalegre. 23
Alphonso of Portugal, Seigneur of Leiria. ibid.
Alphonso of Portugal. 30
Alphonso of Portugal dyed young. 30
Aremburga Countess of Urgel. 13
Adolphe of Cleves, Seigneur of Ravenstein. 43
Alphonso Prince of Portugal. 59
Alphonso Cardinal of Portugal. 66
Anthony of Portugal. 69
Alphonso Prince of Portugal. 73
Anthony of Portugal. 74

Alphonso-Dionysio B. of Portugal 24
Alphonso-Sancto B. of Portugal, Count of Albuquerque. 28
Alphonso B. of Portugal. 33
Alphonso de Cascaes, B. of Portugal. ibid.
Alphonso B. of Portugal, Duke of Braganza. 45
Alphonso B. of Portugal, Duke of Visco. 49

B.

Blanche *of Portugal, Lady of Guadaliara.* pag. 14
Berengaria of Portugal. ibid.
Beatrice of Castille, Queen of Portugal. 21
Beatrix of Castille, Queen of Portugal. 30
Beatrix of Portugal, Queen of Castille. 31
Beatrice of Portugal, Lady of Ravenstein. 43
Beatrice of Portugal, Dutchess of Visco. 44
Blanche of Portugal, died young. 45
Beatrice of Portugal, Dutchess of Visco. 47
Blanche of Portugal, Abbess of Loruano. 23
Beatrix of Portugal, Dutchess of Savoy. 69
Beatrix of Portugal. ibid.

Beatrix B. of Portugal. 34
Beatrice B. of Portugal, Countess of Arundel. 45

C.

Constance *of Portugal, Wife of Gonçalo-Nunez De Lara.* pag. 23
Constance of Portugal. ibid.
Constance of Portugal, Queen of Castille. 27
Constance Manuel, Queen of Portugal. 32
Charlote of Cyprus, Dutchess of Conimbra. 42
Charles of Portugal. 70
Christopher of Portugal. 89

Constance B. of Portugal. 15
Constance B. of Castille. 33

D.

Alphabetical TABLE.

G.

Gilles-Sancto B. of Portugal. pag. 15
Gilles-Alphonso B. of Portugal. 24
George B. of Portugal, Duke of Conimbra. 59

H.

HENRY of Bourgongne Count of Portugal. Chap. I.
HENRY the Cardinal King of Portugal. XVIII.

Henry Prince of Portugal. pag. 8
Henry of Portugal. 13
Henry of Portugal, Duke of Visco. 43

I.

JOHN I. King of Portugal. Chap. XI.
JOHN II. King of Portugal. XIV.
JOHN III. King of Portugal. XVI.
JOHN IV. King of Portugal. XXI.

Jane Countess of Flanders. pag. 11
Isabel of Portugal, Lady of Biscay. 23
Isabel of Portugal, Lady of Albuquerque. ibid.
Isabel of Arragon, Queen of Portugal. 26
John of Portugal. 30
Isabel of Arragon, Dutchess of Conimbra. 41
John of Portugal, Duke of Conimbra. 42
James of Portugal, Cardinal and Archbishop of Lisbon. ibid.
Isabel D' Avalos. 33
Isabel of Conimbra, Queen of Portugal. 42
John of Portugal, Grand Master of the Order of St. James. 44
Isabel of Braganza. ibid.
James of Portugal. ibid.
Isabel of Portugal, Queen of Castille. ibid.
Isabel of Portugal, Dutchess of Bourgongne. 45
John of Portugal, Duke of Visco. 48
James of Portugal, Duke of Visco. ibid.
Isabel of Visco, Dutchess of Braganza. 49
Jane of Portugal, Queen of Castille. 50
John Prince of Portugal, died young. 55
Jane of Portugal, a Nun at Odivelles. ibid.
Isabel of Castille, Queen of Portugal. 64
Isabel of Braganza, Princess of Portugal. 67
John Prince of Portugal. 73
Joane of Austria. ibid.
Isabel of Portugal. 74
Jane Infanta of Portugal. 133
John-Alphonso B. of Portugal. 18
John B. of Portugal. 33
Isabel B. of Portugal, Countess of Gigion. 36

John

An Alphabetical TABLE.

John-Emanuel B. of Portugal, Bishop of Septe. 51

K.

KATHERINE Queen of GREAT Britain. pag. 133
Katherine of Portugal, died young. 49
Katherine of Portugal. 59
Katherine of Portugal, Dutchess of Braganza. 68

L.

LEonor of Portugal, Princess of Denmark. pag. 17.
Leonor of Portugal, Queen of Denmark. ibid.
Leonora of Portugal, Queen of Arragon. 30
Leonora Tellez, Queen of Portugal. 35
Leonora of Visco, Queen of Portugal. 49
Leonora of Portugal the Empress. 50
Leonora of Visco, Queen of Portugal. 58
Leonor of Austria, Queen of Portugal. 65
Lewis of Portugal, Duke of Beia. ibid.
Lucia Queen of Portugal. 132

Leonor B. of Portugal, Wife of Garsia de Souza. 24

M.

MAud of Savoy, Queen of Portugal. pag. 7
Mary of Flanders. 12
Maud of Portugal, Queen of Castille. 14
Maud of Dam-Martin, Countess of Bolongne. 20
Mary of Portugal, Lady of Molina. 23
Mary of Portugal, Queen of Castille and Leon. 30
Mary of Portugal, Lady Marquess of Tortosa. 32
Mary Tellez. 33
Martin Vasquez de Cunha. ibid.
Mary of Castille, Queen of Portugal. 65
Michael Prince of Portugal. ibid.
Mary of Portugal, Princess of Parma. 67
Mary of Portugal. 70
Mary of Portugal. ibid.
Mary of Portugal, Princess of Spain. 74

Martin B. of Portugal, Count of Tristemare. 15
Martin-Alphonso Chicorro B. of Portugal. 24
Mary B. of Portugal. 33
Mary B. of Portugal, Wife of Peter Minho. ibid.
Mary B. of Portugal, Lady Marquess of Villereal. 49

P.

PETER King of Portugal. Chap. IX.
PHILIP II, III, IV. Kings of Spain,
19, 20, 21. Kings of Portugal. XX.

Peter of Portugal, King of Majorca. pag. 13

Philippa of Lancaster, Queen of Portugal. 39
Peter of Portugal, Duke of Corimbra. 40
Peter of Portugal, elected King of Arragon. 41
Philippa of Portugal, a Nun at Odivelles. 42
Philippa of Portugal, never married. 44
Philip Duke of Bourgongue. 45
Peter De Norogna. 36
Philip of Portugal. 49
Philip of Portugal. 71
Peter Infant of Portugal. 133

Peter B. of Portugal. 4
Peter B. of Portugal, Count of Barcellos. 28
Peter B of Portugal, Seigneur De Guerra. 33

R.

ROdrick of Portugal. pag. 15

S.

SANCEO I. King of Portugal. Chap. III.
SANCEO II. King of Portugal. V.
SEBASTIAN King of Portugal. XVII.

Sibille of Flanders, Lady of Beaujeu. pag. 12
Sance of Portugal, Abbess of Lornano. 14
Sance Fernandine De Lara, Lady of Serpe. 17
Sance-Mentie-Lopez De Haro, Queen of Portugal. 19
Sanceo of Castille. 34

T.

TEresa of Castille, Queen of Portugal. pag. 3
Teresa, otherwise called Sance of Portugal. 4
Teresa of Portugal, Countess of Flanders. 8
Teresa of Portugal, Wife of Sanceo-Nunez. 9
Teresa of Portugal, Queen of Leon. 13
Theodosius Prince of Portugal. 132

Teresa-Sancez B. of Portugal. 15

U.

URacca of Portugal, Countess of Trastemare. pag. 4.
Uracca of Portugal, Queen of Leon. 8
Uracca of Castille, Queen of Portugal. 17
Vincent of Portugal. ibid.
Valdemar II. of that Name, King of Denmark, ib.

Uracca B. of Portugal. 15

Y.

YOland of Castille, Lady of Portalegre. pag. 23

FINIS.

THE SECOND BOOK OF THE ROYAL HOUSE OF PORTUGAL,

CONTAINING THE GENEALOGIES

OF THE

Dukes of BRAGANZA and BARCELLOS.

Counts of LEMOS, and Dukes of TAURISANO.

Marquesses of FERREIRA, and Counts of TENTUGAL.

Counts of GELVES, and Dukes of VERAGUA.

Counts of FARO, and of MIRA.

Counts of VIMIOSO.

Dukes of AVEIRO.

Counts of VILLAR.

THE TABLE OF THE SECOND BOOK.

8. PETER King of Portugal.

9. JOHN first of the name, King of Portugal. — DENYS Bastard of Portugal, Lord of Cifuentes.

10. EDWARD King of Portugal. — ALPHONSO B. of Portugal, Duke of Braganza. — FERDINAND of Portugal.

11. ALPHONSO V. of the name, King of Portugal. — ALPHONSO C. of Ourem. — *FERDINAND I. of the name, D. of Braganza. — DENIS Lord of Torres.

12. JOHN II. of the name, King of Portugal. — ALPHONSO of Portugal. — FERDINAND Lord of Villar.

13. GEORGE B. of Portugal, Duke of Conimbra. — FRANCIS B. of Portugal, Count of Vimioso. — BERNARDIN Lord of Villar.

14. JOHN D. of Aueiro. — ALPHONSO. — ALPHONSO I. of the name, Count of Vimioso. — FERDINAND Count of Villar.

15. GEORGE D. of Aueiro. — ALVARO D. of Aueiro. — FRANCIS II. C. de Vimioso. — LEWIS C. de Vimioso. — BERNARDIN de Torres & de Port.

16. JULIAN Dutchess of Aueiro. — GEORGE D. de Tours neufues. — ALPHONSO II. C. de Vimioso, and Marquess of Aguiar. — JOHN de Torres, & de Portugal, Count de Villar.

17. LEWIS II. Count of Vimioso. MICHAEL C. of Vimioso.

DUKES OF BRAGANZA.

11. *FERDINAND I. of the name, Duke of Braganza, Son of Duke Alphonso.

12. FERDINAND II. Duke of Braganza. — ALVARO Seigneur of Ferreira. — ALPHONSO Count of Faro.

13. JAMES Duke of Braganza — DENIS Count of Lemos. — RODERICK Marquess of Ferreira. — GEORGE I. of the name, G. of Gelues. — SANCEO first C. of Odemira.

14. THEODOSIO I. D. of Braganza — FERDINAND I. C. of Lemos. — FRANCIS I. Marq. of Ferreira — ALVARO C. of Gelues — ALPHONSO D. of Portug.

15. JOHN Duke of Braganza. — PETER Couut of Lemos. — NUGNO ALVAREZ. — GEORGE II. Count of Gelues. — NUGNO Duke of Veragua. — SANCEO II. Count of Odemira.

16. THEODOSIO II. D. of Braganza — FERDINAND II. C. of Lemos. — FRANCIS II. Marquess of Ferreira. — LEONORA Countess of Gelues — ALVARO D. of Varagua. — ALPHONSO C. of Odemira.

17. JOHN IV. King of Portugal. — PETER II. C. of Lemos. — FRANCIS D. of Taurifano. — NUGNO II. Marquess of Ferreira, and D. of Cadaval. — PEDRO NUGNO Columb. D. of Veragua. — SANCEO III. Count of Odemira.

18. ALPHONSO VI. King of Portugal. — FRANCIS Duke of Taurifano.

DUKES OF BRAGANZA, and BARCELLOS.

10. ALPHONSO OF PORTUGAL, first Duke of BRAGANZA, and Count of BARCELLOS.

THE House of *Braganza* deriveth its Original from the Royal Family of *Portugal*, and enjoyed more fair and ample Priviledges in this Kingdom, than any other. For those of this House might justly have like Officers, and wear the same Armes as the Kings do. They had their Life-guard, and likewise Heraulds and Kings of Armes, and Power to confer Military Orders. They also held the first place and degree of honour among the Illustrious Houses of this Kingdom, as well because of their High Extraction, the Marriages they have made with several Kings, and Princes of the Blood-Royal, as also by reason of the Rich Seigneuries they have possessed for this Two hundred years. From the Chief or Source of the House, which was this ALPHONSO first Duke of *Braganza*, and Natural Son of King *John* first of the name, are descended several Branches of Dukes, Marquesses, Counts, and other Persons of Quality, which have spread not only in *Portugal*, and *Castille*, but also in *Italy*, and more particularly in the Kingdom of *Naples*; some of which have left the sirname of *Portugal*, and taken the names of those Illustrious Houses into which they have matched; which we find often practised in *Spain*.

PORTU-
GAL-BRA-
GANZA.

D'argent au sautoir de gueules chargé de cinq Escussons de Portugal; un au melieu les autres aux quatre bouts du sautoir.

ALPHONSO was first dignified with the title and quality of Count of *Barcellos*, in the right of his first Wife BEATRICE PEREIRA, she was daughter and heir of *Nugno Alvarez Pereira*, second Constable of *Portugal*, Count of *Arrayalos*, *Barcellos*, and *Ourem*. As for the Dutchy of *Braganza*, he was invested therein by the Infant *Peter* of *Portugal*, Duke of *Conimbra* his Brother; at what time he was Regent of *Portugal*, during the minority of King *Alphonso* V. their Nephew, in the Year, One thousand four hundred forty and two. Sometime after the same King *Alphonso* gave him the Seigneury of *Vimarana*.

Nonius L 9.

Mariana.

1442.

For his second Wife he espoused CONSTANCE OF NO-ROGNA, daughter of *Alphonso* of *Castille* Count of *Gijon*, and of the Coun-

Counteſs *Iſabel* of *Portugal*. But from this ſecond Marriage there came no Children.

Mariana Lib. 21. Cap. 7.

ALPHONSO is charged (by Hiſtorians) with extream ingratitude towards his Brother and Benefactor the Duke of *Conimbra*, and to have been of the number of thoſe that incited King *Alphonſo* to purſue him with Armes, unto the death, as we have informed you before.

ALPHONSO dyed in the Year, *One thouſand four hundred threeſcore and one*, and was inhumed in the great Church at *Chunes*.

His Death 1461.

Children of ALPHONSO Duke of BRAGANZA, and of BEATRICE PEREIRA his firſt Wife.

11. ALPHONSO OF PORTUGAL, Count of OUREM, and Marqueſs of VALENCE, gave original to the Counts of *Vimioſo*, whoſe Genealogy ſhall be deduced in its proper place.

11. FERDINAND OF PORTUGAL, Duke of *Braganza* after his Father, continued the Poſterity.

11. ISABEL OF PORTUGAL or *Braganza*, Eſpouſed to JOHN OF PORTUGAL, a younger Son of King *John* the firſt her Grand-father.

11. FERDINAND I. of the name, Duke of BRAGANZA, Count of ARRAYALOS, and Marqueſs of VILLA-VICIOSA.

HE was ſecond Son of *Alphonſo* of *Portugal* firſt Duke of *Braganza*, and of *Beatrice Pereira* his firſt Wife, and ſucceeded him in the Dutchy. He was alſo Count of *Arrayalos*, and Marqueſs of *Valence*, by the gift of *Alphonſo V.* and Governour of the City of *Septe* in *Affrick*. His Wife JANE DE CASTRO, was daughter and heir of *John de Caſtro* Seigneur of *Cadaval*, and of *Leonor* of *Acugna* his Wife. He received the Honour of Burial in the Church of St. *Auguſtin* at *Villa-vicioſa*, an Abbey which he had founded in that Seigneury.

Children of FERDINAND I. of the name, Duke of BRAGANZA.

12. FERDINAND II. Duke of *Braganza*, whoſe Story followeth in the next Page.

12. JOHN OF BRAGANZA, Marqueſs of *Mont-major*, was Conſtable of the Kingdom of *Portugal*; but having a hand in the Conſpiracy againſt King *John II.* forged by the Duke of *Braganza* his elder Brother, he fled

and Counts of BARCELLOS.

Years of Christ. fled into the Kingdom of *Castille*, where he dyed, without leaving any issue by his Wife ISABEL OF NOROGNA, daughter of *Peter de Norogna*, Arch-bishop of *Lisbonne*.

12. ALVARO OF PORTUGAL, hath given original to the Branch of the Marquesses of FERREIRA, which shall be spoken of in their place.

12. ALPHONSO OF PORTUGAL, Count of FARO, from whom the Counts of MIRA are issued; as you may see hereafter.

12. KATHERINE OF PORTUGAL dyed, having been affianced to JOHN COUTINHO Count of *Marialva*.

12. BEATRICE OF PORTUGAL, Wife to PETER DE MENESES Marquess of *Ville-real*.

12. GUIOMARE DE CASTRO, espoused to HENRY DE MENESES Count of *Loullé*.

12. FERDINAND II. *of the name, Duke of* BRAGANZA, *and* VIMARANA.

AMong the Children of *Ferdinand* first of the name Duke of *Braganza*, and of *Jane de Castro* his Wife, this was the eldest. In the lifetime of his Father he was established Count of *Vimarana* by the gift of King *Alphonso V.* And upon the point of his Marriage to his second Wife ISABEL OF PORTUGAL, daughter of the Infant *Ferdinand* of *Portugal*, he was created Duke of the same place of *Vimarana*.

PORTU-GAL-BRA-GANCE.

The rigorous usage of this Prince, and of other Grandees of the Kingdom, by the Officers of King *John II.* gave ground to his unhappy Conspiracies against the State, which Treason was thus discovered. For when FERDINAND caused search to be made in his Evidences for certain Charters and Priviledges, to get them confirmed, his Secretary found the Letters of Intelligence and Conspiracy, betwixt the Duke his Master, and the Kings of *Castille*, to the prejudice of the King his Soveraign; into whose hands the Secretary delivered them, in the Hope of a Recompence. For some time the King dissembled the discovery, and favourably received the Duke into his Court; but one day, having called him aside, he charged him with his fault, which the Duke would not confess, but on the contrary protested his right intention and fidelity to his service; But not ceasing to continue his Treasons, the King resolved to bring him to a Tryal; where being convicted, and condemned to lose his life, he was beheaded at

His Death. 1483.

Evora, the One and twentieth day of *June*, in the Year, One thousand four hundred fourscore and three, and his Goods were Confiscated. The Dutchess ISABEL his Widow the Queens Sister, sent her three Children into *Castille*, where they were favourably received by the Queen their Aunt. The Body of the Duke was inhumed in the Church of St. *Dominique* of the same City of *Evora*, and afterwards removed to the Convent of St. *Augustine* at *Villa-viciosa*.

Mariana Lib. 24, *cap.* 23.

Bbb   The

Dukes of BRAGANZA.

The first Wife of this Duke *Ferdinand* was LEONOR DE MENESES, daughter of *Peter de Meneses* first Count of *Ville-real*, others say of *Urana*, and of *Margaret* of *Miranda* his Wife; by her he had no Children; but he left issue by his second Wife before mentioned.

Years of Christ.

Children of FERDINAND II. Duke of BRAGANZA, and of ISABEL OF PORTUGAL, his second Wife.

13. JAMES Duke of BRAGANZA, continued the Posterity.

13. PHILIP OF BRAGANZA, was sent into *Castille* by his Mother, when that fatal stroke fell upon his Father, and there dyed without issue. Some believe him to be the eldest Son.

13. DIONYSIO OF PORTUGAL, or BRAGANZA, espoused the Countess of *Lemos*, and in her right was Earl thereof, as we shall inform you in the Deduction of his branch.

13. MARGARET dyed, not having been married.

---

13. JAMES OF PORTUGAL, Duke of BRAGANZA, and Count of BARCELLOS.

PORTU-
GAL-BRA-
GANCE.

Mariana.

Vasconcellius.

HE was eldest Son of *Ferdinand II.* Duke of *Braganza*, and of *Isabel* of *Portugal* his second Wife, and was restored to all his Estates, Honours, and Lordships, by King *Emanuel* his Uncle by the Mothers side, immediately after he came to the Crown of *Portugal*. He made him General of a Fleet, which he sent for *Affrica*, A°, One thousand five hundred and thirteen, where he reduced the City of *Azamor*, which having been tributary to the King of *Portugal*, had thrown off their Yoke; It was sacqued and pillaged by the *Portugueses*, which stroke so great a terrour into the Infidels, that they abandoned to the Christians the Towns of *Tite, Almedina*, and other neighbouring places.

1595.

1513.

This Duke JAMES espoused two Wives; his first was LEONOR DE MENDOZA, daughter of *John de Gusman* Duke of *Medina-Sidonia*, and of *Isabel de Velasco* his Wife.

His first Marriage.

Secondly, He married JANE DE MENDOZA, daughter of *Diego de Mendoza* Grand Alcaide of the City of *Mouron*, and of *Beatrice Suarez* his Wife.

His second Marriage.

Children of JAMES Duke of BRAGANZA, by LEONOR MENDOZA his first Wife.

14. THEODOSIUS OF PORTUGAL, first of the name, Duke of *Braganza*, had issue.

ISA-

and Counts of BARCELLOS.

14. ISABEL OF PORTUGAL, was conjoyned in Marriage with the Infant EDWARD OF PORTUGAL, youngest Son of King *Emanuel*, who, among other Children, had *Edward* of *Portugal* Duke of *Vimarana*, that dyed without issue.

Children of JAMES *Duke of* BRAGANZA, *and of* JANE DE MENDOZA *his second Wife.*

14. JAMES OF PORTUGAL, dyed without issue.

14. CONSTANTINE OF PORTUGAL, was Great Chamberlain to King *John III*. And by him sent Embassadour into *France*, A° 1549. One thousand five hundred forty and nine, where he stood as his Proxy at the Baptizing of *Lewis* of *France* Duke of *Orleans*, second Son of King *Henry II*. He was also honoured with the Dignity of Vice-roy of the *Indies*, and espoused MARY DE MENESES, daughter of *Roderick de Mello* first Marquess of *Ferreira*; and of *Beatrice de Meneses* his second Wife, by whom he had no Children. He dyed in the City of *Estremos*, and was interred in the Church *de las Hagas* at *Villa-viciosa*.

His Marriage.

14. FULGENCE OF PORTUGAL, Prior of *Vimarana*, had issue these Natural Children.

    15. FRANCIS OF BRAGANZA, Canon at *Evora*, Commissary of the Croissade of *Portugal*; and of the Councel of *Portugal*, residing in the Court of the Catholique King at *Madrid*.

    15. ANGELLICA, Abbess of *Villa-viciosa*.

14. THEOTON OF PORTUGAL, Archbishop of *Evora*, was a Prelate of great Virtue. He dyed at *Validolit*, in the Year, One thousand six hundred and two, and his body was interred in the Monastery of St. *Anthony* at *Evora*.

14. JANE OF PORTUGAL, Wife of BERNARDIN DE CARDENAS, Marquess of *Elche*.

14. EUGENIA OF PORTUGAL, espoused to FRANCIS DE MELLO, Marquess of *Ferreira*, her Cosin.

14. MARY and VINCENDA, the one Abbess, the other a Nun at *Villa-viciosa*.

14. THEODOSIUS OF PORTUGAL,
first of the name, Duke of BRAGANZA, and BARCELLOS.

PORTU-GAL-BRA-GANCE.

James Duke of *Braganza*, and *Leonor de Mendoza*, were father and mother of this Duke THEODOSIUS. The King of *Portugal*, *John III.* created him the first Duke of *Barcellos*, a Title which hath ever since been affixed to the eldest Sons of this Royal House of *Braganza*.

His first Wife ISABEL DE CASTRO his Cosin, was daughter of *Dionysius* of *Braganza* Count of *Lemos*, and of *Beatrice de Castro* his Wife.

His second was BEATRICE DE LANCASTRO, another of his Cosins, daughter of *Lewis de Lancastro*, and of *Magdalene de Granada* his Wife.

Children of THEODOSIUS Duke of BRAGANZA, by ISABEL DE CASTRO his first Wife.

15. JOHN OF PORTUGAL, Duke of *Braganza*, succeeded his father in the Dutchy.

Children of THEODOSIUS I. Duke of BRAGANZA, and of BEATRICE DE LANCASTRO his second Wife.

15. JAMES OF PORTUGAL having accompanied *Sebastian* King of *Portugal* at the second Voyage of *Affrica* against the *Moors*, was at the fatal Battel of *Alcacer*, where they were both slain, the Fourth day of *August*, in the Year, One thousand five hundred threescore and eighteen, without having been married. 1578.

15. ISABEL OF PORTUGAL, was espoused unto MICHAEL DE MENESES, first Duke of *Camigna*, and Marquess of *Villa-real*.

15. JOHN

15. JOHN OF PORTUGAL, *first of the name*, Duke *of* BRAGANZA *and* BARCELLOS, Constable *of* PORTUGAL, *and Knight of the* GOLDEN FLEECE.

1578.

His Marriage.

This Duke was eldest Son of *Theodosius* first of the name, Duke of *Braganza*, by *Isabel de Castro* his first Wife. At the time of the Ceremony (performed in *Portugal* in the Month of *August*, One thousand five hundred threescore and eighteen) of the Recognition, and Oath of Allegiance, taken by the *Portugueses* to Cardinal *Henry* in the Quality of King, this same Duke of *Braganza* held the first place, going before him, and carrying the Sword as Constable.

During the life of this King, who was much in years, JOHN Duke of *Braganza*, was one of those Princes which were Competitors for the Crown of *Portugal* in the right of KATHERINE OF PORTUGAL his Wife, daughter of the Infant *Edward*, Son of *Emanuel* King of *Portugal*; In her lay the only right of Succession (*page 68.*) warranted by the Fundamental Laws of this Kingdom (*page 6.*) so that from henceforward the Dukes of *Braganza* did justly wear the Royal Armes of *Portugal* without distinction, the direct Male line being extinguished, and the Kingdom falling to the Collateral of the Dukes of *Braganza* in the right of this *Katherine*.

And because that this Duke JOHN was the prime Grandee of the Kingdom, and his Tenants the most Warlike; and moreover confiding in the good-will which King *Henry* did bear him, he thought himself half in possession of the Estate: But in Fine, he was forced to give place to King *Philip II.* whose best Title lay in the strength of a formidable Army with which he subdued *Portugal*, as you have heard before; who being come to the Crown, continued him in his Estates, gave him the Demonstrations of a high favour, and associated him into the Order of the Knights of the *Golden Fleece*, in the Year, One thousand five hundred fourscore and one.

1481.

His Death.
1582.

He lived not long after, for he left this World in the Year, One thousand five hundred fourscore and two, and was inhumed in the Church of St. *Augustin* of *Villa-viciosa*, with his Predecessors.

PORTU-
GAL-BRA-
GANCE.

D'argent au sautoir de gueules chargé de cinq Escussons de Portugal, un au milieu, & les autres au quatre bouts du sautoir.

Chargez sur le tout d'un Escu de PORTUGAL.

Children of JOHN I. Duke *of* BRAGANZA, *and of* KATHERINE OF PORTUGAL, *his Wife.*

16. THEODOSIUS OF PORTUGAL, second of the name, Duke of *Braganza*, mentioned in the Chapter following.

16. EDWARD OF PORTUGAL, Marquess of *Flechilla*, whose Pedegree is deduced next after this of *Braganza*.

16. ALEXANDER OF PORTUGAL, was Arch-bishop of *Evora*, and Inquisitor General of the Faith in *Portugal*.

16. PHILIP OF PORTUGAL, fourth Son, dyed young.

16. MARY OF PORTUGAL, dyed without having been married.

16. SERAPHINE OF PORTUGAL, espoused unto JOHN-FERNANDEZ PACHECO, Duke of *Ascalona*, and Marquess of *Villena*.

PORTUGAL.
PORTUGAL
D'argent à cinq Escussons d'Azure pris en Croix chacun chargé de cinq besans aussi d'argent posez en sautoir, à la bordure de gueulles chargé de sept chasteaux d'or.
Party de VELASCO.
Coteslaggio.

16. THEODOSIUS OF PORTUGAL, II. of the name, *Duke of* BRAGANZA *and Barcellos, and Constable of Portugal.*

This Prince, eldest Son of Duke *John* by the Dutchess *Katherine* of *Portugal* his Wife, was not past Nine or Ten years old, when, having the Title of Duke of *Barcellos*, he accompanied King *Sebastian* his Cosin, in the second Voyage he undertook into *Affrica* against the *Moors*, 1578. where he was by them made Prisoner at the Battel of *Alcacer*. The Cherif *Muley-Hamet* King of *Morocco*, kept him in durance until that *Philip* II. King of *Spain*, obtained his liberty; who having passed the *Straits* to return into *Portugal*, was detained at St. *Lucar* by the Duke of *Medina-Sidonia*, upon the news of the Death of *Henry* King of *Portugal*, conceiving it would be a matter of importance to the Catholick King his Master, to keep this Prince in durance, as being Son of the principal Pretendants to the Kingdom: whereupon the Duke of *Barcellos* wrote a Letter to his Father the Duke of *Braganza*, that he must not then expect him, and that his detention should not any way prejudice the rights of the Realm, preferring Justice before his own life. This Letter being come into *Portugal*, was by the Duke his Father sent unto the Assembly of Estates at *Almerin*, shewing on the one side the grief for the detainment of this his dear Son; and on the other side, the contentment he received, that in so tender years he was so great a Lover of the good of his Countrey, that he offered, if there were occasion, to sacrifice his Life for the Service of the State. But immediately this fear of the Duke of *Braganza* his Father ceased, for the King of *Spain* commanded that he should have free liberty to depart; which he did as well to avoid the indignation of the *Portuguesses*, as to make a friend of the Duke of *Braganza*.

Vasconcellius.

Not long after THEODOSIUS succeeded the Duke his Father, and still continued the demonstration of his Magnanimity; for when that the Catholick King *Philip* III. and second of the name King of *Portugal*, made his solemn Entry into the City of *Lisbonne*: who willing to shew how much he affected him above all the other Grandees of this Kingdom, and desirous to make him a participant of his Royal Favours, promised that he would grant him whatsoever he would ask; To which the Duke answered, That the Kings of *Portugal* his Predecessors, which were also his Majesties; had so often, and so freely conferred their Benefits upon his House,

House, that there was not any thing remained that he could demand; and if there were, acknowledged to have received a signal Favour from his Majesty if he would vouchsafe to honour and embrace his Subjects of *Portugal* with a fatherly affection, but more especially the Grandées of the Kingdom.

This Duke THEODOSIUS, who was seventh Duke of *Braganza*, and twelfth Constable of *Portugal*, espoused ANNE DE VELASCO, daughter of the Constable of *Castille John-Fernandez de Velasco*, and of the Dutchess of *Frias*, *Mary de Giron* his first Wife.

Children of THEODOSIUS II. Duke of BRAGANZA, by ANNE DE VELASCO his Wife.

17. JOHN II. of the name, eighth Duke of BRAGANZA, crowned King of *Portugal* by the name of *John IV.* and had issue *Alphonso VI.* King of *Portugal*, now Reigning, 1662. of whose Histories and Issue, you may read in the First Book.

17. EDWARD OF PORTUGAL, born the One and thirtieth day of *March*; in the Year of our Salvation, *One thousand six hundred and five*, who coming unto Mans estate, had served the Emperour in his Wars with much gallantry, and no less success; long before his Brother Duke *John* had any thoughts of a Crown; nor did he shew any endeavours to desert the Emperours service, after the news arrived of the Revolt of *Portugal*, but seemed resolved to continue there, till he was betrayed by *Francisco de Mello* a *Portugal*, at that time Ambassador to the Catholique King in the Emperial Court.

This *Mello* notwithstanding he was bound by many strong Obligations to the House of *Braganza*, yet like an ungrateful Villain, having opportunity offered, now resolved to build his fortunes upon their ruine, or at least displeasure; he therefore earnestly sollicited the Emperour to seize upon the person of *Don Duarte*, and deliver him up to the King of *Spain*, alledging of what great concernment the securing of his person would be to the Catholique King; that it much behoved his Imperial Majesty to shew his affection to his brother the Catholique King in this particular, which would not only prove of Interest to *Spain*, but the whole house of *Austria*: That this Prince was the only Prop of the House of *Braganza*; and this was the only means which God had left in the hands of the House of *Austria* to recover the Kingdom of *Portugal*; that it would be a great errour both in prudence and policy to let slip so fair an occasion; for that if he should scape out of their hands, and get to the assistance of his brother, both his personal valour and experience in Warlike affairs, would very much infest the Catholique King.

The Emperour was not only not perswaded by this Discourse of *Mello*'s, but extreamly offended at it, returning him in answer, That he did abhorre and detest so great a breach of publick faith, and violation of all Laws of Hospitality; that it would be both against the liberty of the Empire, and against his own Honour, to imprison a Prince who had committed no fault to the Empire, but rather had laid innumerable Obligations both upon it, and himself.

Nor was the detestation of the Arch-duke *Leopold* to an act so foul and shameful, less than that of his brothers the Emperour; notwithstanding all which, *Mello* was not at all discouraged, but still prosecuted his villanous design, by corrupting with great sums of money the Count of *Tratsmandorf*, and several other Pensioners of the Crown of *Spain*; but they were soon weary of so base and shameful an employment; which made *Mello* think of a more cunning Artifice, which was to perswade the Emperour to hearken to the allurements of one *Diego di Quiroga*, who of a Souldier was turned Monk, and was now Confessor to the Empress: This Father who had often been called to give his judgement in Affairs of State, endeavored by all means possible to perswade the Emperour that he might not only with a good conscience secure the Infante, but that according to the best Rules of Interest of State, he ought to do it.

His Imperial Majesty notwithstanding all these perswasions, was very much unsatisfied in the action, and once fully resolved not to do it; but at length overcome by *Mello's* importunities, and the Ghostly perswasions of *Quiroga*, he was as it were constrained to alter his resolution, and to give order to *Don Lewis Gonzaga*, to go to the Princes quarters at *Leipen*, and summon him to *Ratisbone*.

In the mean time to endeavor to prevent all ill impressions, which an action so hainously wicked, might strike into all bosoms that had either honor or honesty; it was given out abroad, that the Infante *Don Edward* was secretly fled for some misdemeanor from *Leipen*, (when he confident of his own innocency, was in his journey to *Ratisbone*, according to the summons) and thereupon proposal made of Sixteen thousand Crowns, as a reward to any man could bring him either dead or alive; so that the Prince being ignorant of any such thing, very hardly escaped their hands, who out of hopes of the money, had gone in search of him; but missing them, he came to *Ratisbone*; where he was no sooner received, but without any reason given, he was cast into a Common Goal, and all his Servants imprisoned.

Don Edward cast into the Common Goal at Ratisbone.

Don Francisco de Mello having thus far brought his desires to effect, stopped not here, but afresh sollicited the Emperour, that the Prince might be delivered into the *Spaniards* hands, and sent prisoner to *Millain*: but instead of assenting to this, he sends a Messenger to the Infante, assuring him upon his word, that he would not deliver him into the hands of the *Spaniards*, but would speedily procure his liberty and infranchisement.

Yet notwithstanding these fair promises of the Emperours, *Don Edward*'s ill usage in prison daily and hourly increased, nor could he by any means possible get audience of the Emperour, not without reason, for, *No face is more terrible to the offendor, than the face offended*; which made the Prince make his protestation, calling God and man to witness of the injury done him by the Emperour, to whom he was neither subject by Obligation, nor Birth; that when his brother was made King of *Portugal*, he was in the Emperours service, and wholly ignorant of any design of his brothers; that if the King of *Spain* were offended, he should revenge himself upon the person offending; that that business no way concerned the Emperour, &c.

All these Allegations the Emperour confessed to be true, by a Messenger sent to the Infante in prison, again assuring him that he would not deliver him up to his enemies, but that he could not release him for some reason of State: which made *Don Francisco de Sosa Contigno*, Ambassadour extraordinary from *Portugal* to the King of *Sweden*, in the name of the King his Master,

Master, represent at large to the Diet at *Ratisbone*, the whole proceedings, requiring Justice and Liberty for the Infante: But it is in vain to plead against Interest, all the Manifesto's, Protestations, Petitions, and Intercessions made, produced no other effect than the removal of the Infante from place to place, that still as he was the farther off, he might have the harder usage.

But hitherto the Emperour seemed immoveable in his resolution of not delivering up the Infante into the hands of the *Spaniards*, till tempted with what made *Judas* betray his Master, and our blessed Saviour to death, Money; he consented to the breach of his resolve, for upon the promise of Forty thousand Crowns (contrary to the immunities of the Empire, to the Priviledges of Free Princes, to the Law of Nations, and to his Word and Promise so often reiterated) he consented that that Noble and Innocent Prince should be sent whither the Catholique King should think fit; so away he was hurried towards the Castle of *Millain*, there to remain a prisoner.

By the way as he entred into the Spanish Territories, he was received by the Count *de Sirnela* Governour of that Dukedom, where the Emperours Commissary took leave to return, to whom *D. Edward* openly said, *Tell thy Master, that I am more sorry I have served so unworthy a Prince, than to see my self sold a Prisoner into the hands of my enemies; but the just Judge of the world will one day suffer the like dealing towards his children, who are no more priviledged for being of the house of* Austria, *than my self that am of the Blood-Royal of* Portugal, *and Posterity will judge of him and me.*

The Emperour had given instruction to those that Convoyed the Infante, that in case their prisoner made an attempt to escape, they should kill him upon the place: being arrived in *Millain* he was clapt in the Common gate with all the Rogues and *Banditty*, having a Guard lodged with him in his Chamber, so rude, that they would scarce admit him to take his rest; in which Prison he most miserably dyed, upon the Third day of *September*, in the Year of our Lord, One thousand six hundred forty and nine.

His Death.
1649.

Thus was this generous, but unfortunate Prince rewarded, for having left his Countrey, Kindred, Friends, Interest; for having at his own proper cost and charges, served the Empire Eight years, for having alwayes, and upon all occasions ventured his life with the most daring, and yet expecting no other pay but thanks, nor other recompence but Honor.

King *John* was extreamly perplexed at this inhumane barbarism used to his Brother, which he vowed fully to revenge with Arms; but he could for the present do it no otherwise, than defensively, by reason of the continual inroads the *Castillians* made into *Portugal*.

17. ALEXANDER OF PORTUGAL, third Son of *Theodosius II*. Duke of *Braganza*, born the Sixth of *April*, in the Year, One thousand six hundred and seven, and left this World the One and thirtieth of *May*, A° One thousand six hundred thirty and seven.

17. KATHERINE OF PORTUGAL, only daughter of *Theodosius II*. Duke of *Braganza*, came into this World, in the Year, One thousand six hundred and six. She dyed an Infant.

Ddd MAR-

MARQUESSES of FLECHILLA,
And of
XARANDILLA.

16. **EDWARD OF PORTUGAL,** Marquesse *of* FLECHILLA.

PORTU-
GAL-FLE-
CHILLA.

HE was a younger sonne of *John I.* of the name, Duke of *Braganza*, and of the Princesse *Katherine* of *Portugal* his wife, and obtained the honour to be a Grandee of *Spain.* His first wife BEATRICE DE TOLEDO and DE MONROY Lady Marchionesse of *Xarandilla*, was daughter and heir of *John Alvarez de Toledo*, Count of *Oropesa* and *Leitosa*, and of the Countesse *Louise Pimentel*.

In second marriage EDWARD espoused GUIOMAR PARDO Marchionesse of *Magalon*, daughter of *Ares Pardo* Lord of *Magalon*, and of *Louise de la Cerda*, but had no issue by his last marriage.

Children of EDWARD *of* Portugal *Marquesse of* FLECHILLA, *and of* BEATRIX DE TOLEDO *his first wife.*

17. JOHN of PORTUGAL } died both young.
17. FRANCIS of PORTUGAL
17. FERDINAND ALVAREZ DE TOLEDO Marquess of XARANDILLA, &c. continued the Line.

---

17. **FERDINAND ALVAREZ DE TOLEDO,** Monroy and Ayala, *Marquesse of Xarandilla, and Count of Oropesa.*

HE was second son of *Edward* of *Portugal*, Marquess of *Flechilla*, and of *Beatrice de Toledo* his first wife. He espoused MENCIA PIMENTEL, the daughter of *John-Alphonso Pimentel* Count of *Benevent*, by the Countess *Mencia de Cuniga* and *Requesens*. He deceased in the flower of his age, leaving by her two sonnes and a daughter. In the year, *One thousand six hundred and nineteen*, his Grandmother by the Mothers side, in his favour gave up her right and title to the County of *Oropesa*. 1619.

Children

Marquesses of FLECHILLA, *&c.*

Children of FERDINAND ALVAREZ DE TOLEDO, *Count of Oropesa, and of* MENCIA PIMENTEL *his wife.*

18. JOHN DE TOLEDO died young.

18. EDWARD ALVAREZ DE TOLEDO, Count of *Oropesa*, and Viceroy of *Navarre*, married ANNE daughter of *Modica de Cordova* Count of *Alcaudere*.

18. MARIANA DE TOLEDO espoused to PEDRO FAXARDO Marquess *de les yeles*, and *Molina*.

COUNTS OF LEMOS,
AND
MARQUESSES OF SARRIA.

13. DIONYSIUS OF PORTUGAL, Count of LEMOS.

1495.

After that the Duke of *Braganza Ferdinand II.* of that name, his Father had been beheaded, the Dutchess *Isabel* his Widow, sent this Prince DIONYSIUS OF PORTUGAL, their third Son into *Castille*, where he established his Fortune. For the Queen of *Castille Isabel* his Aunt, about the Year, *One thousand five hundred*, procured his Marriage with a rich Heir, whose name was BEATRICE DE CASTRO Countess of LEMOS, daughter of *Roderick de Castro*, and of *Teresa Osorio* his Wife, by whom he had a numerous Issue; she had among other things in Dower, the Lordships of SARRIA, *Castro*, and *Ottero*, which had been given by the Kings. *Mariana* mistakes in making this DIONYSIUS Son of *James* of *Braganza*, contrary to the Evidences and Records of this House, which exactly prove their descent. Their Children took the name of CASTRO, upon the account of their Mother, as is observed often in *Spain*.

His Marriage.
1500.

PORTUGALLEMOS.

Lib. 27. *Cap.* 10.

Children of DIONYSIUS OF PORTUGAL, Count of LEMOS.

14. FERDINAND DE CASTRO first of the name, Count of LEMOS, and Marquess of SARRIA, continued the Posterity.

14. ALPHONSO DE LANCASTRO, Grand Commander of the Order of *Christ*; had also issue, mentioned in his place.

14. PETER DE CASTRO, Bishop of *Cuenca*.

14. LEONOR DE CASTRO, Wife of JAMES-SARMIENTO DE MENDOZA, Count of *Ribadauia*.

14. ISABEL DE CASTRO, first Wife of THEODOSIUS OF PORTUGAL, first of the name, Duke of BRAGANZA her Cosin.

14. ANTONIETTA DE LANCASTRO, married to ALVARO COUTINHO, Marescal of *Portugal*.

14. MENCIA DE LANCASTRO, first Wife of RENE Count of CHALANT in *Savoye*, who had issue *Elizabeth de Chalant* Wife of *Frederick Madruce* Count of *Aue*, and *Arbe*, and Lord of *Beaufremont*.

14. TERESA DE CASTRO dyed before Marriage.

14. CONSTANCE DE CASTRO, a Nun in the Monastery of our Lady at *Lisbonne*.

---

14. FERDINAND DE CASTRO, Count of LEMOS, and Marquess of SARRIA.

PORTUGAL-LEMOS.

TO *Dionysius* Count of *Lemos*, and the Countess *Beatrix de Castro* his Wife, succeeded this FERDINAND their eldest Son, who was sent Embassadour to *Rome* during the Pontificalty of *Paul III*. by the Emperour *Charles V*. who created him Marquess of SARRIA, and the King of *Spain Philip II*. also sent him Embassadour to the Court of *Rome*, where he resided in the time of the Popes *Julius III*. and *Paul IV*. The Princess *Jane* of *Portugal*, Mother of King *Sebastian*, honoured him with the Office of Steward of her Houshold.

He espoused TERESA d'ANDRADA, daughter and heir of *Ferdinand d'Andrada* Count of *Vilalua* and *Andrada*, and of *Frances de Ulloa* and *Zuniga* his Wife.

Children

Children of FERDINAND DE CASTRO Count of LEMOS, and of TERESA d'ANDRADA his Wife.

15. PETER-FERDINAND DE CASTRO, first of that name, Count of LEMOS, of whom we shall speak hereafter.

15. ISABEL DE CASTRO, Wife of RODERICK DE MOSCOSO Count of *Altamira.*

---

15. PETER-FERDINAND DE CASTRO I. of the name, Count of LEMOS, *Andrada,* and *Vilalua,* and Marquefs of *Sarria.*

1580.   HE was Son of *Ferdinand de Caſtro* Count of *Lemos*, and of *Tereſa d'Andrada,* and ſerved the King of *Spain Philip II.* at the Conqueſt of the Kingdom of *Portugal.* PORTU-GAL-LEMOS.

He was twiſe Married, firſt to LEONOR DE LA CUEUA daughter of *Bertrand de la Cueua* Duke of *Albequerque,* and of *Iſabel Giron* his Wife.

Secondly, To TERESA DE BOBADILLA *& de* LA CERDA, daughter of *Peter de Bobadilla* Count of *Chinchon,* and of *Menecia de la Cerda.*

Children of PETER-FERDINAND DE CASTRO Count of LEMOS, and of LEONOR DE LA CUEUA his firſt Wife.

16. FERDINAND-RODERICK DE CASTRO Count of LEMOS, whoſe Story followeth in the next place.

16. BERTRAND DE CASTRO, was never married, but had iſſue three Natural Children. He ſerved the King of *Spain* in *Italy,* the *Indies,* and *Spain.*

   17. JOHN DE CASTRO dyed at *Naples.*

   17. FRANCIS DE CASTRO.

   17. BERTRAND DE CASTRO.

16. TERESA DE CASTRO Wife to GARCIA-HURTADO DE MENDOZA, Marqueſs of *Cagneta.*

16. ISABEL DE CASTRO dyed young.

Children of PETER-FERDINAND DE CASTRO Count of LEMOS, and of TERESA DE BOBADILLA his second Wife.

16. PETER DE CASTRO, Gentleman of the Bed-Chamber to King *Philip III.* married HIERONIMA DE CORDOUA, Lady of Honour to Queen *Margaret* of *Austria*, and daughter of *Roderick de Cordona* Lord of *Palma*, and of *Meneçia de Mendoza* his Wife, from which Marriage came no Children.

16. RODERICK DE CASTRO Canon of *Toledo*, Arch-deacon of *Alcaraz*, and Inquisitor, left three Natural Children; *Viz.*

    17. FELIX
    17. TERESA } DE CASTRO.
    17. ANGELA

16. ANDREW DE CASTRO never married, but left a Bastard Son, named

    17. RODERICK DE CASTRO.

16. JAMES DE CASTRO.

Bastard-Children of PETER-FERDINAND DE CASTRO Count of LEMOS.

16. ANTHONY a Monk of the Order of St. *Benedict*, Abbot of St. *Benet* at *Madrid*, and General of his Order.

16. JOHN DE CASTRO, a Monk also of the same Order, Archbishop of *Otrante*, dyed, being elected Bishop of *Cordona*.

---

16. FERDINAND-RODERICK DE CASTRO Count of LEMOS, and Viceroy of Naples.

PORTU-GAL-LEMOS.

AMong the Children of *Peter-Ferdinand de Castro* Count of *Lemos*, and of *Leonor de la Cueua* his first Wife, he was the eldest. After that King *Philip III.* was come to the Crown of *Spain*, he sent this Count his Embassadour to *Rome* to Pope *Clement VIII.* for to make tender of his obedience, and to have a new investiture in the Kingdom of *Naples*, where this same Earl was also sent Viceroy, and where he deceased in the Year, One thousand six hundred and one.

He

Counts of LEMOS, &c.

He had to Wife KATHERINE DE ZUNIGA DE SANDOVAL, who was daughter of *Francis Royas de Sandoval* Marquess of *Denia*, and of *Isabel Borgia* his Wife, which *Katherine* Countess of *Lemos* was one of the principal Ladies of Honour to the Catholique Queen *Margaret*, Wife of King *Philip III*.

Children of FERDINAND-RODERICK DE CASTRO Count of LEMOS.

17. PETER-FERDINAND DE CASTRO, second of the name, Count of LEMOS, mentioned in the next place.

17. FRANCIS DE CASTRO Duke of *Taurisana*, of whom we shall speak after his Elder Brother, continued the Posterity.

17. FERDINAND DE CASTRO espoused LEONOR DE PORTUGAL, Countess of *Gelves*, Daughter and Heir of *George* of *Portugal* Count of *Gelves*, and of *Bernardine de Vincentelo* his Wife, in whose right he was Count of *Gelves*. They had issue one only Child.

    18. KATHERINE OF PORTUGAL, Countesse of *Gelves*.

---

17. PETER-FERDINAND DE CASTRO, *second of the name, Count of* LEMOS *and Andrada, Marquess of Sarria, and Viceroy of Naples.*

THE King of *Spain, Philip III.* bestowed several Charges and Dignities upon him; for he not only honoured him with the Quality of Gentleman of his Bed-Chamber, but also made him President of the Councel-Royal for the *Indies*, and Viceroy of *Naples*, in the Year, *One thousand six hundred and ten*: As also established him President of the Councel of *Italy*.

His Wife, was KATHERINE DE SANDOVAL, his Cosin-Germane, Daughter of *Francis de Sandoval* and *Royas*, Duke of *Lerme*, by the Dutchess *Katherine de la Cerda* his Wife, by whom he had not any Children.

17. FRANCIS DE CASTRO Duke of TAU-RISANO, Count of Castro, and Viceroy of Naples and Sicilie.

HE was second Son of *Ferdinand-Roderick de Castro* Count of *Lemos*, by *Katherine de Zuniga* and *Sandoval* his Wife; and as his elder Brother, was for his great Experience, employed in important Affairs by the Catholick King: For he not only established him his Viceroy of *Naples*, after the death of his elder Brother, but also of *Sicily*. Afterwards the same King sent him Embassadour to the State of *Venice*, to endeavour a Reconciliation betwixt that Republick, and Pope *Paul V.* to whom FRANCIS DE CASTRO was also sent Embassadour in Ordinary.

He espoused LUCRECE GATINARA LEGNANA, Countess *de Castro* in the Kingdom of *Naples*, only Daughter of *Alexander Gatinara*, Fifth Count of *Castro*, and of *Victoria Caracciol* his Wife.

Children of FRANCIS DE CASTRO, Duke of TAURISANO, &c.

18. FERDINAND DE CASTRO Duke of *Taurisano*, &c. continued the descent.

18. ALEXANDER DE CASTRO.

18. FRANCIS DE CASTRO.

18. KATHERINE and VICTORIA DE CASTRO.

18. CLARA-MARIA DE CASTRO a Nun.

18. ELISE and MARIA DE CASTRO.

18. FERDINAND DE CASTRO Duke of TAURISANO, Count of Castro and Lemos.

HE was eldest Son of *Francis de Castro* Duke of *Taurisano*, and of *Lucrece Gatinara Legnana* his Wife.

His Wife was ANTONIA DE GIRON, the daughter of *Peter Giron* Duke of *Ossuna*, and Marquess of *Pegnafiel*.

Children of FERDINAND DE CASTRO Duke of TAURISANO, Count of Castro and Lemos.

19. PETER DE CASTRO Count of *Antrada*.

14. ALPHON-

14. ALPHONSO DE LANCASTRO.

DIonyſius of *Braganza*, or of *Portugal*, and *Beatrix de Caſtro* Counteſs of *Lemos*, had ſeveral Children, among whom, this ALPHONSO was the ſecond, honoured with the Dignity of great Maſter of the Military Order of *Chriſt* in *Portugal*, and grand Alcaide of *Ovidos*. King *John III*. ſent him Embaſſador to *Rome* unto the Popes *Julius III.* and *Paul IV.* Afterwards he was alſo ſent into *France* to King *Charles IX.* during the Minority of King *Sebaſtian* in the beginning of his Reign. The ſame ALPHONSO was interred in the Monaſtery of the *Carmelites* of *Lisbon*. His Wife, HIERONIMA DE NOROGNA, was Daughter of *James de Norogna*, great Maſter of the Order of *Chriſt*, and of *Philippa Attaida* his Wife; he had by her one Son and a Daughter, which were

PORTUGAL-LANCASTRO.

15. DIONYSIUS DE LANCASTRO mentioned hereafter.

15. PHILIPPA DE LANCASTRO, Wife to MICHAEL DE MENESES Marqueſs of *Villa-real*.

15. DIONYSIUS DE LANCASTRO.

HE was, as his father *Alphonſo*, grand Maſter of the Order of *Chriſt*, and by the King of *Portugal*, *Sebaſtian*, alſo ſent into *France* to King *Charles IX.* about the Year, One thouſand five hundred threeſcore and twelve; then into *Spain* to King *Philip II.* He was alſo nominated by the ſame King *Sebaſtian*, his Embaſſador for *Rome*, to be ſent to Pope *Gregory XIII*. But upon the death of this King in *Affrica*, his Embaſſade ceaſed, and he dyed at *Lisbon*, A°. One thouſand five hundred fourſcore and eighteen, being very much in years: He lieth inhumed in the Monaſtery of St. *Auguſtine*.
By his Wife, ISABEL ENRIQUEZ, Daughter of *Francis Coutinho* ſecond Count of *Redondo*, and of *Mary de Guzman* his Wife; he had theſe Six Children following.

1572.

HisDeath. 1598.

16. ALPHONSO DE LANCASTRO, great Maſter of the Order of *Chriſt*, and grand Alcaide of *Ovidos*. He eſpouſed MARY DE TAUORA, daughter of *Alvaro Perez de Tauora*, and of *Iſabel de Melo* his Wife.

16. FRANCIS DE LANCASTRO, Gentleman-Waiter at the Table, to the Catholick Kings *Philip III.* and *IV.*

16. JOHN DE LANCASTRO Biſhop of *Lamego*, and Chief Chaplain to the King of *Spain Philip III*.

F f f
HIERONIMA

20 Marquesses of FERREIRA,

16. HIERONIMA DE NOROGNA was never married.

16. MARY DE LANCASTRO was espoused to FERDINAND-RODERICK DIEGO MARTINES MASCAREGNAS.

16. IOLAND ENRIQUEZ married to FRANCIS COUTINHO, fourth Count of *Redondo* her Cosin.

MARQUESSES of FERREIRA,
AND
COUNTS of TENTUGAL.

12. *ALVARO DE PORTUGAL*, Lord of *FERREIRA*.

PORTU-GAL-FER-REIRA.

Mong the Children of *Ferdinand* first of the name, Duke of *Braganza*, and of *Jane de Castro* his Wife, this ALVARO was the third. He was President of the Councel Royal in *Castille*, and grand Alcaide of *Seville*, and in *Portugal* also Lord Chief Justice and Chancellor. He espoused PHILIPPA DE MELO Countess of *Olivença*, daughter and heir of *Roderick de Melo* Count of *Olivença*, by *Isabel de Meneses*.

Children of *ALVARO DE PORTUGAL*, Lord of *FERREIRA*.

13. RODERICK DE MELO, and *Portugal*, first Marquess of FERREIRA, continued the Line.

13. GEORGE OF PORTUGAL, Count of GELVES, gave original to the Branch of *Gelves*, hereafter mentioned.

13. ISABEL DE CASTRO, Wife of *Alphonso de* SOTO-MAJOR Count of *Belalcacar*.

13. BEATRIX DE MELO, and *Tentugal*, Dutchess of CONIMBRA, Wife of GEORGE Bastard OF PORTUGAL, Duke of CONIMBRA, and Lord of *Aveiro*.

JANE

13. JANE DE VILLENA married to FRANCIS OF PORTUGAL, Count of VIMIOSO.

13. MARY MANUEL Wife of JOHN DE SILVA second Earl of *Portalegre*.

---

13. RODERICK DE MELO, and Portugal, Marquess of FERREIRA, and Count of Tentugal.

HE was eldest Son of *Alvaro* of *Portugal* Lord of *Ferreira*, and of *Philippa de Melo* his Wife, and for his Memorable Services deserved well the Title of Marquess of *Ferreira*, and Count of *Tentugal*, into which Honours he was Created by the great *Emanuel* King of *Portugal*, his Cosin. He married two Wives.

His first Wife was LEONOR d'ALMEIDA, Daughter of *Francis d'Almeida* Viceroy of the *Indies*, by *Jane Pereira* his Wife.

His second Wife was BEATRIX DE MENESES, Daughter of *Anthony d'Almada* Major General of *Lisbonne*, and of *Mary de Meneses* his Wife. He had issue by both Wives.

Children of RODERICK DE MELO Marquess of FERREIRA, by his first wife.

14. ALVARO DE MELO, dyed in the life-time of his Father, having espoused MARY DE VILLENA, daughter of *John de Silva*, second Count of *Portalegre*, and of *Mary Manuel*. He had one Son bearing his name, which followeth.

15. ALVARO DE MELO, had no Children by his Wife MARY d'ALCACOUA, daughter of *Peter* Count of *Iguana*, and of *Katherine de Sousa*. This *Alvaro* was slain at the Battel of *Alcacer*.

14. FRANCIS DE MELO first of the name, Marquess of *Ferreira*, continued the Posterity.

14. PHILIPPA DE VILLENA Wife of ALVARO DE SYLVA Count of *Portalegre*.

14. JANE DE MELO was a Nun.

Children of RODERICK DE MELO, and of his second Wife.

14. ALVARO DE MELO.

14. MARY DE MENESES espoused to CONSTANTINE DE PORTUGAL, or BRAGANZA, her Cosin: Of whom we have spoken.

---

14. FRANCIS DE MELO, first of the name, Marquess of FERREIRA, and Count of Tentugal.

TO the Marquess of *Ferreira Roderick de Melo*, succeeded this his second Son (the eldest dying before his Father.) He married EUGENIA OF BRAGANZA or PORTUGAL, daughter of *James* Duke of *Braganza*, and of *Jane de Mendoza* his Wife.

Children of FRANCIS DE MELO, Marquess of Ferreira.

15. RODERICK DE MELO second of the name, slain at the Battel of *Alcacer* in *Affrick* with King *Sebastian*, in the Year, One thousand five hundred threescore and eighteen, and left no Children by his Wife KATHERINE DEC'A, daughter of *Alphonso de Norogna*.   1578.

15. NUGNO ALVAREZ DE MELO, Count of *Tentugal*, continued the descent.

15. JOHN DE BRAGANZA, Bishop of *Visco*.

15. CONSTANTINE DE BRAGANZA, espoused MARY DE MENDOZA daughter of *Ferdinand de Meneses*, by *Philippa de Mendoza* his Wife. They had these Children following.

    16. FRANCIS DE MELO, Servant to the Catholick King, Marquess *de la Tour de Laguna*, and Count of *Alcumer*, married ANTONIA DE VILLENA, daughter of *Henry de Sousa* Count of *Miranda*; by whom he had issue N. DE MELO, BEATRIX, and MENTIA.

    16. JOHN DE MELO a *Carmelite* Fryer.

    16. ALVARO DE MELO, Knight of the Order of St. *John*.

    16. FERDINAND DE MELO.

JANE

and Counts of TENTUGAL.

15. JANE DE MENDOZA, Abbess of *Villa-viciosa*.

15. JOSEPH DE MELO, a Natural Son of *Francis* Marquess of *Ferreira*, was Arch-bishop of *Evora*.

15. FRANCIS d'ALMEIDA, also a Natural Son.

---

15. NUGNO ALVAREZ DE MELO, Count of TENTUGAL.

Francis de Melo Marquess of *Ferreira*, and Count of *Tentugal*, and *Eugenia* of *Braganza* or *Portugal* his Wife, were Father and Mother of this Count, who married with MARIANA DE CASTRO daughter of *Roderick de Moscoso* Earl of *Altamira*, and of the Countess *Isabel de Castro* his Wife.

Children of NUGNO ALVAREZ DE MELO.

16. FRANCIS DE MELO second of the name, Marquess of *Ferreira*, continued the Posterity.

16. RODERICK DE MELO Arch-deacon of *Evora*.

16. LEONOR DE MELO, Wife of MANUEL DE MOURA CORTEREAL, second Marquess of *Castelrodrigo*, Gentleman of the Bed-Chamber to the Catholique King, and great Master of *Alcantara*.

16. JANE OF PORTUGAL espoused to MANRIQUEZ DE SILVA Count of *Portalegre*, also Gentleman of the Bed-Chamber to the King of *Spain*, and his grand Master of the Houshold in *Portugal*.

---

16. FRANCIS DE MELO II. of the name, Marquess of FERREIRA, and Count of Tentugal. General of the Melitia to King John IV.

HE was eldest Son of *Nugno Alvarez de Melo* Count of *Tentugal*, by the Countess *Mariana de Castro*. He dyed in the Year, *One thousand six hundred forty and five*; And left no issue by his first Wife MARY DE SANDOVAL his Cosin Germaine, daughter of *Lopez Osorio de Moscoso*, Count of *Altamira*, and of the Countess *Leonor de Sandoval* his Wife.

HisDeath. 1645.

Counts of GELVES,

His second Wife was JANE PIMENTEL daughter of *Anthony Pimentel* Marquess of *Tabara*, by her he had these Children.

17. NUNIUS DE MELO Duke of *Cadaval*, Marquess of *Ferreira*, and Count of *Tentugal*, now living, 1662.

17. THEODOSIUS DE MELO second Son.

COUNTS OF GELVES,
AND
DUKES OF VERAGUA.

13. GEORGE OF PORTUGAL, I. of the name, first Count of GELVES, and Alcaide of Alcacer and Seville.

PORTUGAL-GELVES.

D'argent au sautoir de gueulles chargé de cinq Escussons de Portugal, dount l'un est au melieu du sautoir & les autres aux quatre bouts d'icelui.

OF the two Sons of *Alvaro* of *Portugal*, who was President of the Councel Royal of *Castille*, and of his Wife *Philippa de Melo* Countess of *Olivença*, *Roderick* of *Portugal* first Marquess of *Ferreira*, and Count of *Tentugal*, was the elder, and this GEORGE the younger, who performed so many good and faithful Services for the Emperour *Charles V.* that he honoured him with the Title of Count of GELVES.

The first Wife he espoused was GUIMARE d'ATAIDA and SILVA, daughter of *John de Vasconcellos* second Count of *Penela*, and of the Countess *Mary de Sousa*; by her he had no Children.

His second Wife was ISABEL DE TOLEDO COLOMBO, daughter of *James Colombo* first Duke of *Veragua*, and second Admiral of the *Indies*; and of the Dutchess *Mary de Toledo* his Wife: which *James* was issued from that famous *Christopher Colombus* the *Genevis*, which made discovery of the *West-Indies* under the Reigns of the King and Queen of *Castille* and *Arragon*, *Ferdinand* and *Isabel*.

Children of GEORGE OF PORTUGAL, Count of GELVES, and of ISABEL DE TOLEDO COLOMBO, his second Wife.

14. ALVARO OF PORTUGAL, second Count of GELVES, continued the Line.

14. ANTHONY OF PORTUGAL, a Monk of the Order of St. *Dominique*.

GEORGE

and Dukes of VERAGUA.

14. GEORGE OF PORTUGAL, one of the Four and twenty Magistrates of *Seville*, whose descent shall be mentioned hereafter.

14. JAMES OF PORTUGAL, as his elder Brother, exercised the Charge of one of the Four and twenty of *Seville*, and had to his Wife ISABEL BOTTI daughter of *James Botti* a *Florentine*, by *Anne-Frances Fonti* his Wife, and by her had these Children following;

15. JAMES OF PORTUGAL.

15. ISABEL OF PORTUGAL Wife of JOHN GUTIERREZ TELLO DE SANDOVAL, Knight of the Order of St. *James*.

15. ANNE-FRANCES OF PORTUGAL, conjoyned in Marriage with FRANCIS TELLO DE GUZMAN.

14. LEWIS OF PORTUGAL, fifth Son of *George* Count of *Gelves*, dyed, not having been married.

14. MENCIA DE TOLEDO, by some Records named MARY.

14. PHILIPPA, and ISABEL, her Sisters.

14. ALVARO OF PORTUGAL, Second Count of GELVES.

AMong the Children of *George of Portugal* First of the Name, and First Count of *Gelves*, and of *Isabel de Toledo* his Wife, this was the Eldest, who had two Sons by his Wife LEONOR DE CORDOUA and ARRAGON, Daughter of *Alvaro de Cordova*, grand Chevalier to the Catholick King *Philip II*. which *Alvaro* espoused *Mary* of *Arragon*.

Children of ALVARO OF PORTUGAL, Count of GELVES.

15. GEORGE OF PORTUGAL, Second of the Name, Count of GELVES.

15. NUGNO DE PORTUGAL, Duke of VERAGUA, whose Descent is mentioned after that of his elder Brother.

Ggg 2   15. GEORGE

15. GEORGE OF PORTUGAL, II. of the Name, and Third Count of GELVES.

HE was eldest Son of *Alvaro* of *Portugal*, Second Count of *Gelves*, and of the Countess *Leonor* of *Cordova*, and *Arragon* his Wife, and espoused BERNARDINE VINCENTELO: She was Daughter of *John-Anthony Corso Vincentelo* by *Bridget Corso* his Wife, from which Marriage came only one Daughter following:

16. LEONOR OF PORTUGAL, Countess of GELVES, twice married; first to FERDINAND DE CASTRO her Cosin, Third Son of *Ferdinand-Roderick de Castro* Count of *Lemos*, by whom she had her Daughter *Katherine* of *Portugal* also Countess of *Gelves*.

For her Second Husband, LEONOR OF PORTUGAL, espoused JAMES PIMENTEL Viceroy of *Arragon*, Son of the Marquess of *Tanara*; from this last Marriage there came no Children.

15. NUGNO OF PORTUGAL COLOMBO, Duke of VERAGUA, and Admiral of the Indies.

ALvaro of *Portugal* Count of *Gelves*, and *Leonor de Cordova* and *Arragon* his Wife, were Father and Mother of this Duke of *Veragua*, who was Heir to his great Grandfather *James Colombo* first Duke of *Veragua*; he married with ALDONCE PORTOCARRERO, Daughter of *James de la Bastide*, and had by her Two Sons, and Three Daughters.

Children of NUGNO COLOMBO Duke of VERAGUA.

16. ALVARO OF PORTUGAL COLOMBO, Third Duke of VERAGUA, continued the Descent.

16. CHRISTOPHER OF PORTUGAL, Second Son.

16. LEONOR OF PORTUGAL, one of the Ladies of Honour to the Catholick Queen *Isabel* of *France*.

16. LOVISE OF PORTUGAL, a Nun.

16. PHILIPPA OF PORTUGAL, also a Nun.

16. ALVARO OF PORTUGAL COLOMBO, Third Duke of VERAGUA, Marquess of Jamaica, And Admiral of the Indies.

HE was the eldest Son of *Nugno* of *Portugal Colombo*, Duke of *Veragua*, by *Aldonce Portocarero* his wife, and espoused KATHERINE DE CASTRO; by her he had Issue,

17. PETER-NUNIUS COLOMBUS Duke of VERAGUA now living, A° 1662.

---

14. GEORGE OF PORTUGAL, One of the Four and twenty Magistrates of Sevile.

HE was Third Son of *George* of *Portugal* first of the name, and first Count of *Gelves*, and of his Wife the Countess *Isabel de Toledo Colombo*. He was one of the Four and twenty of *Sevile*. By his Wife GENIEURE BOTTI, daughter of *John Botti*, he left Four Sons and a Daughter, *viz.*

15. GEORGE OF PORTUGAL.

15. JAMES OF PORTUGAL, of whom we shall speak in the next place.

15. ALVARO OF PORTUGAL followed the profession of the Church.

15. CHRISTOPHER OF PORTUGAL, a Monk of the Order of St. *Hierosme*.

15. ISABEL OF PORTUGAL, a Nun in the Abbey of our Lady at *Seville*.

---

14. JAMES OF PORTUGAL, first of the Name.

HE was second Son of *George* of *Portugal* one of the Four and twenty of *Seville*, and had to Wife GUIOMAR-COLOMBO DE TOLEDO, daughter of *Licentio-Hierosme Ortegon*, and of *Frances Colombe*

Iembo his Wife, in whose Right he pretended to the Dutchy of *Veragua*, against *Nugno* of *Portugal* his Cosin, to whom by sentence it was adjudged. The Children of JAMES OF PORTUGAL, were

16. JAMES OF PORTUGAL second of the name, conjoyned by marriage with ISABEL DE MEDINA, and DE GUZMAN.

16. ANTHONY OF PORTUGAL, a Fryer.

16. LEWIS OF PORTUGAL.

16. FRANCES, and ANNE-FRANCES.

16. MARY, PHILIPPA, and ISABEL.

COUNTS OF FARO,
AND OF ODEMIRA.

12. *ALPHONSO OF PORTUGAL*, first of the name, Count of FARO and ODEMIRA.

PORTUGAL-ODEMIRA.

Fter having heretofore written of the Posterity of *Ferdinand II.* of the name, third Duke of *Braganza*, and *Alvaro* of *Portugal* his Brother, from whom are issued the Marquesses of *Ferreira*, and Counts of *Gelves*; it rests now to deduce the Descent of ALPHONSO OF PORTUGAL, who was also their Brother, all Three Sons of the Duke of *Braganza Ferdinand I.* of the name, and of the Dutchess *Jane de Castro* his Wife.

The same ALPHONSO who was Lord of *Faro* in his own right, was created first Count thereof by *Alphonso V.* King of *Portugal*, and at what time the Duke of *Braganza* his Brother, of whom we have written, was punished for having conspired against King *John II.* he fled into *Castille*, where he departed this World, after he had espoused MARY DE NOROGNA Countess of *Odemira*, Daughter and Heir of *Sanceo de Norogna* first Earl of *Odemira*, Lord of *Aveiro* and *Vimieiro*, grand Alcaide of *Estremos*, and of the Countess *Mencia de Sousa* his Wife.

Children of ALPHONSO OF PORTUGAL, Count of FARO and Odemira.

13. SANCEO OF NOROGNA first of the name, Count of ODEMIRA, contiued the Line.

FRAN-

and of ODEMIRA.

13. FRANCIS OF NOROGNA espoused LEONOR MANUEL, daughter of *James Manuel* and *Villena*, Lord of *Cheles*, and of *Major de Silva* his Wife, by whom he had one daughter here mentioned, *viz.*

14. MARY MANUEL Wife of JAMES DE MELO DE FIGUEIREDO, by him she had issue several children.

13. FREDERICK DE NOROGNA, Bishop of *Calaotra* and *Ciguenca*, Arch-bishop of *Sarragoca*, and Viceroy of *Catalonia*.

13. ANTHONY also followed the profession of the Church.

13. FERDINAND DE FARO Lord of *Vimiero*, hath given original to the other Lords and Earls of VIMIERO and FARO, as you may read hereafter.

13. GUIOMARE DE NOROGNA Dutchess of SEGORBIA, Wife of HENRY OF ARRAGON, sirnamed the *Child of Fortune*, who was Son of *Henry* of *Arragon*, great Master of the Order of *Knights* of St. *James*, by *Beatrix Pimentel* his second Wife; which Grand Master was one of the younger Sons of *Ferdinand* of *Castille*, King of *Arragon*, and of *Elianor d'Albuquerque*.

13. MENCIA DE NOROGNO Dutchess of MEDINA CELI, was married to JOHN DE LA CERDA Duke of *Medina Celi*.

13. KATHERINE DE NOROGNA Abbess of *Semide*.

---

13. SANCEO OF NOROGNA, first of the name, Count of Odemira, and Lord of Mortagoa.

TO the Count of *Faro Alphonso* of *Portugal* first of the name, and to the Countess of *Odemira Mary de Norogna* his Wife, succeeded the Earl SANCEO first of the name their eldest Son, who was twice married.

First, He married FRANCES DE SILVA daughter of *James Gil Muniz*, and of *Leonor de Silva* his Wife: By her he had issue Two Sons and a Daughter.

The second Wife of the same Count SANCEO, was ANGELA FABRA daughter of *Gaspar Fabra*; by whom he had also Two Sons and a Daughter.

Children of SANCEO I. of the Name, Count of ODEMIRA, by FRANCES DE SILVA his first Wife.

14. ALPHONSO OF NOROGNA continued the Posterity.

RODE-

Counts of FARO,

14. RODERICK DE NOROGNA was an Ecclesiastick.

14. MENCIA DE NOROGNA espoused to the Count of FRA-QUEZ in *Savoy*.

Children of SANCEO I. Count of ODEMIRA, and of ANGELA FABRA his second Wife.

14. JOHN DE FARO, whose Branch shall be deduced after that of his elder Brother.

14. FREDERICK OF PORTUGAL married (in *Castille*) MARGARET DE BORGIA, Daughter of *John De Borgia* third Duke of *Gandie*, by the Dutchess *Anne De Castro* his Wife, and had this only Daughter following, *viz.*

15. ANNE OF PORTUGAL Wife of RODERICK DE SILVA. Duke of *Prastrana*.

14. JANE MANUEL was conjoined in marriage with JOHN DE LA CERDA Marquess of *Cogolludo*, and Fourth Duke of *Medina Celi*.

14. GUIOMARE DE NOROGNA Wife of JOHN BACA DE LIC,ANA; some Records mention that it was she that was espoused to the Duke of *Medina Celi*.

14. KATHERINE a Natural Daughter of the Count of ODEMIRA *Sanceo I.* was a Nun in the Monastery of *Odivelles*.

---

14. ALPHONSO OF NOROGNA.

IN the life-time of the Count of *Odemira, Sanceo* the first his Father, he was slain by the *Moors*; having before been married to *Mary D' Attaide*, Daughter and Heir of *Nugno-Ferdinand D' Attaide* Lord of *Pena Cova*, Captain of *Cafin*, and of *Jane De Faria* his Wife; from which Marriage came their only Son, which was Count *Sanceo II.* mentioned next following.

---

16. SANCEO DE NOROGNA II. of the Name, Count of ODEMIRA.

HE succeeded his Grandfather *Sanceo De Norogna* first of the Name, and was Fourth Count of ODEMIRA, and grand Alcaide of
Estremos,

Estremos Katherine of *Austria* Queen of *Portugal*, Wife of King *John III*. honoured him with the Office of Steward of her Houshold.

He espoused MARGARET DE SILVA Daughter of *John De Silva* second Count of *Portalegre*; from this marriage there came two Sons and a Daughter.

16. ALPHONSO DE NOROGNA third of the Name, and second Count of ODEMIRA of that Name.

16. NUGNO DE NOROGNA Bishop of *Visco*, and *De La Guarde*.

16. MARY DE NOROGNA Wife of LEWIS D' ATTAIDE Count of *Atouguia*.

---

16. *ALPHONSO DE NOROGNO III. of the Name, and second Count of ODEMIRA of that Name; Lord of Mortaga, and grand Alcaide of Estremos.*

ALPHONSO eldest Son of Count *Sanceo II*. was of the Number of those Lords of *Portugal* that accompanied King *Sebastian* in his second Voyage for *Affrica*, and was slain with him at the fatal Battel of *Alcacer*; in which, besides the King, there dyed Eight or Ten Princes and Lords of the Blood-Royal.

The same ALPHONSO had three Wives; the first was JANE DE VILENA Daughter of *Manuel Telles* Lord of *Ugnon*, by *Margaret De Vilena* his Wife; by whom he had no Children.

His second was JANE DE GUZMAN Daughter of *Peter De Meneses* Captain of *Septe*, and of *Constance De Guzman* his Wife, neither had he Issue by her.

But by YOLAND DE CASTRO his third Wife, Daughter of *Alvaro De Castro*, and of *Anne D' Attaide* his Wife, he had one Son following.

17. SANCEO DE NOROGNA third of the Name, Count of ODEMIRA, Lord of *Mortagoa*, who was also grand Alcaide of *Estremos*, and espoused JULIANA DE LARA, Daughter of *Manuel De Meneses* Duke of *Ville-real*, and of *Mary De Silva* his Wife; by her he had a Daughter, which dyed young.

The same SANCEO deceased in A° One thousand six hundred forty and two.

---

14. *JOHN DE FARO.*

HE was eldest Son descended from the marriage of *Sanceo De Norogna* first of that Name, Count of *Odemira*, and Lord of *Mortagoa*, and of the Countess *Angela Fabra* his second Wife, and took to Wife ISABEL FREIRE Daughter of *Emanuel Freire*, by *Grimanesa de Melo* his Wife, by her he had his only Son, viz.

15. JOHN DE FARO second of the Name, who was conjoined in marriage with MARGARET DE NOROGNA Daughter of *John D' Almeida* by *Lucia D' Ornelas*, by her he had one only Daughter, named,

16. LUCIA DE FARO married to HIEROSME COUTINHO of the Council of State to the Catholick King *Philip III.* in the Kingdom of *Portugal*. They had Issue, PHILIPPA DE COUTINHO married to LEWIS D' ATTAIDA. Count of *Attougia*, and Viceroy of the *Indies*.

LORDS AND COUNTS OF VIMIERO, AND OF FARO.

13. FERDINAND DE FARO Lord of VIMIERO.

PORTU-GAL-VIMIERO.

OF the Children of *Alphonso* of *Portugal* first of the Name, Count of *Faro*, and of *Mary De Norogna* Countess of *Odemira* his Wife, he was the fifth; *Catherine* of *Austria* Queen of *Portugal*, Wife of King *John* the Third, honoured him with the Office of Steward of her Houshold. He left several Children by his Wife ISABEL DE MELO, Daughter of *Gomez De Figueiredo*, by *Leonor De Melo*, viz.

14. FRANCIS DE FARO, who continued the Posterity.

14. DIONYSIUS DE FARO had also Issue, as you shall see hereafter.

14. SANCEO DE FARO died, being elected Bishop of *Leiria*.

14. ALPHONSO ENRIQUEZ Dean of the Chappel-Royal to *Sebastian* King of *Portugal*.

14. MARY DE NOROGNA Wife of JOHN DE MENESES Captain of *Tangier*.

14. MENCIA GUIOMAR, and two other Daughters were Nuns.

14. FRANCIS

14. FRANCIS DE FARO Lord of VIMIERO.

HE was eldest Son of *Ferdinand De Faro*, by *Isabel de Melo* his Wife, and was President of the Council of Affairs to the King of *Portugal Sebastian*.

The first of his Wives MENCIA D' ALBUQUERQUE was Daughter of *George D' Albuquerque*, and of *Anne Enriquez*.

The second, GUIOMARE DE CASTRO was Daughter of *Matthew D' Acugna* Lord of *Pombeiro*, by *Leonor Coutigna*.

The third, was MARY DE MENDOZA the Daughter of *Manuel Cort-real*, and of *Beatrix De Mendoza* his Wife, by her he had no Children.

Children of FRANCIS DE FARO, and of MENCIA D' ALBUQUERQUE his first Wife.

15. FERDINAND ENRIQUEZ whose story followeth in the next place.

15. GEORGE DE FARO was slain at the fatal Battel of *Alcacer*, in the year, *One thousand five hundred threescore and eighteen*.

15. MARY DE NOROGNA espoused to FERDINAND TELLEZ DE MENESES, Governour of the *Indies*, and the *Algarves*.

Children of FRANCIS DE FARO, by GUIOMAR DE CASTRO his second Wife.

15. FRANCIS DE FARO first Count of VIMIERO, of whom we shall speak more fully hereafter.

15. MARIANA DE LANCASTRO, Wife of LEWIS DE SILVA, President of the Council of Affairs to the King of *Spain*, *Philip IV*.

---

15. FERDINAND HENRIQUEZ.

AMong the Children of *Francis de Faro* Lord of *Vimiero*, and of *Mencia d' Albuquerque* his first Wife, he was the eldest, and dyed in the life-time of his Father, having married JANE DE GUZMAN, Daughter of *Alvaro Caraallo* by *Mary de Guzman* his Wife; by her he had these Children following;

16. LEWIS DE FARO never married.

16. MARY DE FARO Wife of MANUEL COUTIGNO.

16. MENCIA DE FARO espoused to PETER ALVAREZ PEREIRA, Counsellour of State to the Catholick King, in the Council of *Portugal* resident in his Court.

16. KATHERINE DE FARO Wife of BLAISE TELLEZ DE MENESES Captain of *Mazagan*.

15. FRANCIS DE FARO Count of VIMIERO.

From the marriage of *Francis de Faro* Lord of *Vimiero*, and of *Guiomar De Castro* his second Wife descended this Count, who was raised to this Dignity by the King of *Spain*, *Philip III*.

He had to Wife MARIANA DE LA GUERRA Daughter of *Peter Lopez De Sousa*, by *Anne De LaGuerra* his Wife, by whom he had Issue Three Sons and a Daughter, *viz.*

16. FERDINAND DE FARO, Lord of *Vimiero*.

16. LEWIS DE FARO, a Monk of the Order of St. *Augustin*.

16. ALPHONSO DE FARO, was also an Ecclesiastick.

16. MARY DE FARO, Wife of RODERICK DE LA CAMARA Captain of the Isle of St. *Michael*.

14. DIONYSIUS DE FARO.

He was second Son of *Ferdinand de Faro* Lord of *Vimiero*, and of *Isabel de Melo* his Wife. And was conjoyned in Marriage with LORISE CABRAL Daughter of *John-Alvarez Camnigna*; by whom he had these two Sons following.

15. JOHN DE FARO, dyed unmarried.

15. STEPHEN Count of FARO and St. *Lewis*, mentioned in the next place.

15. STEPHEN Count of FARO, and of St. Lewis.

Was second Son of *Dionysius de Faro*, by *Lorisa Cabral* his Wife. He was of the Council of Estate to the Catholick King, and also President of the Council of Affairs. *Vasconcellos* writeth that the King of *Spain*, *Philip III.* Created him Count of St. *Lewis*. He espoused GUIOMAR DE CASTRO, Daughter of *John Lobo* Baron of *Alvito*, by *Leonor Mascareguas* his Wife.

Children

Children of STEPHEN Count of FARO, and of LORISA CABRAL his Wife.

16. DIONYSIUS DE FARO, married MAGDALENE DE LANCASTRO, the Daughter of *Alvaro de Lancastro* Duke of *Aveiro* and *Tourneuf*, by her he had issue one Daughter, *viz.*

17. JULIANA DE FARO, was Wife of MICHAEL DE MENESES, Marquess of *Villa-real*, and Duke of *Camigne*.

16. FRANCIS. JOHN. SANCEO. FRANCIS-LEWIS.

16. LUCIA DE FARO Wife of EDWARD DE MENESES Count of *Tarouca*.

16. LEONOR espoused to BERNARDINE DE TAUORA.

COUNTS OF VIMIOSO.

11. ALPHONSO OF PORTUGAL, Count of OUREM, Marquess of *Valence*, and Lord of *Porto de-Mos*.

Alphonso of *Portugal*, first Duke of *Braganza*, Son of King *John I.* and *Beatrix de Pereira* Countess of *Barcellos* and *Ourem* his Wife, had two Sons, of which this was the elder; But deceasing before his father, he succeeded not to the Dutchee; The King of *Portugal, Edward*, his Uncle, sent him Ambassadour to the Senate of *Florence*.

The same Count ALPHONSO having been chosen to Conduct the Princess *Leonor* of *Portugal* to the Emperour *Frederick III.* her Husband, was Created Count of OUREM, and Marquess of *Valence*, by King *Alphonso V.* in the Year, One thousand four hundred and fifty; and 1450. Ten years after dyed at *Tomar*; having had by his Love-Mistress BEA-1460. TRIX DE SOUSA, daughter of *Martin-Alphonso de Sousa*, and of *Yoland Lopez de Tauora*, this his only Son, *viz.*

12. ALPHONSO OF PORTUGAL, was Bishop of *Evora*; and before he followed the Profession of a Church-man, had also by a Lady called DE MACEDON, others say DE MELO, these two Sons following;

13. FRANCIS OF PORTUGAL, first Count of VIMIOSO, mentioned in the next place.

13. MARTIN OF PORTUGAL, Arch-bishop of *Fonchal*, afterwards Bishop of *Algarvie*, and Patriarch of the *Indies*. King *John III.* sent him Ambassadour to Pope *Clement VII.* who made him his *Nuncio* to the Kingdom of *Portugal*. He had two Bastard-Children by KATHERINE DE SOUSA, a Bastard-daughter of *Roderick de Sousa,* viz.

14. ELISHA OF PORTUGAL, was of the Privy-Chamber to the Popes *Pius IV,* and *Gregory XIII.*

14. MARY OF PORTUGAL, second Wife to JAMES DE CASTRO.

---

13. FRANCIS OF PORTUGAL, *first of the name, Count of* VIMIOSO, *and Lord of Aguiar.*

THE King of *Portugal, Emanuel,* honoured him with the Dignity of Count of VIMIOSO, and furthermore instituted him Super-intendant of his Affairs, as did likewise King *John III.* afterward the Prince *Portugal* his Son, made him his High Chamberlain.

He espoused for his first Wife BEATRIX DE VILLENA, daughter of *Roderick Tellez de Meneses* Lord of *Ugnon*, Steward of the Houshold to the Empress *Isabel* of *Portugal,* Wife to the Emperor *Charls V.*

His second Wife was JANE DE VILLENA, daughter of *Alvaro* of *Portugal* of the House of *Tentugal,* and of *Philippa de Melo* Countess of *Olivenza.*

A Daughter of FRANCIS OF PORTUGAL, *Count of Vimioso, by his former Wife.*

14. GUIOMAR DE VILLENA, espoused to FRANCIS DE GAMA second Count of VEDIGUERA, and Admiral of the *Indies.*

Children of FRANCIS OF PORTUGAL, *Count of Vimioso, by his later Wife.*

14. ALPHONSO OF PORTUGAL, Count of VIMIOSO, continued the Posterity.

14. MANUEL OF PORTUGAL had also Children, as you shall see, after we have deduced the Branch of his elder Brother.

14. JOHN OF PORTUGAL, Bishop of *Guarda.*

14. ALPHON-

14. ALPHONSO OF PORTUGAL, first of the name, Count of VIMIOSO.

HE was eldest Son of *Francis* of *Portugal* first Earl of *Vimioso*, by *Jane de Villena* his 2^d Wife, and was, as his father before him, Super-intendant of the Affairs of the Kings of *Portugal*, *John III.* and *Sebastian*, with whom he undertook the Expedition of *Affrick*. The History notes thus much of him; That having been this Kings Chamberlain, and having Command in his first Voyage, he deported himself so ill, that those which emulated his Greatness, took occasion to exclude him the Kings Favour. He behaved himself no better in the second Expedition; For being ambitious, and desirous to regain that Reputation with the King which he had lost, he seconded his will, notwithstanding he knew it to be rash and prejudicial. For the Army being landed in *Affrick*, he perswaded them to make their passage by Land, instead of that by Sea, void of danger, which he did principally out of complacency with the King, whom he observed to be grounded in this opinion, notwithstanding urged and disswaded by many more substantial reasons, from several others: So that he dyed with his Prince at the unfortunate Battel of *Alcacer*.

He was conjoyned by Marriage with LUCIA DE GUZMAN, daughter of *Francis de Guzman* Great Steward of the Houshold to the Infanta *Mary* of *Portugal*, youngest daughter of King *Emanuel*.

Children of ALPHONSO OF PORTUGAL, first of the name, Count of *Vimioso*.

15. FRANCIS OF PORTUGAL second of the name, Count of VIMIOSO, whose Story followeth in the next place.

15. JOHN OF PORTUGAL, a Monk of the Order of St. *Dominick*, a Learned man, was of the Council general of the Inquisition.

15. LEWIS OF PORTUGAL, succeeded his eldest Brother in the County of VIMIOSO.

15. ALVARO OF PORTUGAL, dyed in *Sicilie*.

15. NUGNO-ALVAREZ OF PORTUGAL, was President of the Chamber of *Lisbonne*, and had been One of the Three Governours of *Portugal*. By his Wife and Cosin JANE OF PORTUGAL, daughter of *Manuel* of *Portugal*, and of *Margaret de Mendoza* his second Wife, he had, besides some Children that dyed young, Four Sons, and Two Daughters.

16. LEWIS OF PORTUGAL.

16. JOHN. ALPHONSO. ANTHONY.

16. MARY and MARGARET.

CON-

15. CONSTANCE DE GUZMAN, Abbess of the Monastery of our Lady at *Lisbonne*.

15. BEATRIX DE GUZMAN, also Abbess of the same place.

15. PHILIPPA DE GUZMAN, Prioress of the Monastery of the *Holy Sacrament* at *Lisbonne*.

15. MENCIA and JANE, also Nuns in the Monasteries of *d'Esperanza* at *Lisbonne*, and of St. *Catherine* at *Evora*.

15. FRANCIS OF PORTUGAL, second of the name, Count of VIMIOSO, and Constable of Portugal.

This Count accompanied King *Sebastian* of *Portugal*, to the Battel of *Alcacer*, and was there made a Prisoner, but afterwards finding means to recover his Liberty, and being upon his return into *Portugal*, he there followed the Fortune of Prince *Anthony*, who being declared King, honored him with the Dignity of *Constable* of *Portugal*. He followed this Prince in his Voyage for *France*. 1578. 1580.

Afterwards being at the Naval fight, in A° *One thousand five hundred fourscore and two*, near unto the *Azores*, betwixt the French Army Commanded by the Collonel *Philip Strozzi*, and the Spanish, Conducted by the Marquess of St. *Croix*, Lieutenant General to the King of *Spain*, *Philip II*. This Count of *Vimioso* was so grievously hurt, that he lived but two dayes after the Fight. The Marquess for all he was his Enemy, did much lament and deplore his Fortune, as being his Kinsman. His end was more honorable, than that of any of the other Lords that had followed *Anthony*. He was young, adorned with good parts both of body and mind, and was one that joyned Learning to the Military profession. 1582.

15. LEWIS OF PORTUGAL, Count of VIMIOSO.

His eldest Brother the Count *Francis II*. not having been married, and leaving no Children, this Count succeeded him, and espoused JANE DE MENDOZA daughter of *Ferdinand de Castro* first Count of *Basto*, by the Countess *Philippa de Mendoza* his Wife.

This Count and Countess being touched with a singular Piety, took a holy resolution to forsake the World, and with mutual consent took upon them the Habit of Religious. He entred himself into the Order of St. *Dominick*; and the Countess JANE his Wife Cloystered her self in the Monastery of the *Holy Sacrament* at *Lisbonne*, with the Barefoot Sisters, an Abbey which she and her Husband had founded.

Children

Children of LEWIS OF PORTUGAL, Count of *Vimioso*.

16. ALPHONSO OF PORTUGAL, second of the name, Count of VIMIOSO, continued the Posterity.

16. MICHAEL OF PORTUGAL, Bishop of *Lamego*, Archbishop of *Lisbonne*, Ambassadour from the King of *Portugal*, *John IV*. to Pope *Urban VIII*. Anno 1641. He departed this world in the Year, 1644.

16. FERDINAND OF PORTUGAL, was a Souldier in *Flanders*, where he dyed.

16. LUCIA DE GUZMAN.

16. PHILIPPA DE CASTRO, a Nun with her Mother in the Abbey of the *Holy Sacrament* at *Lisbon*.

---

16. ALPHONSO OF PORTUGAL, second of the name, Count of VIMIOSO.

HE was eldest Son of *Lewis* Count of *Vimioso*, and of *Jane de Mendoza* his Wife: And espoused MARY DE MENDOZA daughter of *Christopher de Mora* first Marquess of *Castle-Rodrigo*, and of the Marchioness *Margaret Corte-real*, by whom he had these Children following:

17. LEWIS OF PORTUGAL, II. of the name, Count of VIMIOSA, was Created Marquess of *Aguiar* by the King of *Portugal*, *John IV*. He dyed without lawful issue.

17. CHRISTOPHER OF PORTUGAL dyed also, not having been married.

17. MICHAEL OF PORTUGAL, Count of VIMIOSO, now living, 1662.

17. JANE. MARGARET. LUCIA. BEATRIX.

---

14. MANUEL OF PORTUGAL.

HE was second Son of *Francis* of *Portugal* first Count of *Vimioso*, by *Jane de Villena* his second Wife. King *John III*. of the name, sent him to the Emperour *Charles V*. to Congratulate with him for his success in the Enterprise of *Algier*; and afterwards King *Henry* sent him also to the King of *Spain*, *Philip II*. to Condole with him for the deplorable Death of King *Sebastian* his Nephews Son. Some time after this MANUEL

NUEL OF PORTUGAL (as did *Francis* second of the name, Count of *Vimioso* his Nephew) followed the Designs and Party of King *Anthony* of *Portugal*, against the same King, *Philip II*.

He married two Wives, first MARY DE VILLENA daughter of *Henry de Meneses*, by *Beatrix de Villena* his Wife.

In second Marriage he took to Wife MARGARET DE MENDOZA daughter of *Manuel Corte-real*, and of *Beatrix de Mendoza* his Wife.

Children of MANUEL OF PORTUGAL, and of MARY DE VILLENA his first Wife.

15. HENRY OF PORTUGAL continued the Posterity.

15. JOHN OF PORTUGAL dyed at the Battel of *Alcacer*, after he had married MAGDALENE DE VILLENA daughter of *Francis de Sousa Tavares*, Captain of *Diu*, and of *Mary de Silva* his Wife; by her he had a Son, and two Daughters following.

    16. LEWIS OF PORTUGAL, dyed at *Septe* with a fall from his Horse.

    16. MARY OF PORTUGAL, Wife of PETER DE MENESES, Grand Alcaide of *Visco*.

    16. JANE OF PORTUGAL, Wife of LOPEZ d'ALMEIDA, Grand Alcaide of *Alcobace*.

15. ALPHONSO OF PORTUGAL, was slain in the Battel of *Alcantara* in the service of *Anthony* King of *Portugal*.

A Daughter of MANUEL OF PORTUGAL, by MARGARET DE MENDOZA his second Wife.

15. JANE OF PORTUGAL, Wife of her Cosin Germain NUGNO ALVAREZ DE PORTUGAL, as you have read before.

---

15. HENRY OF PORTUGAL.

HE was eldest Son of *Manuel* of *Portugal*, by *Mary de Villena* his first Wife; and espoused ANNE ATAIDE daughter of *Anthony Ataide* Count of *Chastaigneraye*, by *Mary de Villena* his Wife, by whom he had issue Four Sons, and Two Daughters. The King of *Portugal*, *Sebastian*, sent him to visit the Emperour *Rodolph II*. to Condole with him for the Death of his father *Maximilian II*. His Children were,

16. MANUEL OF PORTUGAL II. of the name, dyed young in the life-time of his father; having married LUCIA DE VILLENA daughter of *Manuel de Castro* by his Wife *Beatrix de Villena*; by her

her he had two Sons; the elder of which, called by his Grandfathers name, dyed young; the other was,

17. ALVARO OF PORTUGAL.

16. FRANCIS MANUEL.

16. JOHN OF PORTUGAL deceased also in the life-time of his father, having espoused ANTONIETTA DE VILLENA, daughter of *Anthony Corea Batareno.*

16. MARY OF PORTUGAL, Wife of LEWIS d'ALMEIDA.

16. GUIOMAR OF PORTUGAL, was espoused to MANUEL ATAIDE, third Count of *Castaigneraye* her Uncle.

DUKES OF CONIMBRA, AVEIRO, AND TOURSNEUUES.

13. *GEORGE Bastard of PORTUGAL, Duke of CONIMBRA, Lord of Toursneuues, Aveiro, and Mont-Major le Vieil, Grand Master of the Order of Christus and d'Avis.*

His Birth. 1481.

THE King of *Portugal*, *John II.* of the name, had by his Queen *Beatrix* of *Portugal* the Prince *Alphonso* their only Son, who dyed before them in the flower of his age. The same King also begat by *Anne de Mendoza* his Paramore, this Prince GEORGE, who was born about the Year, *One thousand four hundred fourscore and one.* He was affectionately beloved by the King his father, insomuch, that having no lawful issue, he intended after his death to leave him the Crown, which the Grandees of the Kingdom did vigorously oppose, as also the Queen his wife (as we have informed you before.) The Princess (who was transported with a natural Love towards her Friend) would not permit that the Duke of *Beia, Emanuel* of *Portugal* her Brother (who was Heir apparent to the Crown by the right of Blood and Proximity,) should be deprived of his Succession by a Bastard-Son. Nevertheless King *John* having appointed the Prince *Emanuel* for his Successor, recommended this GEORGE to his care, whom he caused to be carefully educated.

After the Death of his father, and that *Emanuel* had taken in hand the Scepter, the young Prince being but Fourteen years old, came and offered him his obedience, where he received a favourable Entertain from this 1495. Great King, who promised to be to him a Father; and for a Testimony

PORTUGAL-AVEIRO.

Mariana Lib. 26. *Cap.* 2. & 33.

Vasconcellos.
Novius Lib.

of his Love, Confirmed to him the Titles and Seigneuries with which the late King had honoured him.

This Duke of *Conimbra* was conjoyned in Marriage with BEATRIX DE MELO AND PORTUGAL, who was Daughter of the great *Alvaro* of *Portugal* branched from the House of *Braganza*, and of *Philippa de Melo* Countess of *Olivenza* his Wife; by her he had several Children, which took the Sir-name of *Lancastro*.

Children of GEORGE OF PORTUGAL, Duke of Conimbra.

14. JOHN DE LANCASTRO, Duke of AVEIRO, continued the Posterity.

14. ALPHONSO DE LANCASTRO, Great Commander of St. *James*, had also issue.

14. LEWIS DE LANCASTRO, Grand Commander *d' Avis*, had likewise Children.

14. JAMES DE LANCASTRO Bishop of *Septe*.

14. HELEN DE LANCASTRO, Commandress of the Monastery of the Order of St. *James*.

14. PHILIPPA
14. MARY } DE LANCASTRO, Nuns, at St. *John* of *Setuval*.
14. ISABEL

Natural Children of GEORGE Duke of Conimbra.

14. GEORGE DE LANCASTRO Grand Prior *d' Avis*.

14. GEORGE DE St. MARY a Monk of the Order of St. *Hierosme*.

14. ANTHONY DE St. MARY a Monk of the Order of St. *Augustine*, and Bishop of *Leiria*.

---

14. JOHN DE LANCASTRO, Duke of AVEIRO, Marquess of *Toursnennes*, and Lord of *Montmor*.

HE was eldest Son of *George* Duke of *Conimbra*, and of *Beatrix de Melo* his Wife. The Title of Duke of *Conimbra* was not continued in his Person; But the King of *Portugal*, *Emanuel*, shewed his affection towards this illustrious Family, which was so near to him, that he Created him

Mar-

Marquess of *Toursneuues*; and King *John III.* raised him to the Dignity of Duke of *Aveiro*. By the Command of the same King, he was to visit the Emperour *Charles V.* to Condole with him upon the Death of his Empress *Isabel* the Infanta of *Portugal*.

He took to Wife JULIANA DE MENESES daughter of *Peter de Meneses*, third Marquess of *Ville-real*, and of the Marchioness *Beatrix de Lara* his Wife.

Children of JOHN Duke of Aveiro.

15. GEORGE DE LANCASTRO second of the name, and second Duke of *Aveiro*.

15. PETER-DIONYSIUS DE LANCASTRO, had to Wife PHILIPPA DE SILVA, daughter of *John de Silva*, heiress of the House of *Portalegre*, and of *Margaret de Silva* his Wife; from which Marriage descended their only daughter JULIANA, who dyed young.

15. JOHN DE LANCASTRO, a Natural Son, was a Monk of the Order of St. *Dominick*.

---

15. GEORGE DE LANCASTRO, second of the name, and second Duke of AVEIRO, and Marquess of Toursneuues.

His Death. 1578.

OF the two Children of *John de Lancastro* Duke of *Aveiro*, by his Wife *Juliana de Meneses*, he was the elder; He accompanied King *Sebastian* in the Voyage of *Affrica*, and was slain at the Battel of *Alcacer*, with many more Princes and Lords of the Blood-Royal of *Portugal*.

His Wife MAGDALENE GIRON, was daughter of *John Tellez Giron* Count of *Urena*, and of *Mary de la Cueua* his Wife.

An only Daughter of GEORGE second Duke of Aveiro.

17. JULIANA DE LANCASTRO, Dutchess of *Aveiro*, was married to her Cosin ALVARO DE LANCASTRO, as we shall shew you more at large hereafter.

---

14. ALPHONSO DE LANCASTRO, Great Commander of St. James.

HE was second Son of *George* Bastard of *Portugal* Duke of *Conimbra*, and of *Beatrix de Melo* his Wife. He espoused YOLAND HENRIQUEZ daughter of *John Coutinho* Earl of *Redondo*, and of the Countess *Isabel Henriquez* his Wife; by her he had four Sons, and six daughters.

Children of ALPHONSO DE LANCASTRO.

15. LEWIS DE LANCASTRO, dyed young.

15. GEORGE DE LANCASTRO, was slain at the Battel of *Alcacer* in *Affrick*, in the Year, One thousand five hundred threescore and eighteen. 1578.

15. ALVARO DE LANCASTRO, Duke of AVEIRO, mentioned in the next place.

15. MANUEL DE LANCASTRO, Great Master of the Order of St. *James*, and Governour of the *Algarvies*, had a Natural Son, which was,

    16. JOHN DE LANCASTRO, a Monk of the Order of St. *Augustine*.

15. ISABEL   15. MARY
15. BEATRIX   15. PHILIPPA } Nuns.
15. HELENE   15. ANNE

15. HIEROSME DE LANCASTRO, a Bastard-Son, was Prior of *Toursneuues*, and had issue CONSTANTINE, ALVARO, and other Natural Children.

---

15. ALVARO DE LANCASTRO, Duke of AVEIRO.

This Duke was fourth Son of *Alphonso de Lancastro* Great Master of St. *James*, and of *Toland Henriquez* his Wife. He took to Wife JULIANA Dutchess of AVEIRO, only daughter, and sole heir of Duke *George II.* by *Magdalene Giron* his Wife: So that the Dutchy went not out of the Family. From this Marriage did descend several Children.

Children of ALVARO DE LANCASTRO, and of the Dutchess JULIANA d'AVEIRO his Wife.

16. GEORGE DE LANCASTRO, Duke of TOURS-NEUUES, espoused ANNE DORIACOLOMNA, daughter of *Andrew Doria* Prince of *Melphi*, and of *Jane Colomna* his Wife. But this Dutchess ANNE dyed without issue.

16. ALPHONSO DE LANCASTRO, Grand Commander of St. *James*.

JOHN

16. JOHN DE LANCASTRO, was a Monk of the Order of St. *Dominick*.

16. MARIANA DE LANCASTRO, a Nun of the Order of St. *Francis*, in the Monastery of our Lady at *Lisbonne*.

16. BEATRIX a Nun of the Order of St. *Dominick*, in the Abbey of St. *John* at *Setubal*.

---

14. LEWIS DE LANCASTRO, *first of the name,* Great Master of the Order d'*Avis*.

1559.

OF the four Sons of *George* Bastard of *Portugal* Duke of *Conimbra*, by the Dutchess *Beatrix de Melo* his Wife, he was the third. He was sent by King *Sebastian*, to the King of *Spain*, *Philip II*. for to Condole with him upon the death of Prince *Charles* his eldest Son, and also for the decease of his third Wife, Queen *Isabel* of *France*.

He married MAGDALENE OF GRANADA daughter of the Infant *John de Granada*, by *Beatrix de Sandoval* his Wife; which Infant was issued from the Blood of the antient Kings of *Granada*.

Children of LEWIS DE LANCASTRO, *first of the name.*

15. LEWIS DE LANCASTRO, second of the name, continued the Posterity.

15. JOHN DE LANCASTRO had also Children, hereafter mentioned.

15. BEATRIX DE LANCASTRO, second Wife of THEODOSIUS OF PORTUGAL, Duke of *Braganza*.

15. ANNE Commandress of *Sanctus*, of the Order of St. *James*.

15. MAGDALENE, Wife of JOHN DE SILVEIRA.

15. MARY espoused JOHN GONCALEZ DE CAMARA, Count of *Callera*.

---

15. LEWIS DE LANCASTRO, II. *of the name,* Great Master d'*Avis*.

HE was the eldest Son of *Lewis de Lancastro* first of the name, by the Infanta *Magdalene de Granada* his Wife; and was of the Council of Estate to the Kings of *Spain*, *Philip II*. and *III*. and Super-intendant of their

their Affairs. He dyed in the Year, *One thousand six hundred and thirteen*; and was interred in the great Chappel of the Monastery of Nuns of St. *John* at *Setubal*.

PHILIPPA DE MENESES his Wife, was daughter of *James de Silveira* second Count of *Sortella*, by *Mary de Meneses* his Wife.

Children of LEWIS DE LANCASTRO, second of the name.

16. FRANCIS-LEWIS DE LANCASTRO, whose Story followeth in the next place.

16. MAGDALENE DE LANCASTRO, Wife of JOHN LOBO, sixth Baron of *Alvito*.

---

16. FRANCIS-LEWIS DE LANCASTRO.

HE succeeded his father and Grand-father *Lewis II*. and *Lewis I*. in the Dignity of Grand Master *d'Avis*; and married PHILIPPA DE MENDOZA daughter of *Manuel de Vasconcellos*, by *Lucia de Mendoza* his Wife.

Children of FRANCIS-LEWIS DE LANCASTRO.

17. LEWIS, and MANUEL.

17. PETER, and VERISSIME.

---

15. JOHN DE LANCASTRO.

AMong the Children of *Lewis de Lancastro* first of the name, great Master *d'Avis*, and of *Magdelene de Grenada* his Wife, he was the second; and had two Wives.

His first Wife was PAULA DE TAUORA daughter of *Lawrence Perez de Tauora*, by *Katherine de Tauora* his Wife.

His second Wife was PHILIPPA DE CASTRO, daughter of *Alphonso de Castelblanco Merino*, Major of *Portugal*, and of *Isabel de Castro*; by her he had no issue; and dyed in the Year, *One thousand six hundred and fourteen*. He lieth buried in the Monastery of St. *Anthony*, of the Order of St. *Francis* in the Province of *Rabida*.

Children of JOHN DE LANCASTRO by his first Wife.

16. LAWRENCE DE LANCASTRO espoused AGNES DE

AVEIRO, and TOURSNEUUES.

DE MENESES, daughter of *Roderick Tellez de Meneses*, Lord of *Ugnon*: By her he had issue

17. JOHN DE LANCASTRO.

16. GEORGE DE LANCASTRO, was slain by the *Infidels* at *Mosambique*.

16. KATHERINE DE LANCASTRO, second Wife of JOHN·MARTINEZ MASCAREGNAS, grand Alcaide of *Mont-Major* the new.

LORDS AND COUNTS OF VILLAR.

9. DIONYSIUS OF PORTUGAL, Lord of CIFUENTES, *Ascalona*, and *Alva de Tormes*.

Mong the natural Children of *Peter* King of *Portugal*, one, which was King *John* the First, came to an Absolute Fortune, being chosen King of *Portugal*, after the Death of King *Ferdinand*; and another, which was this DENIS, whom he begat by *Agnes de Castro*, made his Fortunes in *Castille*, where he was Lord of CIFUENTES, and the other Seigneuries here above-mentioned.

He took to Wife JANE OF CASTILLE, natural daughter of *Henry II*. King of *Castille* and *Leon*.

Children of DIONYSIO OF PORTUGAL, Lord of *Cifuentes*, and of JANE OF CASTILLE his Wife.

10. FERDINAND OF PORTUGAL, Knight of the Order of St. *James*, Commander of *Oreia*, continued the Posterity.

10. PETER OF PORTUGAL, Lord of *Colmeneraio*, had also Children.

10. BEATRIX OF PORTUGAL, founded the Hospital of *Tordesillas*.

10. FERDINAND OF PORTUGAL, Knight of St. James, and Commander of Oreia.

HE was eldest Son of *Denis* of *Portugal* Lord of *Cifuentes*, and lived in *Castille* during the Reign of King *John* the second. He was twice married; his first Wife being MARY DE TORRES, daughter of *Ferdinand Roderick de Torres*, Lord of *Villar* and *Escagnella*, by *Agnes Sollier* his Wife.

For his second Wife FERDINAND OF PORTUGAL espoused ALDARA OSORIO.

A Son of FERDINAND OF PORTUGAL, and of MARY DE TORRES his first Wife.

11. DENIS OF PORTUGAL, Lord of *Torres*, continued the Posterity.

Children of FERDINAND OF PORTUGAL, and of ALDARA OSORIO his second Wife.

11. JAMES OF PORTUGAL, espoused MARY DE VILLENAS, by whom he had several Children.

12. FERDINAND, RAMIRO, and JOHN, dyed all without issue.

12. ALDARA OF PORTUGAL, Wife of LEWIS DE CALA-TAIUD, Lord of *Prouencio*.

12. JANE OF PORTUGAL, espoused to ALPHONSO-SANCHEZ DE CARUAIAL, Lord of *Jodar* and *Touarnela*.

---

11. DENIS, or DIONYSIO OF PORTUGAL, Lord of TORRES.

HE succeeded not in the Lordship of *Villar*, for he dyed in the life-time of *Theresa de Torres* his Cosin German, she was daughter of *Charles* Lord of *Villar* brother to *Mary*, Mother of this DENIS OF PORTUGAL, who espoused ISABEL FAXARDO MANUEL, daughter of *John Manuel*, and of *Mencia Faxardo*; from which Marriage came one only Son mentioned in the next place.

12. **FERDINAND DE TORRES, and PORTUGAL, Lord of VILLAR, Donpardo, and Ecamella.**

HE was only Son of *Denis* of *Portugal* Lord of *Torres*, and of *Isabel Faxardo Manuel* his Wife, and was twice married.

His first Wife was MAGDALENE VILLEGAS, by her he had one daughter, named

13. MARY MANUEL OF PORTUGAL, Wife of ANTHONY DE LA MOTHE in *Mexico*.

The second Wife of FERDINAND DE TORRES, was BEATRIX DE LUXAN, by her he had these Children following:

13. BERNARDINE DE TORRES and PORTUGAL, Lord of VILLAR, continued the Posterity.

13. ISABEL DE TORRES, Wife of JOHN DE VILLEREAL.

13. **BERNARDINE DE TORRES and PORTUGAL, first of the name, Lord of VILLAR and Donpardo.**

AMong the Children of *Ferdinand de Torres*, and *Beatrix de Luxan* his second Wife, this BERNARDINE was the eldest. He espoused MARY DE MEXIA daughter of *Roderick Mexia* Lord *de la Guarde* and St. *Fimia*, by *Mary de Ponce Leon* his Wife.

Children of BERNARDINE DE TORRES, *Lord of Villar.*

14. FERDINAND DE TORRES and PORTUGAL, third of the name, and first Count of VILLAR, had issue

15. BEATRIX DE TORRES, espoused to LEWIS DE CARUAIAL, Lord *de las Velas, Jodar* and *Tonarnela*.

14. FERDINAND DE TORRES and PORTUGAL, third of the name, first Count of VILLAR and Donpardo, and Viceroy of Peru.

HE was Successor of *Bernardine de Torres* Lord of *Villar* his father, and was employed by the King of *Spain*, *Philip II*. who created him first Count of *Villar Donpardo*. He was Viceroy of *Peru*, and was twice married.

He espoused for his first Wife FRANCES DE CARUAIAL, daughter of *Diego de Caruaial*, by *Isabel Osorio*.

His second Marriage was with MARY DE CARILLO DE CORDOUA, daughter of *Fernandez de Cordoua*, by *Isabel Cabeca* his Wife.

Children of FERDINAND DE TORRES Count of Villar, and of FRANCES DE CARUAIAL his first Wife.

15. BERNARDIN DE TORRES and PORTUGAL, continued the Descent.

15. JAMES DE TORRES and PORTUGAL, Knight of St. James.

15. LEWIS DE TORRES.

15. GONCALO MEXIA DE PORTUGAL.

15. FERDINAND DE TORRES and PORTUGAL, of whom we shall speak more amply hereafter.

Children of FERDINAND DE TORRES, Count of Villar, by MARY CARILLO his second Wife.

15. HIEROSME DE TORRES and PORTUGAL, Knight of St. James.

15. JOHN DE TORRES and CORDOUA, Canon of *Jaen*.

15. MANUEL DE TORRES and PORTUGAL.

15. JAMES DE TORRES.

15. BER-

15. BERNARDIN DE TORRES and PORTUGAL.

Ferdinand de Torres and Portugal, first Count of Villar, and Frances de Caruaial his first Wife, had for their eldest Son this BERNARDIN, who dyed in the life-time of his father, having married AGNES MANRIQUE, daughter of Goncalo Mexia Marquess de la Guarde, and of Anne Manrique his Wife; and from their Marriage came these Children following, viz.

16. JOHN DE TORRES and PORTUGAL, Count of VILLAR, whose Story followeth in the next place.

16. BERNARDIN MANRIQUE OF PORTUGAL.

16. FERDINAND DE TORRES and PORTUGAL.

Three Daughters Vailed Nuns.

16. JOHN DE TORRES and PORTUGAL, Count of VILLAR DONPARDO.

He succeeded his Grand-father Count Ferdinand in the Earldom of Villar, being eldest Son of Bernardin de Torres, by Agnes Manriques his Wife, and was made Knight of the Order of Calatraua.
Of the two Wives he espoused, the first was ISABEL CARUAIAL daughter of Alphonso Caruaial, and of Catharine Mexia Lady of Jodar and Touarnela his Wife.
His second Wife was MARY DE MENDOZA, daughter of Bernardin Suarez de Mendoza, fifth Count of Corugua, and of his Wife Mariana de Bacan.

Children of JOHN DE TORRES *and* PORTUGAL, *Count of Villar, by* ISABEL CARUAIAL *his first Wife.*

17. BERNARDIN DE TORRES and PORTUGAL, dyed young.

17. AGNES MANRIQUE DE TORRES and PORTUGAL, espoused to ANTHONY DE CALATAIUD eldest Son of the Count of Real.

Children of JOHN DE TORRES *and* PORTUGAL, *Count of Villar, by* MARY DE MENDOZA *his second Wife.*

17. JOHN-ANTHONY DE TORRES and PORTUGAL

17. FERDINAND.

17. JANE MARY.

---

15. FERDINAND DE TORRES and PORTUGAL.

OF the Five Children of *Ferdinand de Torres* and *Portugal*, first Count of *Villar*, and of the Countess *Frances de Caruaial* his first Wife, this FERDINAND, which was the fifth, was made a Knight of the Order of St. *James*, and married GUIOMAR DE TORRES & CONTRERAS, daughter of *Ruy Dias Torres*, by *Aldonce de Gontreras* his Wife; from which Marriage came two Sons and a daughter.

16. RODERICK DE TORRES and PORTUGAL, was (as his father had been before him) Knight of the Order of St. *James*.

16. LEWIS DE TORRES and PORTUGAL, was one of the Four and twenty Magistrates of *Jaen*.

16. FRANCES DE TORRES and PORTUGAL, was espoused to JOHN PALOMINO HURTADO DE MENDOZA

---

10. PETER OF PORTUGAL, Lord of COLMENERAIO.

DEnis, Bastard-Son of *Peter* King of *Portugal*, left two Sons by his Wife *Jane* of *Castille*, the elder of which was *Ferdinand* of *Portugal*, from whom the Lords and Earls of *Villar* are descended; and the younger, this PETER OF PORTUGAL, which some nevertheless suppose to be born before his brother: But however it was, he espoused ISABEL HENRIQUEZ, by whom had a Son and a daughter, *Viz.*

11. JOHN OF PORTUGAL, Lord of COLMENERAIO, whose Posterity is mentioned in the next place.

11. JANE OF PORTUGAL, Wife of VASCO GONCALES DE CONTRERAS, Lord *de la Puebla* and *Orcaiada*.

---

11. JOHN OF PORTUGAL, Lord of COLMENERAIO.

HE was the only Son of *Peter* of *Portugal*, also Lord of *Colmeneraio*, by *Isabel Henriquez* his Wife, and took to Wife BEATRIX DE LAU-

Lords and Counts of VILLAR.

LAURENCANA; she was descended from the Kingdom of *Leon*. They had issue three Sons and a daughter, *Viz.*

12. FERDINAND OF PORTUGAL, married N. DE QUIADA, and had by her his only daughter,

  13. TERESA HENRIQUEZ OF PORTUGAL, espoused to PETER GONCALES DE MENDOZA.

12. DENIS OF PORTUGAL, a younger Son of *John* Lord of *Colmeneraio*, was an Ecclesiastick.

12. BERNARDIN OF PORTUGAL, married ELUIRA DE MENDOZA, daughter of the Count of *Priego*, and had no issue by her.

12. ISABEL HENRIQUEZ, espoused to FRANCIS Duke DE GUZMAN; so named by *Alphonso Lopez de Haro* in his Book of the Nobility of *Spain*, *Chap. IV.*

FINIS.

www.ingramcontent.com/pod-product-compliance
Lightning Source LLC
Chambersburg PA
CBHW020831230426
43666CB00007B/1180